Churchill: Four Faces and the Man

A. J. P. TAYLOR
The Statesman

ROBERT RHODES JAMES
The Politician

J. H. PLUMB
The Historian

BASIL LIDDELL HART
The Military Strategist

ANTHONY STORR
The Man

BOOK CLUB ASSOCIATES
London

First published in the U.S.A. (as *Churchill Revised*) by
The Dial Press, Inc., 1969
First published in Great Britain 1969
Copyright © The Dial Press, Inc., 1968, 1969
Copyright © A. J. P. Taylor, 1968

This edition published 1969 by
Book Club Associates, 9 Grape Street, London W.C.2,
by arrangement with Allen Lane The Penguin Press

SBN 7139 0091 1

Printed by Cox & Wyman Ltd,
London, Fakenham and Reading

Contents

Contributors

A. J. P. TAYLOR has been a Fellow of Magdalen College, Oxford, from 1938 to the present. His books include *English History 1914–45*, *The First World War*, *The Trouble Makers*, and *The Origins of the Second World War*. He is a frequent contributor to the *Observer*, the *New York Review of Books*, and the *Sunday Express*. Now in charge of the Beaverbrook Library, he is at work on a life of Lord Beaverbrook.

ROBERT RHODES JAMES was born in 1934 and is a Fellow of All Souls College, Oxford. From 1955 to 1964 he was a senior official of the House of Commons. He is the author of *Lord Randolph Churchill* (1959), *Rosebery* (1963), and *Gallipoli* (1965).

J. H. PLUMB, a Fellow of the British Academy and Professor of Modern English History at Cambridge, has published works on a wide range of subjects – including the Italian Renaissance, England in the seventeenth and eighteenth centuries, and the American Revolution – and has contributed to many periodicals in England and America. His major work is a multi-volume life of Sir Robert Walpole, and he is also the general editor of a thirty-volume *History of Human Society*.

BASIL LIDDELL HART was born in 1895 and educated at St Paul's School and Corpus Christi College, Cambridge, where he took the honours course in history. He served on the Western Front in the First World War, and his illustrious career as a contributor to and recorder of modern warfare includes: evolution of the Battle Drill system in 1917; the 'expanding torrent' method of attack that became the basis of the *Blitzkrieg* technique; a role in the modernization of the British Army as consultant to the War Ministry in the twenties and thirties; early advocacy of air power, armoured forces, and amphibious strategy, and authorship of more than thirty books, translated into over two dozen languages. Described as 'the greatest military thinker of the twentieth century', he was knighted in 1966.

ANTHONY STORR was born in 1920 and educated at Winchester and Christ's College, Cambridge. He qualified as a doctor in 1944 and subsequently specialized in psychiatry. He is now in practice as a psychotherapist, reviews regularly for the *Sunday Times*, and has published three books: *The Integrity of the Personality*, *Sexual Deviation*, and *Human Aggression*.

A. J. P. Taylor THE
STATESMAN

Winston Churchill was the subject of much criticism and unpopularity in the course of his long political career. He was dismissed as an adventurer and accused of irresponsibility. Yet he claimed to be a far-sighted statesman of wide views, surveying every problem in detachment, and in time this claim seemed justified by the record. From the beginning, Churchill was a statesman rather than a politician. Most men enter political life at a modest level and grow into statesmanship as they advance. Churchill entered politics at the top. His father had been Chancellor of the Exchequer and was largely responsible for giving the Conservative party a more democratic character. Churchill himself at once moved in the society of Cabinet ministers or of those who were soon to become Cabinet ministers. He became a minister when he was thirty-one and entered the Cabinet when he was thirty-three. He was never a back-bencher in the conventional sense, still less an obedient member of a political party. Essentially he stood alone: neither Tory nor Liberal, aristocrat nor democrat, simply Winston Churchill the statesman. He could be praised as wise, or abused as wrong-headed, but there was no mistaking him.

Churchill was mainly self-educated, and the theme of his education was statesmanship. He read Gibbon, Macaulay, and other great historians, partly in order to emulate their methods, but more to discover how the lessons of the past could be applied to the present. His biographer has described how he worked through old volumes of the *Annual Register*, reading the accounts of Parliamentary debates and noting what he himself would have said on each topic. Later he did much the same in practice. He rarely came to a political dispute with a background of personal experience. His mind was usually virgin soil, and he studied each problem afresh almost in an academic way. He was never content until he had produced a formidable state paper, surveying every aspect of the problem, and his speeches were also exercises in statecraft. He published his first volume of speeches before he was thirty, and by the end of his life eighteen volumes of his speeches stood on the shelves, a record equalled by no other political figure.

His practical knowledge was limited. He had served as a young officer in India and as a war correspondent in the Sudan and South Africa. He often visited the United States. He knew nothing of England beyond the society of political London and the great aristocratic houses. The life of ordinary Englishmen was beyond his ken, until he studied it from outside as the head of some government department. He approached social problems with extreme benevolence, but always with an air of gracious giving. He wished to remove poverty and injustice, not to achieve any fundamental change, and claimed rightly to be at heart a conservative even in his most radical days. His deepest devotion was to England, as she had matured through the ages, and, though it would be unfair to call him a Little Englander, he was never an Imperialist in the ordinary sense. Perhaps Great Englander would be the right term. In his view the British Empire was another form of the benevolence which he sought to practise at home in social affairs. Far from being a source of profit to be exploited, Churchill's Empire was simply the white man's burden – a responsibility imposed by conscience on a great power. Similarly, he did not regard the Dominions as equals, and he saw the Commonwealth (a word he detested) as a family of children, loyally sustaining the venerable mother to whom they owed so much.

Despite the seeming rationality with which his state papers were composed, Churchill was strongly swayed by emotions – usually generous, sometimes the reverse. He responded eagerly to the call of patriotism in the drum-and-trumpet spirit, which coloured his writing of history. He appreciated both the romance of war and its horrors. He believed in concessions from strength, not from weakness. When he was powerful, his benevolence brimmed over. When challenged – either at home or by foreign enemies – he sought total victory first and advocated conciliation only when victory had been won. This was the attitude he adopted in two World Wars, in the Boer War, and in the Irish troubles also. He had the same attitude towards the

British workers: social reforms if they were well-behaved and stern action against them if they dared to strike. He characterized his outlook in an inscription which he devised for a war memorial after the First World War: 'In war, Resolution. In defeat, Defiance. In victory, Magnanimity. In peace, Goodwill.' The inscription was not used, but Churchill set it on the title-page of the six volumes which he wrote after the Second World War.

Churchill was always anxious to learn from expert authorities. In his early days as a minister, he consulted Sidney and Beatrice Webb on social reform. During both World Wars, he turned to scientists as few modern statesmen have done. Tanks were inspired by him in the First World War, and innumerable inventions, culminating in the atomic bomb, were promoted by him in the Second. If he had an intellectual weakness, it was an inability to understand economics. He remained at heart a believer in *laissez-faire* and Free Trade. He could understand social reform, but not socialism. His deeper weakness was impatience, particularly in his earlier years. When he was set on a course, he wanted results at once and was angered by the dead weight of habit. He expected everyone to move at the same rate as himself and, knowing his inner consistency, was not worried by the charges of inconsistency which his impulses towards new enthusiasms often provoked. To others, therefore, he often seemed irresponsible, a reputation which clung to him, not altogether undeservedly, all his life. He combined to the end mature wisdom and boyish zest, a mixture which did not always work out for the best.

The beginnings of Churchill's political career at once showed his unusual qualities. He entered Parliament during the Boer War, with the special distinction of having escaped from Boer captivity. He was something of a war hero. Yet, far from breathing fire, he urged that the defeated Boers be treated with generosity – much to the annoyance of the Conservatives who had elected him. Next, though a former officer in the Army, he went on to criticize the Army estimates and declared that the Royal Navy was Great Britain's sure defence. This was the attitude of an isolationist, even of a Little Englander, not of an imperialist, and he swung still further away from imperialism when he championed Free Trade against Joseph Chamberlain's campaign for Tariff Reform. In 1903 he abandoned the Conservatives and became not merely a Liberal, but a Radical, the close associate of Lloyd George. There was an intellectual consistency in this development, but it was characteristic of Churchill that he had carried it to extremes.

It was also characteristic of Churchill that his Radicalism was self-made. It owed little to the teachings of others, except perhaps for some echoes from his dead father, who had called himself a Tory Democrat. The mainspring of Churchill's Radicalism was generosity: a dislike of Tariff Reform as selfish, and a warm-hearted desire to benefit the poor and distressed. At the Colonial Office, he played a large part in granting responsible government to the Boers and therewith established a friendship with Smuts which lasted for half a century. He imagined that, with this gesture, all bitterness left from the Boer War was dispelled. Later developments were to show that the defeated neither forgave nor forgot so easily.

In 1908 he entered the Cabinet, as a protagonist of social reform. Though he complained that Lloyd George had stolen all the plums, in fact he found plenty to do. In particular the Labour Exchanges which he promoted were a substantial step in aid for the unemployed. But the difference between Churchill's Radicalism and the deeper Radicalism of Lloyd George was already showing. Churchill was merely lessening the edge of economic harshness; Lloyd George aimed at a welfare state which would transform society. The difference was shown even more clearly during an outbreak of large-scale strikes during 1911 and 1912. Lloyd George became the principal conciliator in the Liberal Government and repeatedly made the employers give way. Churchill went into battle against the strikers, reinforcing law and order with the use of troops, and insisting that no concessions should be made until the strikers returned to work. By 1912 Churchill's earlier Radical reputation was dispelled so far as the industrial workers were concerned, and it was never fully restored later, despite his national leadership during the Second World War. Anyone who is puzzled over

Churchill's electoral defeat in 1945 will find much of the explanation in the industrial disputes more than thirty years before.

Churchill's dealings with the advocates of votes for women
showed the same combination of generosity and anger on a
smaller scale. Churchill supported women's franchise with some
enthusiasm, so long as he supplied the enthusiasm. But when
the militant suffragettes began their campaign of violence and
direct action, Churchill was their principal target, and he responded by defying them. Admittedly, there was a peculiarly
feminine logic in a movement which directed its main onslaught
against the supporters of woman suffrage, not against its
opponents. But Churchill's combativeness was easily aroused.
As usual, he was ready to make concessions only from strength.
Threats – and he received many from the suffragettes – were to
him a reason for making no concessions at all. Once provoked,
he provoked others in return, and his wiser impulses were
eclipsed by his pugnacity.

It was in his attitude towards Germany that the Radical
Churchill showed the greatest fluctuations. Churchill was not
anti-German in feeling or policy, as some Englishmen were
becoming at this time. Confident in the overwhelming strength
of the Royal Navy, he wanted to keep clear of foreign entanglements and regarded all countries, including Germany, with the
same aloof benevolence. When the alarm of German naval
building was raised in 1909, Churchill was Lloyd George's chief
ally in refusing to be scared. He opposed the alarm on two
grounds. First, he asserted that the Germans were as pacific as
other nations. Secondly, he claimed, on the basis of technical
advice, that Great Britain could always outbuild any foreign
rival. Churchill sang a different tune when he himself took
charge of the Royal Navy at the end of 1911. Then he became
the advocate of a great ship-building programme and by 1914
was himself locked in conflict with Lloyd George. Again he
could claim to be consistent. He had always been determined
that the Royal Navy should remain supreme and, once convinced that the Germans were challenging this supremacy, he
defied them. This consistency was less convincing to his former

Radical allies. Yet Churchill still held that the naval race was simply due to mutual misunderstanding and believed in 1914 that it could be ended if he had a friendly personal talk with Tirpitz, the head of the German Navy.

One other problem sent Churchill into battle in the years just before the First World War. This was Ireland. Churchill was not an eager Home Ruler by background. Indeed his father had been almost the first to evoke the resistance of Ulster. But when Ulster sought to prevent Home Rule and threatened to rebel against the British Government, Churchill again took up the challenge. He prepared to send ships to Belfast in the hope of overawing Ulster and he also perhaps encouraged the sending of troops. The Unionists accused him of planning a 'pogrom', a charge still disputed by historians. The truth will never be fully known, but it seemed at any rate that Churchill was again answering threats from others by threats and strength of his own.

All these questions were eclipsed by the outbreak of war. Churchill flung himself into combat, whatever his reserves had been before war came. When the generals failed to help the Belgians at Antwerp, Churchill went there himself at the head of a few thousand marines and even asked to be given military command. His sortie was unsuccessful. His impulsiveness had been demonstrated once again. A greater demonstration was to come, the central episode, as it proved, of Churchill's earlier career. Despite a new-found devotion to the French as allies, Churchill doubted whether the war could be won on the Western front, once deadlock had been reached after the battle of the Marne. Where other ministers were barren of strategical ideas, Churchill did not hesitate to give a lead. He sought a back door into Germany and found it at the Dardanelles. An expedition to force the Straits and take Constantinople had every appeal for Churchill. It would rest on British sea power; it was an idea both unexpected and highly ingenious; if successful, it would bring victory without great casualties. The Dardanelles affair showed Churchill at his best and worst. He pressed it relentlessly on the admirals and his ministerial colleagues. He stood forth with the courage and determination of a true leader. Though others acquiesced and some even welcomed the campaign,

Churchill never denied that he was its chief originator, nor would it have gone on so long without his persistence. When it failed, he complained that others had not matched his drive and intensity.

Some of the failure must be attributed to Churchill himself. It was a rush job from first to last. Once Churchill took up the idea, he exaggerated both the ease with which it could be carried through and the rewards which it would bring. There was no inquiry into the means available. Churchill merely assumed that battleships could force the Straits unaided. When this failed, he assumed that there was a powerful army available for Gallipoli and assumed also that this inhospitable peninsula presented no formidable military obstacles. Beyond this, he assumed also that the fall of Constantinople would inflict a mortal blow on Germany. All these assumptions were wrong. The Navy failed. The Army failed. Even if they had succeeded, it is difficult to see what they would have accomplished. Churchill in fact embarked on a rash gamble and then brushed aside the difficulties without consideration. As always with Churchill, when he wanted something, he was convinced that he could have it, and he convinced others also. Those who succumbed to his promptings bore their share of responsibility, but it is not surprising that they shifted the blame on to Churchill once the campaign failed. He on his side did not shrink from responsibility. If anything, he grasped at it impatiently and too readily.

Failure at Gallipoli ruined Churchill for the duration of the First World War and saddled him with a reputation for hasty, though brilliant, improvisations. He left office and served on the Western front. When he again became a minister, it was as one of Lloyd George's subordinates, not as a leader of policy and an inspirer of strategy. Only when the war ended did he rise again to the rank of statesman. Though he had acquiesced in Lloyd George's policy of the 'knock-out blow', he was among the first to preach reconciliation with Germany as soon as she had been defeated. He was eager to send food for the hungry German people. He opposed the idea of collecting reparations for many years to come. He urged that Germany be admitted without delay into the League of Nations. With him, generosity followed hard on victory. As usual, also, he underrated the speed with which most men could change from one mood to the other.

It was, however, a different question which brought Churchill once more into prominence and notoriety. In the past, he had been friendly towards Russia, believing, as his father had done, that she should control Constantinople and the Straits. During the war he responded warmly to the somewhat tattered romance of Holy Russia and her tsar. He was the more indignant when the Bolshevik revolution overthrew these traditions. Again he had a romantic vision, this time one of horror and repugnance. He was convinced that the Bolsheviks aimed at the destruction of European civilization and imagined that somewhere millions of patriotic loyal Russians were longing for release. He sent military aid to the White counter-revolutionaries and favoured intervention on the largest scale. What really provoked him in the Bolsheviks was their rejection of the values in which he believed. They dared to repudiate the legacy of past centuries. Therefore, they must be crushed by force. Once roused, he attributed to the Bolsheviks the most evil and far-reaching designs. He soon extended the same attitude to events at home and saw in every industrial dispute the hidden hand of Moscow. With Churchill there was never a half-way house and, since the Bolsheviks were clearly not friendly, he treated them as implacable enemies.

Churchill still showed many Radical impulses and strokes of generosity. He sympathized for instance with the anxiety of the soldiers to return home and imposed haste in demobilization on a lethargic War Office. He advocated a 'capital levy' to diminish the fortunes made by profiteering during the war. In 1921, he worked closely with Lloyd George in reaching an agreement with Sinn Fein and himself established a warm friendship with Michael Collins – another example of how with Churchill yesterday's enemy became the friend of today. More often, however, his Radicalism was overshadowed by a pugnacious determination to maintain the greatness of the British Empire. He intervened constantly in foreign affairs, much to the annoyance of Lord Curzon, the Foreign Secretary, and he cared little for Lloyd George's strivings for general appeasement, particularly when these were extended even to Soviet Russia.

He set up a new sphere of influence for Great Britain and himself in the Middle East. This originated partly in the accident which made him Colonial Secretary, responsible particularly for Palestine and Mesopotamia. It also had deeper roots. Imperial power extending from Gibraltar to the Persian Gulf was another version of the policy which had produced the attempt on the Dardanelles. It rested on the Royal Navy and on a great military base in Egypt, and it implied an indifference to European affairs, which Churchill had often felt. The war against Germany had been for him an almost irrelevant distraction; a war to be fought and then forgotten. Imperial greatness was the enduring reality. Churchill's efforts established Great Britain as the predominant power in the Middle East, at any rate until the end of the Second World War. In Palestine, he was more nearly successful in reconciling Jews and Arabs than any other British statesman proved to be. Sustained by T.E. Lawrence, he won the friendship of the Arab rulers in Iraq and Transjordan. He sought reconciliation with the new national Turkey, led by Kemal Pasha – another former enemy whom he wished to turn into a friend. Churchill's old desire to give Constantinople to Russia was now forgotten. The Turks became in his eyes the guardians of civilization against the Bolsheviks.

The Turkish problem ended with a curiously Churchillian twist. Lloyd George wished to support the Greeks against the Turks. Churchill opposed this policy to the utmost of his endeavour. In 1922 the Greek Army was routed. The victorious Turks advanced to the Straits and threatened the British garrison there. Lloyd George was ready to fight, and the prospect of fighting captivated Churchill also, even in a war which he thought mistaken. Or maybe the Turks, by threatening instead of pleading, temporarily forfeited, like others, their claim on his generosity. At any rate, in this Chanak crisis, as it was called, Churchill once more became a warmonger in appearance. The British people were weary of war. They refused to support Lloyd George. The Conservative party turned against him, and he fell from power for ever. Churchill fell with him.

Thus ended the first epoch of Churchill's life as a statesman. He had held high office, with a two-year interruption, from 1905 to 1922, a record surpassed only by Lloyd George himself. He had been Home Secretary, First Lord of the Admiralty, Minister of Munitions, Secretary for War, and Colonial Secretary. He had been second only to Lloyd George in inaugurating social welfare. He had reformed the prisons. He had prepared the Royal Navy for its victories in the war. He had initiated a brilliant, though unsuccessful, stroke of strategy at the Dardanelles. He had established a new British Empire in the Middle East. These were only his more official achievements. He had also contributed to the pacification of Ireland. He had set out broad principles of foreign policy, particularly in regard to Germany and Soviet Russia. If a statesman be judged by the breadth of his interests and by the weight of his public utterances, Churchill should have stood in the front rank. Instead, his reputation was low. In 1922 only Lloyd George was more distrusted as a statesman, and Churchill's defeat at the general election was almost universally applauded by men of all parties.

For Churchill, despite his great qualities, lacked one gift essential to a statesman: he did not know how to put himself across. He had no intimate political friends except Birkenhead, Lloyd George, and perhaps Beaverbrook – men as erratic and as much distrusted as himself. He never understood how his readiness to give a lead and to pronounce on every subject irritated his colleagues. Curzon, for instance, complained of his trespassing into foreign affairs. Both Asquith and Lloyd George remarked that Churchill behaved as though he were Prime Minister. Bonar Law put it more bluntly. When asked whether he would rather have Churchill for or against him, he replied: 'Against, every time.' Again, Churchill never considered party or the need to conciliate his supporters. He regarded party as an instrument for putting him into office, not as an association which he should serve. He had left the Conservatives for the Liberals and was soon to become a Conservative again. Essentially he was always an Independent Constitutionalist, the description which he gave himself between 1922 and 1924.

He had no doubt of his own consistency. He was always ambitious to serve the greatness of the British Empire and to promote the principles of democracy and ordered freedom. The consistency was less obvious to others. He had been friendly to the workers and hostile to the trade unions; against great naval expenditure and then for it; friendly to Germany, hostile to her, and then friendly again; hostile to Turkey, and then friendly. He had denounced the House of Lords and was soon to champion its remaining privileges. He had supported votes for women and was soon to oppose a further extension of female suffrage. By 1922 anti-Bolshevism was the only cause to which he seemed indissolubly wedded, and even this did not last for ever. His record was blotted by impulsive acts of folly or bad temper: Tonypandy, where he was accused of sending troops against strikers; Sidney Street, where he directed an attack on a probably mythical anarchist; Antwerp; and worst of all, Gallipoli. The blame was often undeserved: certainly at Tonypandy, where he actually held the troops back; perhaps at Gallipoli. But the record stuck. He had become, in the popular view, a man who could never resist a fight. This was true. Churchill had almost an excess of courage. Certainly he had more courage than calculation. Also, he was easily roused by opposition. In Beaverbrook's words: 'Churchill on the top of the wave has in him the stuff of which tyrants are made.'

Here again, Churchill never understood the effect which he had on others. Though he fought with passionate intensity, it was always with good feeling, often almost in fun. When he argued persistently, he expected others to answer with equal persistence. Thus he blamed Asquith and Kitchener for acquiescing in the Gallipoli expedition if they did not really believe in it. Then as later he did not allow for the fact that men might agree with him merely in order to end the argument. Similarly, when Churchill knocked a man down, this was a preliminary to picking him up and treating him with generosity. The Boers, the Germans, the Irish, the trade unions were expected to forget in the twinkling of an eye the violence which Churchill had levelled against them. Hardship and failure were gradually to impose on Churchill greater patience and moderation. At heart he never learned wisdom, at any rate not the wisdom of the serpent.

Churchill was left high and dry by Lloyd George's fall and his own. His attempt to rattle the anti-Bolshevik drum produced little response. He had no principle tying him to the Liberal party except Free Trade and therefore easily returned to the Conservatives in 1924 when they renounced Protection. He was now the humble suitor of Stanley Baldwin, the man who had overthrown the Lloyd George Government. Churchill became Chancellor of the Exchequer. He did not distinguish himself in the conduct of Great Britain's financial affairs. His most substantial step was to carry through the return to the gold standard at the pre-war parity in 1925. This is often held to have had a disastrous effect on Great Britain's economic position, though perhaps its influence has been exaggerated. Churchill did not grasp the economic arguments one way or the other. What determined him was again a romantic devotion to British greatness. The pound would once more 'look the dollar in the face'; the days of Queen Victoria would be restored. Apart from this stroke, Churchill's conduct of finance produced many ingenious and somewhat irresponsible expedients – a series, one might say, of minor, though in this case relatively harmless, Gallipolis.

Churchill did not, however, confine himself to budgets and the details of finance. Once more, he ranged over every field as though he were Prime Minister. In foreign affairs he had again become an isolationist. Now that the war was won, Great Britain, he believed, should wash her hands of European affairs and rest secure on the Royal Navy. He made permanent the instruction to the service chiefs that they need not plan for a major war in the next ten years. He was thus mainly responsible for the extensive British disarmament which he was later to denounce bitterly. He opposed the guarantee of the Franco-German frontier which Austen Chamberlain gave by the treaty of Locarno. Churchill sympathized, in benevolent detachment, with the aggrieved and discontented countries – so long as they did not challenge British interests. He admired Mussolini, both as a patriot and as the supposed saviour of Italy from Bolshevism. A little later, he declared his hope that, if the British people were ever defeated in war, they would find a revivalist leader of the stature of Hitler. He dismissed the League of Nations as a useless and undesirable barrier against national independence and patriotic wars. In short, his foreign outlook was a compound of romantic enthusiasms, far removed from the general disillusionment of the post-war period.

In home affairs Churchill was equally romantic and equally combative. The question of the coal industry overshadowed all others. As the industry declined, the owners tried to save them-selves by demanding lower wages and longer hours. The mine-workers resisted. Churchill sympathized with the miners. He believed that they had been badly treated both by successive governments and by the owners. But once the miners fought back, Churchill's sympathy was forfeit, and still more so when the other unions prepared a general strike in their support. The general strike itself appeared to Churchill as his finest hour. Where Baldwin sought conciliation and compromise, Churchill strove to transform the general strike into civil war. He referred to the workers as 'the enemy', brought armed troops into the streets of London, and wished to make the unions illegal. It was the old pattern: a romantic charge into battle against the imagi-nary enemy of Bolshevism. Fortunately, neither Baldwin nor the trade union leaders were inclined to mount the barricades. The general strike passed over without grave social disturbance, and Baldwin did his best to restore good feeling. Churchill for his part had completed the estrangement between himself and the industrial workers, who were after all a substantial part of the British people.

Throughout the five years of the Conservative Government, from 1924 to 1929, there was a running undercurrent of conflict between Baldwin and Churchill. Baldwin wanted to win over the working class and to make the Labour party fully at home in the constitutional courses as a preliminary to crushing them. Churchill wanted to treat Labour as an irreconcilable enemy. Again, it was a question of fight first and conciliate, perhaps, afterwards. As in other matters, the British people were in no mood for a fight. The one cause which might have injected some passion into politics was Protection. But Churchill was debarred from using this weapon against Baldwin by his own belief in

Free Trade. He sought some other topic which might shatter the complacent calm of the Baldwin era.

He believed that he had found this topic of controversy in India. All parties were committed to a policy of gradual concession towards India which would culminate in the grant of Dominion status. The only dispute, it seemed, was over the rate at which to go. Churchill himself had been for conciliation so long as it was a matter of generosity, resting on strength. When the Indian nationalists, led by Gandhi, began to practise non-violent resistance and actually to defy the British Raj, Churchill took up the challenge. He remembered the India of his youth and looked with romantic admiration on the Indian princes. India became Churchill's obsession. On this issue, he broke with Baldwin, abandoned his high position in the Conservative party, and went into solitary opposition. This was a period of grave crisis. The world was ravaged by the Great Depression. There were nearly three million unemployed in Great Britain. In 1931 a National Government was formed to save the pound and instead was forced to abandon the gold standard. Abroad, the security established after the First World War crumbled. Hitler and the Nazis were marching to victory in Germany. Meanwhile, Churchill, who had often shown himself a statesman of great wisdom, could only reiterate his devotion to the Indian princes and his opposition to all constitutional concession. This was romantic loyalty perhaps of a Jacobite kind, but not one likely to win a response from the British people.

It has puzzled later observers that Churchill was disregarded when dangers and difficulties accumulated for Great Britain. Baldwin and Ramsay MacDonald, the two leaders of the day, have been blamed for their sloth and blindness, and the British people have been blamed as well. These charges have some justification. But the fault lay also with Churchill himself. He lost all hold on British opinion by his intemperate opposition over India. The British people would not respond to the romantic call of Imperial glory. Rightly or wrongly, they were committed to the cause of constitutional concession, and Churchill's resistance seemed to them irrelevant obscurantism. He was the more diminished because on the great economic questions of the moment he had nothing to say. He remained silent during the interminable debates over unemployment, Protection, and economic recovery. This was in striking contrast to Lloyd George, who, although equally isolated, produced a rich stock of creative ideas.

Churchill was drawn back to foreign affairs almost as a side issue, an interruption in his Indian campaign. Soon after the First World War, he laid down the principle: 'The redress of the grievances of the vanquished should precede the disarmament of the victors.' Hence, he had urged this redress during the 1920s. Instead the Disarmament Conference opened in 1932, with Germany still aggrieved. In practical terms, France was being asked to disarm and to accept a permanent inferiority as against Germany. The British Government continued to press this policy on France, even when Hitler came to power with the avowed aim of making Germany again the greatest power in Europe. Once more, Churchill stood almost alone in opposing disarmament and all that went with it. In particular, he sounded the alarm at the increase of the German Air Force and called for a large increase in the Royal Air Force, just as he had advocated a great increase of the Royal Navy before 1914.

Churchill was again on an unpopular path. His alarm at the German Air Force had some foundation, though his actual figures were exaggerated – as the similar figures about the German Navy had been exaggerated before 1914. Then British public opinion had been ready to maintain naval supremacy at all costs. Now public opinion tended to regard great armaments – even their own – as a cause of war. Churchill imagined that both British and French would respond to the call of greatness as they had done in the past. As always, it was difficult for him to grasp that others, apart from a few despised figures, were not as courageous and combative as himself. In the eyes of most people, Churchill's outlook seemed to be purely negative: a mere maintenance of the armed supremacy which had followed the First World War. The moral climate of the time had turned, however mistakenly, against the old ideas of the balance of power and Imperial greatness. If Germany had to be opposed, it had to be in the name of supposedly higher causes.

These causes existed. The one which had most appeal to men of moderate opinion was the League of Nations and its off-spring, collective security. States, it was believed, should settle their disputes peacefully through the League of Nations, and the pacific countries should somehow stand together against aggression. Churchill, too, supported collective resistance to the aggressor, but not when it was presented in the Wilsonian phrases of the League of Nations. Hence he remained aloof when the Japanese invaded Manchuria. In 1935 the League was put to its great test. Italy attacked Abyssinia, and the League attempted to assert collective security by imposing economic sanctions against the aggressor, who happened conveniently to be also Fascist. Churchill was less concerned about democracy abroad and, in the last resort, preferred Fascism to Bolshevism. He remained silent throughout the Abyssinian crisis from a reluctance to commit himself one way or the other. He admired Mussolini; he wanted to enlist Mussolini's aid against Hitler; he disliked the paraphernalia of the League of Nations.

The British Government seemed to betray the League by endorsing the Hoare–Laval plan, which gave Mussolini most of what he wanted. British opinion was roused. There was perhaps a brief chance of overthrowing Baldwin. Churchill was not there to take it. The crisis passed. Mussolini marched on to triumph. The prestige of the League was irremediably destroyed.

A new opportunity offered in March 1936 when Hitler re-occupied the Rhineland. This time, Churchill took it. He had never felt for Hitler the sympathy which he felt for Mussolini. He was now indignant that Hitler, as he supposed, was daring to threaten British security in the air; and if others were indignant with Hitler for other reasons – as that he had destroyed the trade unions or persecuted the Socialists and the Jews – he was prepared to share these indignations also. Now faced with terri-ble dangers, he was even prepared to espouse belatedly the principles of collective security. Arms and the Covenant became his cry. He seemed to be at last in tune with a broad current of public opinion. He was recapturing popularity and support such as he had not enjoyed for many years. Churchill won this position only to throw it away by a new gesture of romantic enthusiasm, and the great issues of foreign policy were temporarily dwarfed in Churchill's mind by the marital troubles of King Edward VIII.

There was little element of statesmanship in Churchill's championing of the King's cause. If, as has been suggested, he calculated that Baldwin could be defeated on this question, he showed himself lacking in statecraft or at any rate in political judgement. British opinion, so far as it can be assessed, was decisively against the King. Even now, when standards have changed, it is difficult to understand how anyone could expect Edward VIII to plan marriage with a woman who was still married to someone else and yet retain his throne. Churchill was beyond all such calculations. Though he had no long-standing ties with the King or personal obligations, he could not resist the appeal of romantic loyalty. Churchill flung himself into battle on the King's side and continued to fight even when the King himself had given up the day as lost. There are some occasions when the wise course for a statesman is to remain silent. This was not in Churchill's nature. In December 1936 when Edward VIII abdicated, Baldwin was triumphant. Churchill was again solitary and discredited.

Churchill did not recover easily from this failure. During 1937 he believed that opportunity had passed him by. He believed also that the period of danger was almost over. British rearmament was now beginning to develop, though more slowly than Churchill wanted. Once Great Britain had restored equality, or something near it, in the air, she would be again secure and could once more offer Germany concessions from strength – the policy which Churchill had always advocated. For Churchill, too, favoured appeasement, once it did not spring from weakness. He, too, believed that there was no irremediable cause of war and that war, if it came, would be, as he in fact called it, 'unnecessary'. There was a further reason for Churchill's relative silence. The overriding issue in foreign affairs between 1936 and 1938 was the civil war in Spain, where the Left-wing Republican Government was contending with a Nationalist rebellion, led by Franco and massively supported by two Fascist powers, Italy and Germany.

Here was the great conflict between democracy and Fascism, or so it seemed to many idealists in Great Britain. Churchill could not take sides. Emotionally he sympathized with the Nationalists against the Reds. On the other hand, he did not want to see an extension of German power. He accepted the policy of non-intervention put forward by the British Government and continued to support it when it was openly disregarded by the Fascist powers. He even implied, against the facts, that Soviet Russia was cheating more grossly on the Republican side. Only in 1939, when all was over, did he belatedly acknowledge that the Republic, with all its faults, had been the cause of freedom. Franco's victory did not in fact have the evil consequences predicted for it, at any rate so far as British interests were concerned. Nevertheless, Churchill had failed to become the champion of democracy against Fascism, as many British people wanted.

All this was eclipsed when Hitler began his march to European domination in 1938, first with the annexation of Austria and then with the virtual destruction of Czechoslovakia. Earlier Churchill had concentrated on rearmament. Now he began to propound policy. He assumed that Great Britain, with an overwhelmingly powerful navy and an increasing air force, was herself secure. Therefore she should take the lead in setting up a coalition against the aggressor. Behind this assertion was a series of assumptions which were less clearly stated. Great Britain's contribution, apart from the moral example, would be naval blockade and perhaps aerial bombardment of Germany. She would not be expected to provide a large land-army, the great mistake, in Churchill's eyes, of the First World War. Churchill's central assumption was that others were eagerly waiting to be led. France, Russia, and all the states of east-central Europe would merge their armed forces in a great coalition as soon as they were invited to do so. As a final assumption, Churchill was sure that this coalition would be easily victorious against Germany or, more probably, would deter her without fighting at all. Once this supremacy was acknowledged, concessions to Germany would follow, and she would be welcomed back into the happy European family.

Churchill was again believing what he wanted to believe, and not on the basis of much knowledge. There were some elements in France which favoured resistance, though they were to show themselves singularly ineffective, and the French Army was no more than a defensive weapon, despite its glamorous appearance. Soviet Russia, once the centre of international revolution, had become, in Churchill's opinion, both peaceful and co-operative, simply because it was necessary for the Grand Alliance that she should be so. Many others in England held a similar view about Russia, people who not long before had been denounced by Churchill as the dupes or agents of Communist tyranny. Now he forgot 'the baboonery of Bolshevism' in his anxiety for Russian aid.

There was abundant evidence that the rulers of Soviet Russia were alert to the danger from Germany, but this did not make them eager to bring the danger down on their own heads, still less to engage in war for the sake of the distrusted capitalist powers, Great Britain and France. As to the lesser states who were to be enlisted, their behaviour was witness enough that each hoped to pass the burden on to his neighbour. Churchill sometimes recognized this and spoke sternly of refusing to aid those who on their side refused to co-operate. Since the aid was offered for reasons of practical strategy, and not from altruism, the threat was empty. Churchill seems also to have believed that every associate, however small, brought an addition of strength. The experience of the First World War had already shown that small states were usually a burden, not an asset, and the experience of the Second War was to confirm this, though the burden was often inevitable.

The essence of Churchill's policy was a defensive alliance of the contented powers. He reinforced it with an appeal to the great ideals of freedom and justice, thus assuming against the evidence that all the non-aggressive powers enjoyed something like the blessings of the British Constitution. The democracy which he professed was in practice not much more than a preservation of things as they were, and freedom meant similarly the preservation of sovereign independence by each state. Churchill had no vision of a new Europe, still less of a new world. He wanted to get back to the old one. Even Germany was not to be weakened or destroyed. Once the German people had tamed their dictator or shaken him off, they would settle down in happy harmony with the Western Powers, and Europe, thus consolidated, would be again secure from the interference of Soviet Russia.

The strategy which Churchill advocated from the summer of 1938 until the outbreak of war, and indeed after it, was equally traditional. Great Britain had followed it, much to her advantage, throughout the long wars against Bourbon France and Napoleon. The continental powers, with their large armies, had done most of the fighting on land, while Great Britain, controlling the seas, provided economic aid and moral encouragement. This policy had been abandoned during the First World War, when Great Britain had built up an army of continental size and had borne, for a time, the main brunt of land warfare. Churchill had opposed this course, as Gallipoli bore witness, and he did not propose to repeat it now. Even in 1939 he was insisting that a large army was unnecessary and that compulsory military service, which he came to favour, should be adopted in order to impress Great Britain's foreign friends, rather than for any practical purpose.

The Grand Alliance which Churchill envisaged was confined to Europe and was indeed a specifically anti-German combination. He continued to hope that Italy would somehow return to her friends of the First World War, and he was even more confident that Great Britain would remain neutral in the Far East, benevolently sympathizing with both China and Japan. On the other hand, he attached ever-increasing importance to close relations between Great Britain and the United States and himself addressed direct appeals to American opinion. He did not at this time seek an alliance with the United States, perhaps recognizing that it was impossible in the prevailing mood of isolationism. In any case, he thought it unnecessary. He was convinced that the peaceful European countries would more than hold their own against Hitler, particularly if they could draw freely on the United States for raw materials and munitions. The Americans need not fear that they would be involved. They had only to look on the good cause with a friendly eye.

Churchill stressed, indeed exaggerated, Germany's preparations for war and believed mistakenly that everything there was being sacrificed for the sake of armaments. This led him into an equal exaggeration on the other side. Believing as he did that life in Germany was being conducted under almost intolerable strain, he expected that the increased demands of actual war would cause the Nazi system to break down of itself. This misjudgement was shared by many qualified observers. Paradoxically it was the main cause of Churchill's strength. His confidence that victory, though perhaps not easy, was certain in time inspired others, and appeasement seemed to be unnecessary as well as dishonourable. Churchill's arguments mattered less than the tone in which he said them, and his voice ultimately made him, in British eyes, the architect of victory. He was less successful in spreading the same confidence to potential allies across the Channel.

Statesmen have not only to devise a policy. They must also consider how to carry it out. Most of those who wished to oppose Nazi Germany were equally opposed to the Conservative or so-called National Government in Great Britain. They imagined that a change of policy could be brought about only by some sort of Left-wing upheaval. Churchill had no sympathy with this view. His aim was to win over the Conservative members of Parliament, and even the Conservative ministers, not to destroy them. Since the Conservatives had an overwhelming majority in the House of Commons, this was no doubt tactically wise. But it was more than a matter of tactics. Churchill was as much a Conservative as those in power, indeed more so. He wanted to save old England, not to lead a Left-wing revolution. The danger from Hitler united Churchill and his like with the Left, just as it created later an alliance with Soviet Russia. But Churchill intended, once Hitler was defeated, that everything should be put back as it was before, at home and abroad.

The outbreak of war in September 1939 brought Churchill back to office at last, as First Lord of the Admiralty. He became,

without demur, the colleague of men whose policy he had denounced. He did not ask them to repudiate that policy: events
had done it for him. In any case, as always with Churchill, bygones were bygones. Once a situation changed, he forgot or put
aside what had gone before. As a minister, Churchill was welcomed as a symbol of energy rather than of policy. He was expected to provide the dynamism which war needed and which
Chamberlain's government clearly lacked. His pugnacity, previously unwelcome, now sounded a popular note, and he became
the living pledge that the war would not be merely the continu-
ation of peace by other means. Though he tried to be on his best
behaviour after the disappointments of previous years, his
nature was too strong for him. He could not resist ranging over
all the problems of government, and Neville Chamberlain, too,
soon found himself complaining that Churchill behaved as
though he were already Prime Minister.

Much of Churchill's promptings concerned simply a more
energetic conduct of the war, abroad and at home. There were
also two independent contributions to policy, both anticipating
what was to come. Neville Chamberlain regarded the two world
powers, Soviet Russia and the United States, with cool dislike.
Churchill prepared to win them over. He opened a private correspondence with President Roosevelt and established, at any
rate in his own opinion, a close personal friendship. Here again
was his old belief that international relations could be shaped by
individual sentiments and human affection. This belief was
widely shared by Englishmen so far as America was concerned.
Churchill stood more alone in his attitude towards Soviet Russia. The Nazi-Soviet pact and Russia's subsequent neutrality
provoked a general revival of anti-Bolshevism, which extended
even into the Labour party. Churchill, the original anti-
Bolshevik, was now less affected by it. Though he deplored that
Soviet Russia was not an ally, he insisted that she still represented a balance against Hitler and foresaw the time when
Germany and Russia would be enemies. He even applauded the
occupation of Poland's eastern lands by the Red Armies, as
barring Hitler's road to the east. When Churchill wanted something, he assumed that he could have it; and from the beginning

of the Second World War, he assumed that he could ultimately have alliances with Russia and America, even though he did not know how to get them.

Churchill showed the same restraint and concentration when Russia attacked Finland. Most Allied leaders wished to aid Finland, even at the risk of war with Russia – a war which some of them would have welcomed. Churchill had no sympathy with this lunatic project. On the other hand, he could not resist the attraction of a smart stroke, a way round on the Gallipoli model. According to his ingenious plan, the Allied troops, dispatched to aid Finland, would not reach their objective, but would instead wreck the sources of German iron ore in northern Sweden and Norway. It was perhaps fortunate that the Finns made peace with Russia before this idea could be tested against events. The abortive project left a legacy in the shape of a continuing Allied interest in the extreme north, and Churchill welcomed the German invasion of Norway on 8 April. He believed that the Germans were now exposed to British sea power and made prophecies of success more extravagant than any given by Neville Chamberlain. The prophecies were belied. Sea power was ineffective without control of the air. Failure to appreciate this illustrated yet again the curious contradiction in Churchill's nature as a strategist. He had repeatedly emphasized the importance of air power, more so perhaps than any other civilian statesman. Yet when it came to action, he could not resist the call of tradition and romance, and imagined that the Royal Navy could still assert the old supremacy unaided. The mistake of the Norwegian campaign was to be repeated in the Mediterranean, and still more disastrously at Singapore.

The failure in Norway at last provoked revolt among Conservative members of the House of Commons, and on 10 May Churchill found himself Prime Minister at the head of a real National Government. He attained supreme power without intrigue – at any rate on his own part. Moreover, the new Government was as little changed as possible from the old one. There was no proscription of the appeasers and not much reward for their opponents, and the Conservatives still held most of the principal posts, with Chamberlain himself in second place. This

was the sort of National Government which Churchill had always projected, and, though the Left might grumble, any less
Conservative Government would have had difficulty in commanding the support of administrators and businessmen, a
consideration overlooked by those who wanted to make some
sort of Popular Front revolution. There were shifts of political
balance later in the war, usually towards the Left, but Churchill
had ensured his essential principle at the start: there were to be
no political or social changes beyond what the needs of war dictated.

Churchill was supported by men of all parties, and he held
supreme power so long as he enjoyed the national confidence.
All his life had been an unconscious preparation for this hour,
and his qualities as a statesman must be judged principally from
the way in which he discharged his trust during the Second
World War. On the vital point of strategic control, he did better
than Lloyd George in the First World War and probably better
than any national leader except Stalin in the Second. By making
himself Minister of Defence, he established his authority over
the chiefs of staff and thus secured unity of strategic direction,
or something near it. His direction of civil affairs was less sure
and was certainly not exercised through the War Cabinet, a
body which seems to have acted only as an occasional court of
appeal. Ministers and committees were left to do much what
they thought best, with occasional interference or arbitration
from Churchill when things went wrong. None of the advances
in social or financial policy made during the war owed anything
to Churchill except a distant approval.

Churchill also claimed the supreme direction of foreign affairs.
This he attained partly by personal intimacy with Anthony
Eden, who was Foreign Secretary for most of the war, and
partly by going his own way, regardless of expert opinion in the
Foreign Office. Churchill's foreign policy was of his own devising,
a mixture of impulse and matured thought. His influencing of
public opinion was also an odd story. Official organizations,
from the Ministry of Information to the political parties, tried
to take a defined line, and Churchill made guerrilla raids into
publicity by means of radio addresses – addresses at first enor-

mously popular, later both less effective and out of tune with what most people were thinking. Essentially Churchill, despite his radio success, did not like political discussion except in the House of Commons and, to a lesser extent, the newspapers. He believed that ordinary people should get on with their work and rely on him to guard their freedom, just as he believed that other ranks in the services should be content with the position which the Tommies had accepted during his own remote days in the Army. If Churchill had had his way, and he did to a considerable extent, the Second World War would have been conducted in Great Britain by officers and gentlemen, the sluice gates being opened only enough to admit trade union officials also.

Churchill, though somewhat of a tyrant, imposed his will more by discussion than by dictation. He never wearied of argument and would even yield when faced with equal persistence. He has described his method in an engaging phrase: 'All I wanted was compliance with my wishes after reasonable discussion.' It was compliance he wanted all the same, and those who opposed his ideas too persistently paid the penalty. Thus Wavell and Auchinleck in turn forfeited the command in the Middle East for failing to provide an offensive when Churchill needed one. Nor did he tolerate rivals near his political throne. Halifax, the only possible alternative as Prime Minister among the Conservatives, was early deported to Washington as ambassador, and Stafford Cripps, a possible Labour alternative later on, was similarly manoeuvred into obscurity. Churchill treated Eden as a favourite son rather than as a competitor for power, and in this his judgement was correct. The most successful ministers were former civil servants or non-party experts, men accustomed to obey a master.

The one exception was Ernest Bevin, Minister of Labour, whom Churchill treated as a more or less independent power. Bevin had a strong enough personality to insist on this. As well, Churchill for once recognized that soft words were not enough to remove the distrust which his own past actions had caused. Though he never understood the working-class hostility towards him, he realized that it was there, and this made him dependent

on Bevin to some extent. The treatment of labour was an outstanding success in the Second World War. Churchill's contribution was to leave the topic to Bevin.

With these limitations, Churchill held the supreme direction
of British policy. The strategy of the war was his – at any
rate so far as this strategy was determined from the British side.
He also intruded into the detailed operations of war and, when
told that Hitler constantly interfered with his generals, replied:
'I do the same.' Great Britain has never known any such civilian direction of war except perhaps in the case of the elder Pitt.
This was a unique achievement among modern British statesmen. Churchill at once defined British war aims, or rather he
laid down a single aim: the total defeat of Hitler and the undo-
ing of all Germany's conquests. When he came to write his account of the war, he implied that this definition was hardly necessary and that the entire nation was united in pursuing total
victory or, put the other way round, unconditional surrender by
the Germans. It is unlikely that he played such a modest part.
Despite Churchill's assertion that negotiations with Hitler were
never discussed by the War Cabinet, it is now known that Halifax raised the topic on 27 May. In fact Churchill was showing his
usual generosity when he gave the impression that all his associates were as resolute as himself, and his cover for them perhaps
appears less surprising, if it be borne in mind that the weaker
vessels were Conservatives, members of the party which Churchill led.

There are other indications that Churchill's extremism was
not universally shared. Obscure approaches for peace were made
towards Hitler in the summer of 1940, and the Foreign Office
held out against repudiating the Munich settlement until 1942.
In regard to Churchill himself, there can be no doubt. Compromise with Hitler could only have been made under some
other leader. Churchill remarked: 'I have only one aim in life,
the defeat of Hitler, and this makes things very simple for me.'
The remark was not, of course, quite true. He wished to preserve
the independence and greatness of the British Empire so far as
he could and even wished to preserve the existing social structure. But these wishes were firmly subordinated to his main aim.

In this, Churchill probably interpreted aright the spirit of the British people. His popularity rested on many causes: his pre-war advocacy of resistance, his endearing ways, his rhetorical utterances. But it rested most of all on the universal belief that he was the certain guarantee against weakness or compromise and that he would shrink from no sacrifice for the sake of victory. There were those after the war who regretted this firmness and its consequences. Churchill was blamed where he had earlier been praised. The blame was misapplied. Churchill and the British people were at one. 'Victory at all costs' was the programme of all except a few leading politicians and, if the British people paid an excessive price for victory, they did it with their eyes open.

Churchill gave a new resolution to the British. He tried to give the same resolution to the French, as their armies crumbled before the German invaders. In this he was unsuccessful. He could not easily shake off the illusions about French strength which he had held before the war and tended to imagine that a few ringing phrases in counsel would restore French spirits. Like others, he was overwhelmed by events and could not weigh calmly the situation which would follow France's defeat. If he had had his way, British fighter squadrons would have been sent unavailingly to France, and victory in the Battle of Britain would have been jeopardized. Dowding, the head of fighter command, resisted this generous impulse – a resistance which Churchill did not forgive. The fighter squadrons did not go to France. Later attempts to invigorate the French, such as the offer of political union, were not of Churchill's doing.

On the other hand, Churchill exaggerated the eagerness of Frenchmen to resume the war against Hitler after the Franco-German armistice had been made. When De Gaulle came to London, Churchill saw in him the man around whom the French Empire and many Frenchmen at home would rally. His enthusiasm for De Gaulle led him into some wild ventures, of which the expedition to Dakar was the first. Churchill himself lamented later that he had to bear a Cross – the Cross of Lor-raine. Nevertheless his support for De Gaulle remained un-shaken, despite many quarrels, and it followed inevitably from the similarity of their outlooks. De Gaulle, too, represented a cause of traditional greatness and loyalty, without much infusion of modern political ideas. By a curious irony, this cause ultimately triumphed in France, the defeated country, and was rejected in Great Britain, the victor.

Churchill fully accepted responsibility for the attack on the French fleet at Oran, in order to prevent its falling into German hands. The attack has sometimes been presented as a demonstration of British resolve, unfortunately at the expense of an old ally, to continue the war at all costs. The explanation is probably simpler: justified refusal to trust Hitler's word and further refusal, perhaps less justified, to admit that there could be any third course between resistance and surrender. Like most English people, Churchill never appreciated that collaboration with Hitler, however mistaken it turned out, could be advocated for genuinely patriotic reasons – as, after all, it had been in Great Britain until the outbreak of war. Churchill's judgement in such matters was both romantic and innocent. He regarded the British cause as the cause of freedom and national independence all over the world and therefore dismissed those who failed to support it as traitors. He supposed that this view was universally held and that in every country an indignant majority of eager patriots was held down by German agents. Churchill was easily led on from this to exaggerate greatly both the extent of resistance to the Germans and its effectiveness. However, in times of great peril it does no harm if men, even in the highest places, are buoyed up by false hopes.

The British mood in the summer of 1940 was strangely cheerful, and Churchill was cheerful with it. The defeat of the German Air Force, which is known as the Battle of Britain, owed little to Churchill except a generous admiration. He was inspired by this victory and used it to inspire others. For once, he did nothing wrong. Every speech was right. Every emphasis was right. He made people alert and active without making them fearful. Those summer months established Churchill's ultimate popularity. His position did not rest on a belief that he would always be right or that he possessed a superior wisdom. But he had spoken for the nation in a moment of emotional unity. Probably he could have exploited his position more if he had been less emotionally involved. A more calculating statesman would have deliberately engrossed personal power. Churchill tended to assume that the mood of national exaltation would last and that he would always be equally in tune with his fellow countrymen.

There was a more practical side to Churchill's activities in the course of 1940, and this set a clearer test for his statesmanship. Churchill, like the British people, was not content to survive. Even at the moment of greatest danger, he was thinking of ultimate victory. The first plans for victory were actually drawn on 27 May, the very day when the chances of German invasion were also seriously weighed. By the late summer the Germans controlled all the resources of Europe, either directly or indirectly. They had conquered or won over most of the continent up to the Soviet frontier, and Soviet Russia was lavish in supplying them. The German Empire had far greater resources than Great Britain, even if the Dominions were counted in, far greater manpower, and a more secure strategic position. Yet British policy never relapsed into a purely defensive attitude.

In a sense, this followed logically from the refusal to seek a compromise with Hitler. Since it was inconceivable that the war would last for ever, the only alternative to defeat was victory. Churchill himself never lost faith that this victory was not only desirable but possible, and he imposed this faith on the less confident. His faith was in part emotional or even mystical: a stubborn belief in the British Empire and its latent power. If victory did not wait on British arms, Churchill's lifework was meaningless. His faith had also rational grounds. He foresaw that the two neutral powers, Soviet Russia and the United States, would ultimately be drawn into war against Hitler, as Great Britain had been, and he hoped to accelerate the process. Once more, he believed that something would happen because he wanted it to happen, and in this case his belief proved true.

Nevertheless, Churchill misjudged, to some extent, the factors working in Great Britain's favour. Fortified by his own American background and experience, he supposed that nearly all Americans were pro-British and that an Anglo-Saxon alliance was in the making. He never understood that even those Americans who wished to defeat Hitler were not equally anxious to save the British Empire. Again, he overrated the power of personal relations. Having easily developed an emotional attachment to President Roosevelt, he imagined that the President had a similar emotional attachment to him. This was a mistake. Though Roosevelt often used emotion, he was not swayed by it. He needed Great Britain for America's security. Otherwise he remained uninvolved.

Towards Soviet Russia, Churchill had no emotional commitments. He did not suppose that Soviet policy would be determined by anything except practical considerations. On the other hand, he had largely discarded the anti-Soviet prejudices which had earlier dominated his mind and which many Conservatives still held. He did not fear that Nazi Germany and Soviet Russia would develop a genuine co-operation simply because they were both totalitarian states. Such ideological considerations were outside his ken. Nor did he seriously fear at this time that Soviet Russia was anxious to promote international Communism. If anything, he underrated Soviet strength, as most people, including the Soviet leaders, did at the time. Churchill expected that the United States would make the major contribution towards defeating Hitler and that Soviet Russia would provide at best a diversion.

These were refinements of the general assumption that Russia and America would be drawn into the war. There was, however, a further quality in Churchill's thought. He was not content to wait for the two neutral powers. He wanted Great Britain to win on her own and sometimes believed that this could be done. Hence there were two Churchills in the period when Great Britain stood on her own, and these two Churchills continued even when she had great allies. One was the Churchill who worked for the Grand Alliance and held it together. The other Churchill directed a purely British strategy which had little relationship to the alliance.

British strategy for independent victory had two aims. The first was the bombing of Germany. Between the wars many experts had preached that bombing, unaided by land-armies, could

win future wars, and the R.A.F. had been designed specifically
for this purpose. As events proved, it was not well designed. It
had neither the strength nor the equipment with which to
achieve a decisive result. Nevertheless, the pursuit of a bombing
victory went on all through the war, and Churchill did much to
promote it. No doubt the most powerful motive was simply the
lack of any alternative. If the British did not drop bombs on
Germany, there was nothing they could do against her. But it
was also a new version of the insular strategy in which Churchill
had always essentially believed. British industrial power was to
produce the bombers needed for victory, as in earlier times it
had produced the Royal Navy. The Army took second place.
The mass army of the First World War would not be needed.
The British Army would enter the continent only to restore
order when Germany had already collapsed.

Bombing strategy involved a moral judgement for which
Churchill later was sometimes condemned. Originally bombing
was to be directed solely against industrial targets and lines of
communication. This precision proved impossible. Bombing
became indiscriminate, at first by accident and then avowedly.
The object was the destruction of German morale, in other
words the killing of German civilians. The Germans themselves
had a bad record in killing civilians and were not entitled to
raise moral objections on their side. But it caused some disquiet
in British circles which would have liked the war to be conducted in a high-minded way. Churchill himself was often un-
easy, particularly as he did not share Bomber Command's
wholehearted conviction of success. Rulers in other countries –
not only Hitler, but also Stalin, Roosevelt, and later Truman –
were ready to use methods equally destructive and equally bar-
barous. Churchill at least had the redeeming quality of disliking
what he was compelled to do. Though he, too, waged war ruthlessly, he remained a humane man.

Churchill's heart was more deeply committed to the other
aspect of British strategy. This was war in the Mediterranean.
Like much else, it grew up partly by chance. The British and
French navies had co-operated in the Mediterranean when
France was still in the war. The larger part of the Royal Navy

was at Alexandria; another force was at Gibraltar. Since the Germans had few capital ships, these forces were not needed at home. In previous wars, the British had kept the Mediterranean open for their shipping. During the First World War, they had continued to use the Suez Canal as their main route to India and the Far East. But when Italy entered the war and France fell out, the Mediterranean could no longer be used by British ships, and it remained closed until May 1943. British forces, however, remained in Egypt, ostensibly for a negative purpose: they barred Hitler's route to the oil of the Middle East. This was a precaution against an imaginary danger. Hitler's strategy, so far as he had one, was purely continental. If he ever contemplated Middle Eastern oil, he proposed to reach it by means of southern Russia and the Caucasus. His activities in the Mediterranean, such as assistance to Italy and the conquest of Greece, were defensive answers to British attacks, not preparations for an advance of his own.

Egypt as the starting point for a British offensive was indeed Churchill's idea. He was always anxious to renew the strategy which had failed at Gallipoli. With indomitable persistence, he pursued the dream that Turkey could be drawn into the war. Then the combined British and Turkish armies would sweep through the Balkans, picking up other allies on the way. Germany would be defeated from the rear or at least brought to an acceptable compromise. This was a strange fantasy. At one moment, Churchill was insisting that victory would be hard and prolonged even if Russia and America were in the war. At another, he was dreaming that it would be easy if only Turkey – a country without either modern resources or a modern army – became an ally. There is no explaining such a contradiction. Churchill remained himself even in his years of supreme responsibility. In one part of his nature, he was a clear-sighted realist, facing the problems of modern war with precise calculation and long-term preparation. In the other part, he was still a gambler and an impulsive boy, for ever hoping that some ingenious twist would work a miracle after all. Everyone else looked back to Gallipoli as a failure. Churchill remembered it as a short-cut to success.

The Turkish alliance was never achieved for any serious purpose, though Churchill pursued it throughout with unflagging persistence. Instead, the Mediterranean became the field of conflict with Italy. This had not been intended by either Churchill or Mussolini. Mussolini had entered the war only because he thought that it was already won, and he knew that Italy was not equipped for war on any large scale. Churchill had little sympathy with the idea that the war was a general crusade against Fascism and would have tolerated Mussolini just as he tolerated Franco. He wrote later: 'Even when the issue of the war became certain Mussolini would have been welcomed by the Allies.' However, Mussolini was trapped on the German side, first in the hope of victory, later by fear of German might. The British had to fight Italy whether they wanted to or not, and they were in a position to do so. The naval war in the Mediterranean and the war in the desert provided victories which revived the spirit of the British people and helped to restore British prestige in the world. Churchill's own stock rose with each desert victory and sank with each defeat.

Thus Churchill's own inclination and the pressure of events combined to make North Africa the pivot of British strategy. Churchill needed victories for their own sake, in order to maintain his position at home. But he never relinquished his ultimate objective of a Balkan offensive. Even when the Mediterranean campaign extended from North Africa to Italy, the defeat of Italy was a secondary consideration in his mind. Italy was to be simply an alternative starting place for a Balkan advance. In the actual conduct of the campaign, Churchill displayed the mixture of wisdom and rashness which he had always shown. He 'prodded' the British commanders into premature offensives. He encouraged, though he did not alone promote, the rash expedition to Greece, which was supposed to enhance the British name and instead brought humiliating disaster. He counted unthinkingly on the ability of British sea power to hold Crete and shared responsibility for that disaster also.

There were larger prices to pay for Churchill's Mediterranean

obsession. Preparations for a landing on the European continent
had to take second place. This was not unwelcome to Churchill
nor indeed to his military advisers. He steadily opposed a
repetition of the large-scale land combats which had marked
the First World War and remained confident that some other
way could be found of bringing Germany to collapse. Perhaps
bombing would succeed; perhaps a back door would be opened.
If not, maybe economic difficulties or subversion in the occupied
countries would produce the desired result. Europe was not the
only field of operations to be sacrificed. The Far East had also
to be neglected, despite the growing danger from Japan; and
Churchill, who had extolled the glories of the British Raj, in
fact took the decisions which brought down Great Britain's Far
Eastern power. The decisions were no doubt imposed by events,
but Churchill as ever threw himself wholeheartedly into what
lay nearest at hand, particularly when it accorded with his own
inclination. For the sake of North Africa, Churchill had to
gamble that Japan would not enter the war.

This gamble could not be openly stated. Churchill never lost
sight of American friendship as the overriding means of British
salvation. Here he found the right combination. On the one
hand he emphasized Great Britain's determination to go on
with the war. On the other, he hinted that she could not go on,
let alone win, without American aid. It was his aim to get British
and American affairs, in his own phrase, 'somewhat mixed up'.
Roosevelt had the same aim with a different context. He, too,
wanted to keep Great Britain going, but not necessarily to
maintain British greatness. The most important decision of
Churchill's career, and indeed of modern British history, was
made in the early days of 1941. By accepting Lend-Lease, the
British gave up all attempt to maintain their economic independence and looked to America for the resources which would
enable them to continue the war. As Keynes said: 'We threw
good housekeeping to the winds.' Churchill mistook calculation
for generosity in American policy and supposed that the United
States would restore Great Britain to her former position
when the war was over. But once more he had little choice. The
British people were ready to sacrifice the future for the

sake of the present, and Churchill had to make the best of things.

Though Churchill secured Lend-Lease, he failed to draw the United States into the war. Roosevelt was ready to accept Churchill's claim that Great Britain could win on her own and perhaps believed it. Events provided a different ally. On 22 June 1941 Hitler invaded Soviet Russia. The same evening Churchill announced British support for Russia. This, too, was a great decision. It was a repudiation, at any rate until the war was over, of the old British dream that Germany and Russia could be somehow played off against each other. Again the decision was implicit in the line which Churchill had taken ever since the rise of Hitler and again it was imposed upon him in part by the will of the British people. It was a great decision all the same. Originally it meant no more than a readiness to keep Russia going until Great Britain and America were in a position to win the war. But it had to be maintained even when it meant that Soviet Russia would outstrip all European powers, including Great Britain herself.

Most military experts, both British and American, at first expected that Germany would defeat Soviet Russia within a relatively short time. Churchill, and Roosevelt too, were slightly more confident than their advisers – an indication that the two men shared a confident temperament and assumed that things would go well in the end. But for a long time neither weighed seriously the consequences of a Russian victory. It is significant that at the Atlantic meeting of August 1941 the subject of Soviet Russia was hardly mentioned. Probably Beaverbrook was the only leading man in either country who seriously believed that the Soviet card was the winning one to play. Churchill was still intent on drawing the United States into the war, and he tried to reassert British prestige in the Far East as a means of attracting American favour. His promise that, if Japan attacked the United States, a British declaration of war would follow within the hour, was intended to provoke a corresponding American promise in return, which it failed to do. The promise also assumed that there was a real threat behind it and that British power in the Far East could actually help to deter

Japan. Probably no British policy could have prevented a Japanese attack. But Churchill, intoxicated with high-sounding phrases, invited this attack on what was in fact a defenceless Empire.

The Japanese attack on Pearl Harbor did what both Churchill and Hitler had failed to do: it brought the United States into the war. Churchill now had a double preoccupation. On the one hand, he had to enlist the main weight of American strength in the European theatre of war, though without jeopardizing the British Empire in the Far East. On the other, he had to ensure that this strength was directed towards the Mediterranean and not to north-west Europe. These two themes dominated Anglo-American relations for most of the war. Agreement was easily reached in regard to the first. Roosevelt and most of his generals accepted Germany as the main enemy, and even the American admirals who wished to concentrate on fighting Japan wished to conduct a more or less private war, unhampered by allies. Dispute over the second was more prolonged and was eventually decided, as such disputes often are, by logistics, not by argument. Though the Americans always favoured landing in north-west Europe, they lacked the forces with which to undertake it, and the British, who perhaps had the forces, did not believe that it was possible. Hence, by the summer of 1942, action in the Mediterranean was accepted by the Americans for want of anything better. Thus Churchill imposed his strategy on his potentially stronger ally. The war continued to be waged against Italy, not against Germany, and the most considerable success was the overthrow of Mussolini, an outcome which Churchill had never intended.

Against this, Churchill, the champion of the British Raj, was the man who in fact presided over its fall. Many men and many governments shared responsibility for the neglect of Singapore. Churchill completed what others had begun. The vital need at Singapore was for fighter aircraft, and this need could not be met because of the British obsession with heavy bombers. Churchill's individual contribution to the disaster at Singapore was the dispatch of two mighty warships, which were intended to deter the Japanese by a 'vague menace'. Lacking air cover,

they were sunk by the Japanese within two days of the outbreak of war. Everything at Singapore from the sending of
the two ships to the final capitulation reproduced Gallipoli in
a defensive form. Words took the place of action. Rhetoric
was substituted for reality. It is strange how Churchill, who
at one moment appreciated the decisive importance of air
power, at another imagined that the Japanese could be
checked by a vague menace and the shadow of an Imperial
name.

In the earlier part of 1942, Allied strategy hardly existed, at
Singapore or elsewhere, except as a series of improvised re-
sponses to grave dangers. The situation changed in the course of
the year, as the three great Allies stabilized their position – the
Americans in the Pacific, the British west of Alexandria, the
Russians at Stalingrad. Thereafter the Allies not only began to
prepare their own offensive plans, they also began to think,
however vaguely, in terms of a coalition war. The battle of El
Alamein was the last independent victory of British forces, and
even it was won largely with American weapons. Churchill had
now to show his capacity as a coalition statesman. Ever since
May 1940, he had enjoyed supreme authority, despite occasional
alarms. By 1943 he had two equals and was indeed hard-pressed
to keep up with them.

No one, Churchill least of all, ever formally decided that
Great Britain should continue to assert her position as a world
power. This was taken for granted, much as continuing the war
had been taken for granted in 1940. A more modest British
statesman than Churchill might have been less determined
about it and might have husbanded some British strength for
the future. Great Britain, largely thanks to Churchill, kept in
the front rank almost until the end of the war and exhausted
her resources in doing so. The original decision to accept Lend-
Lease was pressed to its logical conclusion. Great Britain abandoned the remnants of her export trade at America's behest and
accumulated a vast debt in the form of sterling balances.
Churchill's faith in American good will was inexhaustible. He
assumed that somehow the United States would restore the
British Empire to its former greatness, or maybe he thought

that the Empire would again become great of itself, once the Axis threat was removed. In a sense, there were no Anglo-American relations during the war. There was only Churchill's personal connexion with Roosevelt.

Anglo-Soviet relations were more important. By 1943 it was clear that Soviet Russia would emerge from the war as a formidable power, and her future position in Europe became Churchill's preoccupation, second only to the defeat of Hitler. There is still some dispute on this subject, a dispute not clarified by Churchill's own writings later. According to one version, Churchill was alarmed at the growth of Soviet power and tried to take precautions against it, if not in 1942 at least well before the end of the war. There are even those who suggest that Churchill would have liked to maintain a strong Germany as a barrier and balance against Russia. It is hard to sustain this view from contemporary records. Churchill never wavered from his determination that Nazi Germany must be utterly defeated. At the same time, he was concerned to strike some clear bargain with Soviet Russia before the war ended. This was his main, perhaps his only, disagreement with Roosevelt, who, in his usual evasive way, wanted to keep the situation open until the war ended.

Churchill's policy, brutally put, was partition. Assuming an American withdrawal from Europe, as Roosevelt's statements gave him every reason to do, he aimed at a division of Europe into British and Soviet spheres of influence. So far as we can tell, Stalin welcomed the idea and certainly applied it emphatically during the British intervention against the Communists in Greece. Yet partition never came near to working out successfully. The underlying assumptions were too different. Churchill assumed that the countries of western Europe would produce peaceful democratic governments if they were allowed to do so. Stalin assumed that the countries of eastern Europe would produce governments hostile to Soviet Russia unless prevented from doing so. Both assumptions proved reasonably true. There was a curious exception. Yugoslavia, the one country where Soviet and British influence was supposed to be equal, was also the one country which produced a Communist government thoroughly independent of Soviet Russia. Churchill's Second World War statesmanship has at least Tito to its credit.

Churchill had no European policy in any wider sense. His outlook was purely negative: the defeat of Germany. Then everything should be left to go back much as it was before. He had no faith that a new democratic spirit was being produced by the Resistance or that national antagonisms had been eroded by the experience of war. His ideas for a future Germany, such as the elimination of Prussia, had no more than an antiquarian interest. His scepticism was not unjustified, and no one did any better in planning the future. On the other hand, his old generosity also reasserted itself. Though he had made many fierce threats of vengeance against the Nazis during the war, he abandoned this attitude when Stalin and Roosevelt were still talking of killing 50,000 Germans. Churchill regarded the post-war trials of German leaders with extreme distaste and remarked to his military adviser: 'You and I must take care not to lose the next war' – the only fit comment on the Nuremberg proceedings.

With Churchill it was always one thing at a time. So long as Hitler had to be defeated, he thought virtually of nothing else. Once this defeat became certain, he was the first to talk of restoring Germany and even envisaged rearming the Germans against Russia before the war was actually over. Sounding the alarm had become a habit with him and, having risen by championing liberty against Hitler, he could not resist repeating the performance against Stalin. There was again, to borrow Churchill's phrase, an unnecessary war – this time cold and largely Churchill's doing. There may have been an element of more serious calculation in Churchill's new line. He never wavered from his desire to draw the United States fully into European affairs. This had to be done on an idealistic basis so long as Roosevelt was alive. After Roosevelt's death, idealism lost its force. Anti-Bolshevism and the Red Peril took its place, and Churchill turned this to Europe's advantage. Since he himself believed in this Peril and even imagined that a Labour Government would bring to Great Britain all the horrors of the Gestapo, the alarm came easily to him. Yet even this was not the end. In his last senile days as Prime Minister, Churchill once more announced the need for reconciliation with Soviet Russia and in particular emphasized that he was the man to accomplish it. Here was a last touch of the grandiose approach which Churchill had always shown to events. He lived for crisis. He profited from crisis. And when crisis did not exist, he strove to invent it.

Churchill was a rich character, exasperating in his earlier days, endearing and even admirable as the years went by. He incorporated the resolve of the British people at what was probably the last great moment in their history, and no Englishman who lived through 1940 can regard him dispassionately. In those days patriotism was enough, and Churchill provided it abundantly. Despite his many apparent aberrations, he never wavered in devotion to the British cause. All else, from isolation at one end of the scale to collective security at the other, were no more than means to this end. Palmerston, another great Englishman, once said: 'England has no eternal friends and no eternal enemies. Only her interests are eternal.' Churchill would have endorsed this with one exception, especially as he grew older. His devotion to the United States was almost as great as that to the British Empire, and he placed his faith for the future in the increasing unity of what he called the English-speaking peoples.

Fundamentally his outlook was sombre. He did not share the contemporary belief in universal improvement nor did he await the coming of some secular Heaven on Earth. He strove to ameliorate hardships without ever expecting that they could be finally removed. But he had also a combative cheerfulness which broke through the gloom, particularly when things were at their worst. He drew inspiration from disasters and inspired others also. In the direction of war, he was often rash and impetuous. A long catalogue of impatient blunders can be drawn against him. But the fact remains that he won the Second World War. Perhaps he paid an excessive price, but the British people agreed with Churchill that the price was worth paying.

As Prime Minister, Churchill often declared that he was the servant of the House of Commons, and his practice showed that this was true. What he served was the traditional institution, as embodied in his own writings and those of other romantically minded historians. Churchill did not serve the contemporary House of Commons and still less did he serve the British people. Rather he expected the people, like himself, to serve the traditional values of Constitution and Empire which had been handed down to them – or manufactured by historians. Churchill used words as weapons of power and was also enslaved by them. He took Macaulay's rhetoric and his own as reality and often sacrificed human beings for the sake of glittering phrases.

Behind the façade of a cheeky individualism, he' was essentially conservative. He had great courage, an almost inexhaustible energy, and a generosity of spirit which could disarm all but the most implacable of opponents. He was fertile in expedients and remained unbowed by adversity. It is difficult to discern in him any element of creative statesmanship. He responded to events with infinite adaptability and persistent enthusiasm. But he had to be driven from without. Churchill had no vision for the future, only a tenacious defence of the past. The British people raised him up, and he failed them. The British ruling classes did their best to keep him down, and he preserved them. He is best described by words which were written about Bismarck in old age: 'He was no beginning, but an end, a grandiose final chord – a fulfiller, not a prophet.' Perhaps Churchill was the penalty people paid for reading history.

Robert Rhodes James THE
POLITICIAN

Winston Churchill was a career politician, a man who devoted himself for his entire adult life to the profession of politics. 'He was,' as Lord Beaverbrook has written, 'in every sense a professional politician, having trained himself for his vocation.' His other achievements and attainments – notably his writing – were essential adjuncts to that career, but were not in serious competition with it. At one point, at the outset of the Great War, it seemed that the profession of arms had profound attractions for him; and yet, within three months of enforced absence from the political world after November 1915, he was eager to return to it.

Perhaps this was not an advantage. Perhaps it would have been better had he worked and lived longer in a non-political environment, and had he not spent his life in the atmosphere of Whitehall and Westminster. But the fact was that politics were his life almost from the beginning.

For he was born into politics, as were the younger Pitt and Fox. As with them, his early political interests, ambitions, and attitudes were shaped by filial devotion and admiration. The influence of the neurotic, brilliant, wayward, tragic father whom he hardly knew must be accounted the first of those factors that impelled him towards a political career from an early age and dominated his first political attitudes.

The background to his entry into the House of Commons as Conservative member for Oldham at the end of 1900 when he was just twenty-six was itself of importance. Lord Randolph Churchill had been dead for only five years, and many members had keen – and sometimes hostile – recollections of him. Lord Randolph's son was manifestly an adventurer and an opportunist. As such, and with little else beyond his own enterprise, courage, and ability to rely upon to make his fortunes, it was sometimes necessary to cut corners with a sharpness that did not endear him universally. Unlike many soldiers of fortune, he had been fully prepared to put his own life to the hazard, but the aura of the adventurer dimmed the very real and remarkable military, literary, and political achievements that stood to his credit when he entered Parliament.

It was to be a very long time before he shook off these early prejudices against him. As his career advanced, he could have complained in Disraeli's words that 'when I was a young and struggling man they taunted me with being an adventurer. Now that I have succeeded they still bring the same reproach against me'. But, as with Disraeli, the reproach was not without foundation.

As a young man he made no attempt to conceal his ambition. What was attractive in the man was unwise in the politician. There is a common misconception to the effect that, in England, Youth and Ambition are regarded with approval. In reality, Youth is considered to be a regrettable interlude to be borne with appropriate patience and modesty; Ambition is tolerable only if it is decently concealed. The young Churchill infringed both these canons. He was brash, egocentric, wholly absorbed in his political career, and unashamedly on the make. He had not appreciated – nor perhaps did he ever appreciate – the importance of humbug in British politics. 'He has that scorn of concealment that belongs to a caste which never doubts itself,' the Liberal journalist A. G. Gardiner wrote of him in 1908. A Parliamentary colleague and contemporary subsequently wrote of him that 'in the 1900 Parliament Churchill made no attempt to dispel the suspicion and dislike with which he was regarded by the majority of the House of Commons. He seemed to enjoy causing resentment. He appeared to have, in modern parlance, a "chip on his shoulder" when in the Chamber itself or in the Lobbies.'[1]

What was difficult to see in the young Churchill, as in his father, was any specific objective in his life save that of an intense personal ambition. Beatrice Webb commented in 1903 that he was 'bound to be unpopular – too unpleasant a flavour with his restless, self-regarding personality and lack of moral or intellectual refinement.' But she, unlike many others, also saw his qualities: 'But his pluck, courage, resourcefulness, and great tradition may carry him far unless he knocks himself to pieces like his father.'[2]

The final qualification was significant. Between 1901 and 1905 it seemed that Churchill was intent upon re-creating his father's career: fighting his enemies, battling for his policies, and repeating his errors. He took at once an individualistic stance; he launched a crusade for Economy; he adopted attitudes towards Imperial and military commitments that were out of sympathy with traditional Conservative views; by his membership in a group of Conservative free-lances who called themselves the 'Hughligans' in honour of Lord Hugh Cecil, one of their members, he revived memories of Lord Randolph's 'Fourth Party' of 1880–83; even in his dress he followed his father's lead. Above all, in his attitude towards the Conservative hierarchy there were strong echoes of Lord Randolph's iconoclasm. The fact that he was, throughout this period, writing Lord Randolph's biography was not without significance.

From the very beginning his approach was aggressive, and he fully appreciated the importance of gaining a name by assailing the biggest men. His sense of the dramatic was, however, intuitive; like his father, he was a man to whom the centre of the stage was both natural and essential. 'The applause of the House,' Lloyd George wrote of him in a private letter in 1907, 'is the very breath of his nostrils. He is just like an actor. He likes the limelight and the approbation of the pit.'[3]

The quickest, and the most perilous, path to the political limelight is to occupy it by assailing an established political figure. This had been proved by Lord Randolph and, more recently, by Lloyd George himself. Churchill began by assailing St John Brodrick, Secretary of State for War, in much the same way that Lord Randolph had sharpened his dialectical teeth on the hapless Mr Sclater-Booth. Then he became one of the most vigorous critics of Joseph Chamberlain after the latter had thrown contemporary politics into utter confusion by his dramatic espousal of Tariff Reform in 1903 and resignation from

the Unionist Government* of which he had been, although not
Prime Minister, the dominant figure. Long before Churchill left
the Conservatives in 1904 over the issue of Tariff Reform he had
been a persistent critic of the Government he had been elected to
support.

The violence of his early political utterances was in itself
remarkable. In the 1900 election campaign he had described the
Liberals as 'prigs, prudes, and faddists', and had declared that
the Liberal party was 'hiding from the public view like a toad
in a hole, but when it stands forth in all its hideousness the Tories will have to hew the filthy object limb from limb'. By 1903
a very different picture had emerged! His assaults on the Balfour Government became increasingly harsh, and those on
Balfour himself were particularly severe. He accused Balfour of
'gross, unpardonable ignorance'; he attacked him for his
'slipshod, slapdash, haphazard manner of doing business'; he
declared that 'the dignity of a Prime Minister, like a lady's
virtue, is not susceptible of partial diminution'. And then:

To keep in office for a few more weeks and months there is no principle which the Government are not prepared to betray, and no
quantity of dust and filth they are not prepared to eat.

In these circumstances it was not surprising that the Conservatives regarded him with all the antipathy reserved in the
House of Commons for the renegade, nor that the Liberals eyed
their new recruit with some reservation. As the veteran Parliamentary commentator, H. W. Lucy, wrote at the time:

Winston Churchill may be safely counted upon to make himself
quite as disagreeable on the Liberal side as he did on the Unionist.
But he will always be handicapped by the aversion that always per-

* After the split in the Liberal ranks over Home Rule for Ireland in
1886, the dissident Liberals, led by Lord Hartington and Chamberlain,
had gradually been drawn into alliance with the Conservatives. The
phrase 'the Unionist Alliance' was Lord Randolph's, but it was not
really until 1895, when the last Salisbury Government contained the
leading Liberal Unionists, that the alliance was formalized. But
although this party was called 'the Unionist party' until 1922, in this
essay I have used the word 'Conservative' throughout.

tains to a man who, in whatsoever honourable circumstances, has turned his coat.*

Churchill's tactics, and his shift of party allegiance, won him substantial advantages. From the fall of the Balfour Government in December 1905 until May 1915 Britain was ruled by Liberal governments. Throughout this period Churchill was in office and, after the middle of 1908, in high office. These were years of high attainment and success. But the personal and political animosities that he had aroused during his brief and spectacular advance in 1900–1905 were to stalk him relentlessly, were to temporarily destroy him in 1915, and were never to be wholly eradicated. In politics, both individuals and parties have long memories. Churchill, within five years of active politics, had arrived – but at a price.

It was already apparent by the end of 1905, when he first received office as Parliamentary Under-Secretary at the Colonial Office, that Churchill was not merely an attractive speaker but was showing signs of becoming a very formidable one. This part of his political equipment was of such importance throughout his career that it merits a substantial digression at this point.

The spoken and written word is the politician's essential public weapon, and it is one of the curiosities of modern politics that there is such a conspicuous failure to develop this weapon. It is true that the modern House of Commons style is 'conversational', and that thundering oratory is regarded with scepticism. It is also true that Grand Oratory, like Grand Opera, is rarely suited to the English temperament, and that the pace of modern political life militates against the careful and lengthy preparation that men like Lord Randolph, Rosebery, Asquith, and Churchill devoted to their major pronouncements. But it is strange that so little care and attention is given to the art of

*H. W. Lucy, *The Balfourian Parliament*, p. 322. For Campbell-Bannerman's lack of excitement over Churchill's defection, see Spender, *Campbell-Bannerman*, vol. II, p. 131. Sir Henry Campbell-Bannerman (1836–1908) had been leader of the Liberal party since the end of 1898; he was Prime Minister from December 1905 until his death in 1908.

public oratory. In this, Churchill may be said to have been behind his time. Yet, when one compares the impact of his personality upon his contemporaries with that of a man of the high
ability of Leo Amery – whose speeches were usually excellent in
content but dull in form and delivery and almost invariably too
long – the crucial importance of his oratorical powers upon his
political fortunes can be best appreciated.

It is well known that Churchill was not a natural impromptu
speaker. In addition to his voice impediment – an inability to
pronounce the letter 's', which gave his speech a slurred and
unattractive sound – he experienced considerable difficulty in
thinking when on his feet in the Commons and even on the
public platform. 'I had never the practice which comes to
young men at the University of speaking in small debating
societies impromptu on all sorts of subjects,' he has written,
adding that for many years he was unable to say anything in
public that he had not written out beforehand and learned by
heart. Fortunately, learning by heart was an attribute at which
he had always excelled.

Thus, from the outset he had to attempt to anticipate the
mood of the House of Commons or a public meeting and to
impose his prepared views and arguments. To do this in the
Commons, which was then, as it is now, the most volatile, critical, and inconstant audience in the world, presented difficulties
of such magnitude that it would ordinarily have proved fatal to
Parliamentary ambitions. But the fact – and the frank recognition of the fact – gave Churchill's speeches their careful and well-
planned character. It would be foolish to claim that Churchill
never made a bad speech; it is true to say that he rarely, if ever,
made a slovenly one. How strange that this most articulate of
men – of whose private conversation Lord Boothby has written
that 'It can be said of Churchill, as it was of Burns, that his
conversation is better than anything he has ever written; and
those who have not had the opportunity of listening to it can
hardly appreciate the full quality of the man '[4] – should be in
public so completely dependent upon prior preparation. It was
all the more remarkable when it is realized that all his books and
articles after *The River War* were, in whole or in substantial

part, dictated; and that, in his own words, 'I lived from mouth to hand.'

Thus, when one talks of Churchill's oratory, an important qualification must be made. Gladstone once wrote that 'I wish you knew the state of total impotence to which I should be reduced if there were no echo to the accents of my own voice.' For Churchill, the task was always to provide the echo – or at least to provide *for* it. This caused some famous disasters, but on the whole it became a powerful advantage. It has been rightly said of Lloyd George, and by a warm admirer, that 'his real fault was his desire to please his audience – his weakness was an extreme responsiveness to atmosphere and in place of an immovable candour a too adroit opportunism'.[5] This criticism could not be applied to Churchill.

In a remarkable early portrait of the young Churchill, written in 1898, G. W. Stevens wrote that 'He has not studied to make himself a demagogue. He was born a demagogue, and he happens to know it. The master strain in his character is the rhetorician.' In one respect this was not correct; Churchill *had* studied rhetoric, and had written in 1897 an essay entitled 'The Scaffolding of Rhetoric', in which he put forward his views on the power wielded by the orator and his techniques, which merits reading.[6] His views anticipated what he wrote in his only novel, *Savrola* – a greatly neglected self-portrait – in 1900:

He ... knew that nothing good can be obtained without effort. These impromptu feats of oratory existed only in the minds of the listeners; the flowers of rhetoric were hothouse plants.

It may be argued whether this characteristic of Churchill's speaking was in the long run a disadvantage or an asset; what cannot be contraverted is the fact that he faced and overcame a temperamental feature of his personality and indeed turned it to advantage. This required courage and application, and to the end he was dependent upon careful preparation for any major speech. It could be said of him that he wrote his speeches and spoke his books. What Sir Harold Nicolson has called 'the combination of great flights of oratory with sudden swoops into the intimate and controversial', which eventually became the outstanding feature of Churchill's speaking technique, had to be worked for.

His first major speech in the Commons, a devastating attack on Brodrick on 12 May 1901, took six weeks to prepare; in his own words, 'I learnt it so thoroughly off by heart that it hardly mattered where I began it or how I turned it.'* It was a sensational success, and an examination of Churchill's style reveals the careful preparation. Of Brodrick's plan to create six Army Corps, of which three were to be held ready for dispatch abroad, Churchill said:

The Secretary of State for War knows – none better than he – that it will not make us secure, and that if we went to war with any great Power his three Army Corps would scarcely serve as a vanguard. If we are hated, they will not make us loved. If we are in danger, they will not make us safe. They are enough to irritate; they are not enough to overawe. Yet, while they cannot make us invulnerable, they may very likely make us venturesome.

In this particular campaign, Churchill made a number of remarkably mature and powerful speeches. One extract may be taken to demonstrate this:

Europe is now groaning beneath the weight of armies. There is scarcely a single important Government whose finances are not embarrassed; there is not a Parliament or a people from whom the cry of weariness has not been wrung. . . . What a pity it would be if, just at the moment when there is good hope of a change, our statesmen were to commit us to the old and vicious policy! Is it not a much more splendid dream that this realm of England . . . should be found bold enough and strong enough to send forth on the wings of honest purpose the message which the Russian Emperor tried vainly to proclaim: that the cruel and clanking struggle of armaments is drawing to a close, and that with the New Century has come a clearer and calmer sky?

---

* Curiously enough, H. W. Lucy described this as Churchill's maiden speech; which had in fact been delivered some three months before. But although Lucy considered that 'Winston Churchill is not likely to eclipse the fame of Randolph', he was struck by the fact that in an hour-long speech Churchill never looked at his notes (*The Balfourian Parliament*, pp. 62–4).

Churchill was still under thirty years of age when he delivered this judgement.

Already in his writings as well as in his speeches, the dominating aspect of the rhetorician was becoming evident. 'In nearly every case,' Charles Masterman wrote a few years later, 'an *idea* enters his head from outside. It then rolls round the hollow of his brain, collecting strength like a snowball. Then, after whirling winds of *rhetoric*, he becomes convinced that it is *right*; and denounces everyone who criticises it. He is in the Greek sense a Rhetorician, the slave of the words which his mind forms about ideas. He sets ideas to Rhetoric as musicians set theirs to music. And he can convince himself of almost every truth if it is once allowed thus to start on its wild career through his rhetorical machinery.' This judgement, although severe, had much truth in it, even in 1910; it had an even greater force in the 1930s, and it is instructive to compare the magnificent controlled rhetoric in *The World Crisis* with passages in *Marlborough*; by this stage Churchill's writings, like his paintings, tended to be over-obsessed by glaring colours.

It would be easy to over-simplify this matter. Churchill was not bombastic, nor was he ever demagogic in the full sense of the word. But the rhetorician – in private as well as in public – was never far absent. It is difficult indeed to improve upon the comment of Sir Isaiah Berlin that 'Churchill is preoccupied by his own vivid world, and it is doubtful how far he has ever been aware of what actually goes on in the heads or hearts of others. He does not react, he acts; he does not mirror, he affects others and alters them to his own powerful measure'.[7]

There are many perils in the rhetorical approach, of which the principal one is that it can in time lose its impact. In 1921 Gardiner wrote sharply of Churchill, but again with some justification: 'He does not want to hear your views. He does not want to disturb the beautiful clarity of his thought by the tiresome reminders of the other side. What has he to do with the other side when his side is the right side? He is not arguing with you; he is telling you.' It is possible to discern some impatience with Churchill's rhetoric before 1914; but it was to be in the inter-war years that this became something more than impatience. His voice had been exhorting, cajoling, ordering, thundering, for nearly forty years; it was not surprising that men turned with relief to other voices and other styles.

The word 'style' requires emphasis. Churchill was brought up at the close of the Antonine Age of British Parliamentary oratory. The dramatic changes in the structure of British politics after the First World War, and the establishment of the universal suffrage which Churchill so much deplored and disliked, resulted in a subtle but important alteration to the plane on which political controversy was conducted. Furthermore, there was a new medium of public communication, the radio, which required entirely different techniques from the formal mass-meetings of late Victorian and Edwardian politics. It is one thing for the listener to be shouted at in the meeting hall; quite another when the listener is seated comfortably in his own home. Baldwin, Roosevelt, and King George V brought to the new medium styles that were wholly attuned to it. Churchill, like Lloyd George and MacDonald, found considerable difficulty in doing so; indeed, it is doubtful if he ever really succeeded, save in the darkest moments of the war when the rhetorical tone was for once appropriate.

Churchill's equipment was formidable, not least in invective and in raillery. By 1905 he had stung the Conservatives on several occasions; between 1905 and 1914 he was to do so again and again. Except on isolated occasions, his early invective lacked the essential ingredient of cruelty, and he was at his most effective when he made deliberate use of humour and sarcasm. His application to every major speech was such that he came armed with facts and figures and arguments carefully developed. In the early years they were often too obviously carefully developed, and his first speech as a Minister early in 1906 was a famous disaster. He was more successful on later occasions, and quickly overcame the bad effects of this initial setback to his ministerial career. But the peril of a repetition always remained. Read today, it is a good speech; it certainly seemed so when rehearsed to his new secretary, Edward Marsh[8]; but it was fatally ill-tuned to the mood of the House, and significantly, even when he realized that he was marching towards a fiasco, there could be no departure from the set speech.

Oratory is not merely a matter of technique, and it is impossible to divorce what Rosebery called 'the character breathing through the sentences' from the impact of a speech. Nevertheless, the technique itself is of supreme importance, and in Churchill's case it also revealed much of the character of the man. In the early essay on rhetoric to which reference has already been made, he wrote: 'Abandoned by his party, betrayed by his friends, stripped of his offices, whoever can command this power is still formidable.' The truth of this was to be seen throughout Churchill's career, and never more vividly than in the 1930s. And, when his hour finally came, he was exceptionally well equipped.

By the time of Churchill's entry into ministerial office in December of 1905, he had changed parties once, and had incurred deep dislike on this account. To a very exceptional and remarkable extent, Churchill stood apart from party in the sense that he had no permanent commitment to any. Few men could indulge in the exchange of party acerbities with greater vigour, yet he always regarded party as essential in the sense that the horse is essential to the rider. Perhaps unhappily, modern political confederations resent such attitudes, particularly as Churchill's shifts of allegiance were never unconnected with his personal interests. Parties like to use men; they intensely dislike being used. 'To his imperious spirit,' as Gardiner commented in 1911, 'a party is only an instrument.' The lines of Pope that he applied to his father were equally applicable to him:

> Sworn to no master, of no sect am I;
> As drives the storm, at any door I knock.

This lack of total commitment to any party, manifested by his perennial interest in what Asquith once called 'strange coalitions and odd regroupings', goes some way towards explaining many of the vicissitudes of his career after 1905.

Churchill's relationship with the Conservative party was stormy almost throughout his career. Between 1901 and 1904 he was a turbulent rebel within their ranks; for the next decade he was among their most vigorous opponents; in the Lloyd George Coalition between 1917 and 1922 he was a colleague, but never viewed with enthusiasm by the Conservatives; in 1924 he rejoined the Conservative party, but broke with the leadership in 1930 and henceforward, until war broke out in 1939, was once again a rebel. It was not altogether to be wondered at that, as Churchill wrote in the late 1920s, 'the Conservatives have never liked nor trusted me'. The feeling was reciprocated. In 1940 their mutual interests brought them together in what was something considerably less than a love match, and, to the end, the Conservative party and Churchill viewed each other with wariness.

But, even in the Liberal period of his career, from 1904 until 1915, Churchill's conservatism was a fundamental feature of his political attitudes. When Asquith succeeded the dying Campbell-Bannerman in 1908, he at once promoted Churchill to the Cabinet as President of the Board of Trade. Churchill flung himself into the cause of social reform with characteristic ardour and determination, and his achievements were considerable. The establishment of Labour Exchanges in 1909; the measures to curb the excesses of 'sweated' labour; the Miners Accidents Act, 1910, and the Coal Mines Act of 1911, owed much to his direct intervention and energy, and constituted, as the author of the Labour Exchange project, William Beveridge, has written, 'a striking illustration of how much the personality of the Minister in a few critical months may change the course of social legislation'.[9] Together with Lloyd George, Churchill provided the most vigorous approach to social injustices in the 1905–14 Liberal Government, in his periods at the Board of Trade (1908–10) and the Home Office (1910–11).

Nevertheless, there were many Liberals who wondered how deep all this went. Charles Masterman, who worked under Churchill at the Home Office, wrote of him that 'he desired in Britain a state of things where a benign upper class dispensed benefits to an industrious, *bien pensant*, and grateful working class'. These suspicions deepened when Churchill went to the Admiralty in 1911, but they had received considerable justification before that turning point.

Churchill's Liberalism may be examined in his speeches, and particularly those that he published in *Liberalism and the Social Problem* in 1909. Churchill, in company with all Liberals, had the problem of retaining in a single political structure what might be loosely called the 'old' Liberal party and the new Labour party. This was not – and was not to be until 1918 – a separate party with a separate programme; but it already contained individuals and attitudes that clashed with traditional Liberal philosophies and policies.

In October 1906, at Glasgow, he declared that 'the fortunes and the interests of Liberalism and Labour are inseparably interwoven. They rise by the same forces, they face the same enemies, they are affected by the same dangers'. The theme that he expounded in this speech, and in many later ones, was that the moderateness of Liberal reforms would ensure success, whereas extremism would imperil it: 'By gradual steps, by steady effort from day to day, from year to year, Liberalism enlists hundreds of thousands upon the side of progress and popular democratic reform whom militant Socialism would drive into violent Tory reaction. That is why the Tory party hate us. . . . The cause of the Liberal party is the cause of the left-out millions.' The State, he argued, had real responsibilities – up to a point. Thus, competition and free enterprise should not be impaired, but 'the consequences of failure' could be mitigated: 'We do not want to pull down the structures of science and civilisation, but to spread a net over the abyss.'

The principal interest of these speeches lies in their increasing insistence upon the maintenance of the structure of society and the importance of 'gradualness'. His attitudes began to harden as early as 1909, when serious industrial unrest began to cause real concern, but in 1908, in the course of the by-election at

Dundee occasioned by his defeat in Manchester,* he delivered an assault on Socialism which merits quotation:

Liberalism is not Socialism, and never will be. There is a great gulf fixed. It is not a gulf of method, it is a gulf of principle. . . . Socialism seeks to pull down wealth; Liberalism seeks to raise up poverty. Socialism would destroy private interests; Liberalism would preserve private interests in the only way in which they can be safely and justly preserved, namely by reconciling them with public right. Socialism would kill enterprise; Liberalism would rescue enterprise from the trammels of privilege and preference. . . . Socialism exalts the rule; Liberalism exalts the man. Socialism attacks capital; Liberalism attacks monopoly.

Disillusionment with Churchill in the Labour party and in parts of the Liberal party was not based on his assaults on Socialism – which were echoed by Lloyd George and other Liberal ministers – so much as on his conduct of a serious railway strike early in 1911. Shortly before this, in a potentially dangerous situation in the South Wales coalfields, Churchill had acted with restraint and skill; troops were made available, but their employment was strictly controlled. In the rail strike, however, his conduct was far less easy to explain or defend, and it was the kind of action that provoked Lloyd George's comparison of him to an apparently sane chauffeur who drives with great skill for months and then suddenly takes the car over a precipice. Without waiting for appeals from the local authorities, Churchill mobilized fifty thousand troops supplied with twenty rounds of ammunition each, and dispatched them to all strategic points. This was a decisive incident, as it demonstrated one aspect of Churchill's personality that had already occasioned some disquiet in a party dedicated to 'Peace, Retrenchment, and Re-

---

* Under the situation that existed until 1922, all ministers had to vacate their seats and seek re-election. Churchill was defeated at North-West Manchester, but found succour at Dundee. The passions against Churchill in the Conservative party may be glimpsed from the ecstatic comment of the *Daily Telegraph*: 'Churchill out – language fails us just when it is most needed. We have all been yearning for this to happen, with a yearning beyond utterance. Figures – oh, yes, there are figures, but who cares for figures to-day? Winston Churchill is out, OUT, OUT!'

form'. Immediately before the strike there had occurred the episode known as 'the siege of Sidney Street', in which Churchill had personally superintended military operations against a gang of desperadoes taking refuge in a house in the East End of London. It was all very colourful and dramatic, but it seemed to many commentators to be excessively so. The railway strike intervention was described by Ramsay MacDonald at the time as 'diabolical', and the general reaction of Labour was vehement. In George Isaacs' words, 'his reputation with organized labour suffered a severe blow', and it was significant that the Conservative press applauded his actions, whereas it had attacked his policy of restraint in South Wales. The Liberal press was dismayed. Gardiner, in the *Daily News*, was particularly scathing about his tendency to exaggerate situations, 'the tendency that sent artillery down to Sidney Street and during the railway strike dispatched the military hither and thither as though Armageddon were upon us'. Lloyd George intervened to restore the situation, but this was a real turning point in Churchill's relations with Labour. It was wholly unfair that Churchill should have been blamed for the deaths of two miners at Tonypandy, but by some inexplicable transference of responsibility and distortion of memory, his actions in the railway dispute were applied to those in the South Wales dispute. 'Tonypandy' was to enter Labour mythology, and it has remained an astonishingly enduring legend.

On another major item Churchill changed his views very drastically between 1900 and 1910. His early attitudes to expenditure on the Army have been referred to; in 1908 he was Lloyd George's most vigorous ally in his battle against increased Navy expenditure. But these attitudes were changing before the Agadir Crisis of 1911. Realization of the direction in which German policies were moving provoked a new understanding of the warnings of the Navy and the soldiers. Characteristically, he swung from one extreme to the other. 'Once I got drawn in,' as he has written, 'it dominated all other interests in my mind. For seven years I was to think of little else. Liberal politics, the People's Budget, Free Trade, Peace, Retrenchment and Reform – all the war cries of our election struggles began to seem unreal

in the presence of this new pre-occupation. Only Ireland held
her place among the grim realities which came one after another
into view.'

Churchill's move from the Home Office to the Admiralty in
August 1911 marked the decisive end of the 'social reform' period. The break was so complete, and his absorption with his
new task so total, that it inevitably revived the suspicions that
his commitment to the cause of social reform had been shallow,
and even opportunist. This was unfair; but the change did reveal one important aspect of Churchill's character which has
rarely received adequate attention, and which was well expressed by Lord Esher in 1917:

He handles great subjects in rhythmical language, and becomes
quickly enslaved by his own phrases. He deceives himself into the
belief that he takes broad views, when his mind is fixed upon one
comparatively small aspect of the question.

This decline in his position in the Liberal party was accompanied with a further heightening of the mistrust felt towards
him in the Conservative ranks. The immediate cause was the
Irish Question, which at the beginning of 1912 had entered a
new and violent phase with the introduction of the third Home
Rule Bill.

The division between the main parties – and it was a deep
and wide one indeed – concerned the future of the nine counties
of Ulster. In 1886 Lord Randolph had declared 'Ulster will
fight: Ulster will be right'. This was again the cry of Ireland in
1912 when threatened with subordination to Southern Ireland
in an Irish Parliament. The Ulstermen had a new leader at
Westminster, Sir Edward Carson. The new Conservative leader
– who had succeeded Balfour in November 1911 – was Andrew
Bonar Law, who was deeply committed, personally and politically, to the maintenance of Ulster's ties with Britain. It
was, from the outset, a bitter, exhausting, and dangerous
dispute; it was to get progressively more bitter, exhausting, and
dangerous.

As Lord Randolph's son, Churchill was in a difficult position.
In private, he anticipated the necessity of separate treatment

for Ulster. In public, however, his attitudes were belligerent and indeed appeared to be deliberately provocative. A visit to Belfast in March 1912 was courageous, but hardly calculated to calm the passions in that fevered city. It was, however, his intervention early in 1914 that really evoked Ulster, and Conservative, bitterness.

In this episode it is important to see things as they appeared rather than as actual facts. He delivered a remarkably defiant and even bullying speech at Bradford in the middle of March, in which he in effect dared the Ulstermen to stand in the way of the Government, and declared that 'there are worse things than bloodshed, even on an extended scale', and ended: 'Let us go forward, and put these grave matters to the proof.' This was immediately followed by the movement of warships to the west coast of Scotland and the dispatch of destroyers to the area. There then ensued the so-called Curragh Mutiny, in which Churchill's close friend J. E. B. Seely, the Secretary for War, played a prominent but foolish part.* In the end, Ulster and Conservative feeling were enraged; the warships were withdrawn; Seely was humiliated and outwitted by the soldiers, and obliged to resign; and the chances of a peaceful settlement of the Irish Question, never good at the best of times, suffered a severe blow.

In all this, as Churchill has admitted with characteristic frankness, he was seeking to ingratiate himself with his party. Home Rule – whether for Ireland or India – was never a cause to which he warmed naturally. His repudiation of the Conservative attacks on him as 'a vote of censure by the criminal classes upon the police' was very much to the point, but not calculated to lower the temperature. As one of his colleagues had once remarked, Churchill 'did not exactly walk about with an oil-can'.

These domestic controversies were not wholly submerged by the outbreak of war with Germany in August 1914. The political temperature in Britain had been rising steadily since 1905, and the ill-feeling between the Liberals and Conservatives could not be removed by an Act of Oblivion. Party warfare was officially

* For a good brief account of the episode, see A.P. Ryan, *Mutiny at the Curragh*.

abandoned, but the former antipathies and mistrust still smouldered.

The events of the war at sea in the first three months of the war came as a considerable shock to the British public; perhaps they had expected too much; certainly they had never expected what actually happened. The *Goeben* and *Breslau* evaded Allied warships in the Mediterranean and reached Constantinople, the first decisive step in the series of events that was to bring Turkey into the war at the end of October. On 22 September, three British cruisers were sunk by a single submarine in the North Sea. Admiral von Spee's squadron completely destroyed a small British force at Coronel. In the Indian Ocean the cruiser *Emden* paralysed the movement of British ships. In December a German cruiser force shelled three east coast towns, killing 137 people and injuring 592. The Cabinet deemed it prudent to suppress the publication of the loss of the battleship *Audacious*, and passed what was in effect a vote of censure on the Royal Navy. From criticism of the Navy it was only a short step to censuring the First Lord of the Admiralty.

These events were embarrassments rather than a dire threat to British naval supremacy, but they caused considerable consternation. The First Sea Lord, Prince Louis of Battenberg, was hounded from office by a vicious press campaign, and Churchill took the opportunity to recall the aged Lord Fisher from his retirement. The initial results of this remarkable combination were excellent, but it was not long before serious differences of outlook between the two men became evident, and Fisher maintained his close contacts with the Conservative leaders. 'Churchill co-opted Fisher to relieve the pressure against himself,' Beaverbrook has written, 'but he had no intention of letting anyone else rule the roost. Here, then, were two strong men of incompatible tempers both bent on an autocracy.'[10]

These naval reverses, very unfairly, had done Churchill's reputation considerable harm, and he was exposed to severe criticism in the Conservative press, particularly from *The Times* and the *Morning Post*. But what really undermined his positions in the Cabinet and in the Admiralty were two other incidents.

The French proposed in September that a British force should land at Dunkirk to stage a demonstration that might alarm the Germans about their right flank. Churchill, at Kitchener's* request, took command of the operation. A mixed force of marines and yeomanry carried out an elaborate charade which became derided as the 'Dunkirk Circus'. It was the kind of operation that Churchill relished, but others, including Asquith, were less amused, and the 'Circus' was concluded.

This was only a preliminary to the storm of criticism that fell on Churchill for his part in the defence of Antwerp in October. Much of this criticism was even more unfair than that he had received over the Dunkirk episode, but he did not help matters by the air of melodrama that he injected into the affair. He arrived at Antwerp, in the account of one startled observer, in 'undress Trinity House uniform', making an entrance that 're-minded me for all the world of a scene in a melodrama when the hero dashes up bare-headed on a foam-flecked horse and saves the heroine, or the old homestead, or the family fortune, as the case may be'. He arrived on 3 October, and on the next day offered to resign his Cabinet post to take command. This offer, when read out to the Cabinet, only provoked 'roars of incredulous laughter', and he was recalled to London. Melodrama was followed by disaster. Antwerp fell, and more than 2,500 men of the newly formed and largely untrained Royal Naval Division – one of Churchill's own creations, already a bone of contention between himself and the War Office, and viewed with less than enthusiasm by some senior officers at the Admiralty – were lost either as battle casualties or interned in neutral Holland. Controversy still continues as to whether the defence of Antwerp for a few vital days owed very much to the contribution of the Royal Naval Division. In any event, at the time the brunt of public disillusion fell on Churchill.† He himself subsequently appreciated the strength of the criticism of his conduct: 'Those who are charged with the direction of supreme affairs must sit

* Lord Kitchener of Khartoum (1850–1916) had been made Secretary of State for War at the outbreak of war.

† For some of these criticisms, see A. J. Marder, *From the Dreadnought to Scapa Flow*, vol. II, pp. 83–5.

on the mountain-tops of control; they must never descend into the valleys of direct physical and personal action.'

These episodes illuminated Churchill's eagerness – amounting, in the view of some, to a mania – to establish a military reputation. His excitement and ardour for action – and fame – also brought periods of dejection and depression. His feverish activity, often high-handed conduct, and manifest enjoyment of drama evoked serious apprehensions among his service advisers and Cabinet colleagues about his judgement and stability. By the end of 1914 these apprehensions were widespread in the Admiralty, the Navy, the Cabinet, and – above all – in the Conservative Opposition. Absorbed in his great work, dominated by the war, he was totally unaware of the abrupt decline in his reputation. As Beaverbrook has written:

His attitude from August 1914 onwards was a noble one, too noble to be wise. He cared for the success of the British arms, especially in so far as they could be achieved by the Admiralty, and for nothing else. His passion for this aim was pure, self-devoted, and all-devouring. He failed to remember that he was a politician and as such treading a slippery path; he forgot his political tactics. . . . As he worked devotedly at his own job, the currents of political opinion slipped by him unnoticed.[11]

This was the vital background to the tragic Dardanelles campaign of 1915. The campaign itself lies outside the scope of this account, but the broad outlines must be given.

At the end of 1914, with the Western front established in a trench system that writhed from the Channel coast to the Swiss frontier, the possibilities of attack elsewhere were canvassed by Lloyd George and the Secretary to the War Council (which had been set up early in November), Maurice Hankey. Their comments were fortified in December by a Russian appeal for a diversion against the Turks. Churchill was very sympathetic to the views of Lloyd George and Hankey, and he had already urged a naval attack on the Dardanelles without success. He now renewed his arguments, and fortified them with the opinion of the admiral commanding the British force in the Aegean. The War Council was greatly taken by the proposal, which Churchill urged with all his skill and ardour. Lord Fisher's attitude veered from reluctant support to outright opposition, but Churchill persuaded him to support the venture. On 19 February, the naval bombardment opened. Operating in characteristically bad weather, with in the main obsolete warships, and meeting increasing resistance, the naval attack was checked. Churchill urged the dispatch of troops to the area, *not* to force the Dardanelles (as he implies in his own account) but for subsequent operations. Kitchener eventually (10 March) agreed to the dispatch of his last Regular Division (the 29th) to the Middle East, and two days later appointed General Sir Ian Hamilton, a close friend of Churchill's, to command the Mediterranean Expeditionary Force. Hamilton arrived at the Dardanelles on 18 March, just in time to see the great naval attack launched by Admiral de Robeck end in virtual disaster. Out of nine battleships engaged, three were sunk and three crippled: six out of nine is a lot. Turkish losses, save in heavy shells, were negligible. The vital minefields, the object of the operation, were not touched. On 22 March, Hamilton and de Robeck agreed on a joint naval and military attack, originally intended for 12 April, but eventually launched on 25 April. Churchill was dismayed by this decision – which was taken by the men on the spot, and not by the Cabinet or the War Council – and he subsequently made great play with the low reserves of ammunition that the Turks possessed. But, as the minutes of the War Council reveal, he did not consider that Hamilton's army of some seventy thousand British, French, and Dominion troops would experience much difficulty.

They did get ashore on the Gallipoli Peninsula, but by 9 May had suffered some twenty thousand casualties and were definitely halted. The British had now acquired another major front, at a time when they had barely sufficient resources to handle one. Most ominously of all from Fisher's point of view, three more battleships had been lost – two from German submarine attack. Other episodes propelled Fisher towards resignation. By 14 May the Government was in the middle of a major ministerial crisis.

The check at the Dardanelles and Fisher's resignation coincided with a disastrous reverse on the Western front, which was ascribed by the commander-in-chief (Sir John French) to a shortage of shells. By itself, the 'shells scandal' would probably not have brought the Government down; the decisive episode was Fisher's resignation, speedily communicated to Bonar Law.

The precariousness of Churchill's position was now exposed. Lloyd George was an eager advocate of a Coalition, to which Asquith consented as a regrettable necessity. The removal of Churchill from the Admiralty was a *sine qua non* for Conservative participation. Churchill vainly, and even desperately, fought to save himself, but the Conservatives were implacable. Asquith had no choice in the matter, but Churchill never really forgave him for his downfall. Like most politicians, he could not accept the fact that he had encompassed his own ruin.

In fact, Asquith did quite well for him in the circumstances. Churchill stayed in the Government (as Chancellor of the Duchy of Lancaster), with membership in the newly formed Dardanelles Committee. Within two weeks of his departure from the Admiralty he had persuaded the new Government to reinforce Hamilton substantially at Gallipoli.

This was the first reverse Churchill suffered in his political career. Until the storm broke, he had had no conception of the strength and the extent of the personal hostility against him. Of all his Cabinet colleagues, only Kitchener called to express his condolences. Admiral Beatty commented that 'the Navy breathes freer now it is rid of the succubus Churchill'; Admiral Wemyss – at the Dardanelles – was to write that his name would be handed down to posterity as that of a man 'who undertook an operation of whose requirements he was entirely ignorant'; Admiral Jellicoe described him as 'a public danger to the Empire'; the King described him curtly as 'impossible'.* In the

---

* The censure was not quite universal. J. L. Garvin struck a different note when he wrote in the *Observer* on 23 May: 'He is young. He has lion-hearted courage. No number of enemies can fight down his ability and force. His hour of triumph will come.' And F. S. Oliver wrote in a private letter: 'The only two men who really seem to understand that we are at war are Winston and Lloyd George. Both have faults which disgust one peculiarly at the present time, but there is a reality about them, and they are in earnest, which the others aren't.' But such supporters were few indeed.

late 1920s and the 1930s, the harsh judgements delivered against Churchill for the Dardanelles campaign were amended, and subsequently became so amended that the balance has been taken too far in his favour. It was unfair that he should have borne the full responsibility, but there was a certain amount of rough justice in the overwhelming tide of feeling against him. As he himself wrote more than thirty years later: 'I was ruined for the time being over the Dardanelles, and a supreme enterprise was cast away, through my trying to carry out a major and combined operation of war from a subordinate position. Men are ill-advised to try such ventures.'

Churchill's fall from the Admiralty was the prelude to his complete political ostracism. He has vividly described his own reaction:

Like a sea-beast fished up from the depths, or a diver too suddenly hoisted, my veins threatened to burst from the fall in pressure. . . . At a moment when every fibre of my being was inflamed to action, I was forced to remain a spectator of the tragedy, placed cruelly in a front seat.

The Gallipoli campaign reached its climax in August 1915. After prodigious effort and sacrifice, the British and Dominion forces failed in their attempt to seize the decisive heights of Sari Bair; 'the terrible summits', as Churchill subsequently wrote, 'flamed unconquered'. From this point the voices of those ministers never enthusiastic about the Dardanelles became more insistent in favour of withdrawal. Churchill fought against evacuation throughout the autumn, and the records of the Dardanelles Committee demonstrate his isolation. By November the die was almost cast. When Asquith reorganized the Dardanelles Committee into a new central body, Churchill was excluded from the new War Committee. His position in the Coalition had never been a happy one, and his relations with the Conservative leaders – notably Bonar Law – had not been smooth.

Churchill accordingly resigned, and made a defiant speech in the Commons before setting off to France to serve in the trenches. His speech was listened to with sympathy, but he fell virtually unmourned. It was unfortunate that in the speech he referred to Gallipoli as 'a legitimate war gamble'. So, perhaps, it had been, but the statement gave an impression of lack of remorse or sense of personal responsibility for the emphatic reverse suffered at the Dardanelles.

Churchill's period at the front with 'those magnificent Grenadiers' lasted for six months. This was an unhappy period of his political career. In March 1916 he returned to the House of Commons to deliver an attack on the Government that included the extraordinary proposal that Lord Fisher should be recalled to the Admiralty! Much of the good impression created by his departure to the war was eradicated by this hapless speech, which gave the strong impression of a deeply resentful and deeply ambitious man capable of using any opportunity to effect his own return to office. It was with difficulty that he was persuaded to return to France, and it was not surprising that his few remaining political friends viewed his conduct with despair.

There could be no question but that Churchill's capacities were ill-used in the Army, and he was right to make the definite return to politics in the summer of 1916. But he remained an outsider. In the complicated intrigues that resulted in Lloyd George's accession to the premiership in December 1916, Churchill played only a minor role; a violent clash with Bonar Law at Beaverbrook's house* in November emphasized the gulf that remained between himself and the Conservative leader.

Nevertheless, no Prime Minister – and certainly not one as acutely conscious of the precariousness of his position as Lloyd George – could view with equanimity the presence on the back benches of this formidable personality. Law always took the view that Churchill was far preferable as an opponent than as a colleague, but Lloyd George was acutely conscious not only of Churchill's abilities but of his position in the Liberal party, now divided into two camps after Asquith's fall. On 10 May 1917, Churchill eclipsed Lloyd George in debate; Lloyd George at once resolved to brave the Conservative wrath and secure Churchill.

* It is admirably described by Beaverbrook in *Politicians and the War*, pp. 306–8.

The extent of the Conservatives' dismay and anger at this step gives a vivid portrait of the dislike and distrust with which they regarded Churchill. So intense was the opposition that for a time it seemed as if the Coalition were in jeopardy. It is to Lloyd George himself that we look for the best analysis of this Conservative alarm:

Here was their explanation. His mind was a powerful machine, but there lay hidden in its material or make-up some obscure defect which prevented it from always running true. They could not tell what it was. When the mechanism went wrong, its very power made the action disastrous, not only to himself but to the causes in which he was engaged and the men with whom he was co-operating.

Churchill's alignment with Lloyd George was a decisive moment in his career. The old Liberal party was riven in twain, and in the 1918 general election it was to be destroyed for ever. The Liberals who followed Lloyd George had to accept the fact that they were dependent upon Conservative support for their political existence. Lloyd George was a Prime Minister without a party, and his supremacy rested upon the strength of his personal authority and political adroitness and, above all, the support of the Conservatives.

These weaknesses in the position of the Lloyd George Liberals were not evident at the time. Indeed, it seemed that the great Centre party which had attracted Lloyd George and Churchill for so long had materialized. The Asquithian Liberals were shattered in the 1918 election – Asquith himself being in the ranks of the defeated – while those who had followed Lloyd George sailed on victoriously and triumphantly, enjoying office and power, and giving an impression of permanence and even impregnability. The fundamental insecurity of their position was not made apparent until, in October 1922, the Coalition and its leader dramatically vanished.

The story of the decline of the prestige and position of the Lloyd George Coalition is of considerable importance in any study of Churchill's career, and the part that he played in that decline has tended to receive inadequate attention. The dominant characteristics of the Coalition, in which were faithfully reflected the character of its leader, were opportunism, cynicism, and an almost obsessional desire to live excitingly. Its eventual downfall was less the consequence of a failure of policies than a failure of character. It succeeded in alienating virtually every sizeable interest and section of the nation. It dismally failed to build, as Lloyd George had promised, 'a nation fit for heroes to live in'. It embarked upon, and then withdrew from, military intervention in Russia against the Bolsheviks. It attempted, and failed, to rule Ireland by force. Its record was scarred by a degree of corruption and cynical use of the honours system that was without parallel in modern British political history. Much of the responsibility for this must lie with Lloyd George personally; as Harold Laski wrote in 1919 of him, 'he seems determined to sacrifice upon the altar of his private ambition the whole spirit of our public life'. It was not long before such feelings were developing within the Conservative party.

Churchill's work at the Ministry of Munitions since his return to the Government in 1917 had been competently done; in January 1919 he became Secretary of State for War and Air, and his career entered one of its most controversial periods.

The first point of divergence between Churchill and the rest of the Cabinet concerned the future of British forces in Russia. These forces had been introduced in wartime conditions, and, at the time, there had been no question of 'intervention'. It was clearly in the interests of the Allies in the summer of 1918 that all possible aid and comfort should be given to those Russians who were prepared to oppose a régime that had made peace with the Germans and who were prepared to fight on. After the defeat of Germany, however, the future of these forces became a matter of high policy.

As the papers of the Coalition Cabinet become available, the extent of Churchill's personal commitment to the anti-Bolshevik cause is extensively documented. The skill with which, in *The Aftermath*, he indulges in selective quotation from these documents may be admired as an exercise in special pleading rather more than as an instance of historical objectivity. In this episode he frequently found himself opposed by Lloyd George, who was highly sceptical about the military intervention from the outset, and by Bonar Law and Austen Chamberlain (Chancellor of the Exchequer). For a time, Churchill managed to maintain the intervention – on one occasion by acting contrary to the decision of the Cabinet on the grounds that it was purely a War Office responsibility – but the pressure against continuing intervention inside and outside the Government became too strong.

The Russian intervention marked another stage in Churchill's alienation from Labour. Initially, Labour had not taken a favourable view of the Bolshevik Revolution, as it had brought down a government with which most Labour leaders had been in considerable sympathy. But as the months passed, and the intervention continued, regret at the downfall of Kerensky was replaced by increasing support for the Bolshevik Government. No minister expressed loathing of 'the foul baboonery' of Bolshevism more articulately than Churchill, and by the end of 1919 he was the principal target of the agitation in the Labour and trade union movement against the maintenance of a British presence in Russia. The T.U.C.'s Council of Action specifically named Churchill as the prime proponent of the policy, and it was correct. The policy of intervention – if, indeed, such a series of half-decisions can really be called a policy – was quietly abandoned, but Churchill's part in this hapless adventure, and the violence of his language, were not forgotten.

Churchill's part in the attempt to coerce Ireland was of less direct influence upon his reputation at the time. The vigour of his language in Cabinet, and the extent of his commitment to a policy of military suppression, come as a surprise. His public statements were considerably less belligerent, and although he did a complete volte-face in 1921, so did many other ministers. The Irish Treaty of December 1921 won the Government few new friends, and made it – particularly on the Conservative benches – many new enemies. Perhaps this tardy repentance deserved no better.

By the summer of 1922 the Coalition was in serious jeopardy. Bonar Law had retired on grounds of ill health a year earlier, but was still in public life, and Conservative disillusion with Lloyd George began to group around this diffident, cautious man. Austen Chamberlain, who had replaced Law as Conservative leader, was fatally out of touch with party feeling; Churchill's great friend Lord Birkenhead (F.E.Smith) was, if anything, even further out of touch. The selling of honours for party fund purposes was becoming a public scandal. The economy, after a brief post-war boom, had slumped disastrously. Lloyd George had become, so far as the House of Commons was concerned, virtually an absentee Prime Minister. In these dark and lowering circumstances, it only needed one final step to bring the Coalition down.

Once again, Churchill was implicated. He had not been responsible for Lloyd George's pro-Greek policies, and had been a moderate influence when a Turkish nationalist movement led by Mustapha Kemal (Ataturk) threatened the Greek position in Turkey-in-Asia. But when the triumphant Kemalist forces threatened the neutral zones at the Dardanelles, Churchill was in the fore of those who advocated military resistance.

What became known to history as 'the Chanak Incident' of September 1922 completed the ruin of the Coalition. The nation, to its amazement, awoke to discover itself almost at war. The Dominion Prime Ministers read an appeal for assistance, drafted by Churchill, in the newspapers before they received it officially; not surprisingly, their reactions were bleak. The British senior commander at Constantinople, General Harington, turned a Nelsonic blind eye to the Cabinet's order to deliver an ultimatum to the Kemalist Government. The crisis passed, but it destroyed the Coalition.

The Coalition fell largely through hubris. Austen Chamberlain, in order to quell the revolt in the Conservatives, called a party meeting. The tactic boomeranged disastrously. The party voted to leave the Coalition, and followed the advice of Bonar Law and Baldwin – the hitherto unregarded President of the Board of Trade – rather than that of Chamberlain. At the Carlton Club Meeting of 19 October 1922, the Coalition crashed to disaster; by the afternoon Lloyd George was no longer Prime Minister. Bonar Law replaced him. At this critical moment, Churchill was prostrated by acute appendicitis, 'and in the morning when I recovered consciousness I learned that the

Lloyd George Government had resigned, and that I had lost not only my appendix but my office'; within a few weeks he had lost his seat in Parliament as well. Dundee decisively rejected him. The country turned emphatically away from the Coalition and all that it had stood for. After over twenty years in the House of Commons, most of them in high office, Churchill was in the political wilderness – without a seat, without a party, without a leader, and without a following.

The results of Churchill's career up to October 1922 were, in terms of position and reputation, remarkably meagre. The Conservatives rejoiced at his defeat. So did Labour. So did the Asquithian Liberals. Politically, he had no home to go to.

Among his political contemporaries, with the exception of Lloyd George, his experience of high office was unequalled. His personality was attractive, and, as Beaverbrook has written, 'always free from rancour and never treacherous'. He had, like Lord Randolph, the showman's knack of always remaining in the public eye. He was wholly untouched by any breath of personal or political scandal. His abilities in the Commons or on the public platform were formidable. *The World Crisis* – his first major literary work since his biography of his father – was an astonishing achievement. On any plane, it was evident that Churchill was a figure of the very first rank.

But all this, politically, added up to surprisingly little. The vigour with which he entered every controversy, the robustness of his language, and the dexterity with which he appeared to shift his allegiances were partly responsible. Yet there was something else, not easy to define, that made men distrust and dislike him. The general estimate held of Churchill in the early 1920s was hostile. What we may loosely call 'the Churchill magic' had a repellent as well as an attractive quality, and at this stage – and for many years to come – the former was dominant. He was widely regarded as unreliable and prone to exaggeration. It is probable that there were others in addition to Lloyd George who wondered if there were not a strain of insanity in the Churchill family, and who recalled that Lord

Randolph had died insane but did not know the real cause.* Even those who did go this far would have echoed, perhaps in less kindly tones, Lord Derby's comment that: 'I believe in Winston's capability if only he were a bit more steady. But you never know what kite he is going to fly next.'

A study of contemporary estimates of Churchill emphasizes the difficulty many people found in specifying their mistrust of him with any exactness. The most frequent criticism was to the effect that the time had passed for 'a daring pilot in extremity, pleased with the danger when the waves went high', who 'sought the storms, but for a calm unfit', and who would, above all, 'steer too nigh the sands to boast his wit'. Calmer times required calmer men. So ran the argument. 'What sensible man,' a hostile biographer demanded in 1931, 'is going to place confidence in Mr Churchill in any situation which needs cool-headedness, moderation and tact?'[12] The same point was made by a personal friend but a political opponent, Arthur Ponsonby, in a private letter to Edward Marsh:

He is so far and away the most talented man in political life besides being charming and a 'gentleman' (a rarish bird these days). But this does not prevent me from feeling politically that he is a great danger, largely because of his love of crises and faulty judgment. He once said to me years ago 'I like things to happen, and if they don't happen I like to make them happen.'[13]

Churchill himself was genuinely surprised, both in 1915 and 1922, by the discovery of how many enemies he had. 'I have never joined in an intrigue', he is reported to have said. 'Everything I have got I have fought for. And yet I have been more hated than anybody.' 'Hated' was perhaps too strong a description; 'deeply distrusted' would have been more apposite.

The immediate problem for Churchill after the débâcle of 1922 was to find himself a party and a seat in Parliament. His position was exceedingly vulnerable. 'He failed in 1915,' as

---

* Lord Randolph had died of general paralysis of the insane. (See Randolph S. Churchill, *Winston S. Churchill*, companion vol. I, part 1, pp. 542–3.)

Beaverbrook has written, 'because he showed himself too confident to be prudent. He neither tied the Liberals to him nor
conciliated the Tories.' This comment had equal application in
the early 1920s.

The political situation in the two years following the fall of
the Lloyd George Coalition and the establishment of a Conservative Government headed by Bonar Law was exceptionally
confused. Those Conservatives who had supported the Coalition –
notably Austen Chamberlain, Balfour, and Birkenhead – stood
aloof from the new Government. There was a chance of reunion
when Baldwin succeeded the dying Law in May 1923, but it
was not taken. Although the Liberals made a show at unity
when it seemed that Free Trade was in peril, the acuteness
of the division between Lloyd George and Asquith could
not be long concealed by any stage-managed reconcil-
iations. The position of Liberalism, furthermore, was being
steadily eroded by the dramatically expanding Labour
party.

As has been emphasized, Churchill's attitudes were essentially Conservative. The Mastermans had seen, in 1910, 'the
aboriginal and unchangeable Tory in him'; now, the spectre of
'the foul baboonery' of Bolshevism abroad and Socialism at
home impelled him even more sharply in this direction. In the
Dundee campaign of 1922, when opposed by E.D.Morel, the
Communist Willie Gallagher, and the 'quaint and hen-dim figure' of the Prohibitionist Mr Scrymgeour (who won), Churchill declared that 'Mr Gallagher is only Mr Morel without the
courage of his convictions, and Trotsky is only Mr Gallagher
with the power to murder those whom he cannot convince'. It
was perhaps not altogether surprising that his principal meeting
in that campaign had had to be abandoned amid wild scenes of
uproar and tumult.

Churchill's movement to the Right did not go undetected.
'His tendency is all to the Right,' Beaverbrook wrote to Lloyd
George in March 1922, 'and his principles are becoming
more Tory.' A commentator in *The Times* had noted in
1920:

He has latterly become more Conservative, less from conviction than from the hardening of his political arteries. His Liberal velleities have dried up, the generous impulses of youth throb more slowly, and apart from some intellectual gristle his only connections with Liberalism are personal.

For the present, however, the movement towards the Conservative party had to be cautious. Had Bonar Law lived, it is doubtful whether the movement could ever have taken place.

Political historians often underestimate the importance of *luck* in politics. Between October 1922 and November 1924 there were no less than three general elections, of which certainly one – that of December 1923, called by Baldwin to seek approval of a more Protectionist policy – was unexpected, and probably unnecessary. At this election Churchill stood as a Liberal Free Trader at West Leicester and was defeated by four thousand votes. It was a fortunate escape. When the election dust cleared, the result was indecisive. Asquith's decision to support Labour, and in effect put in the first Labour Government, was a decisive moment for Churchill. In January 1920, in the course of a vigorous assault on Bolshevism and Socialism, he declared that Labour was 'quite unfitted for the responsibility of Government'. On the morrow of Asquith's announcement, he said in a public letter (17 January 1924):

The enthronement in office of a Socialist government will be a serious national misfortune such as has usually befallen great states only on the morrow of defeat in war. It will delay the return of prosperity, it will open a period of increasing political confusion and disturbance, it will place both the Liberal and Labour parties in a thoroughly false position. . . . Strife and tumults, deepening and darkening, will be the only consequence of minority Socialist rule.

He was now, in fact if not in name, a Conservative again. He shared – and perhaps believed in it more than many Conservatives – the fear of Socialism and Bolshevism. Belief in private enterprise lay at the core of his being. During the war he had been in favour of draconian measures to meet the crisis, but he had stopped short of anything approaching government ownership of industry. 'I do not believe in socialistic production, but in private enterprise and private thrift regulated and sustained by private interest.'[14]

Thus it was not surprising to find him, early in 1924, standing as 'an Independent and Anti-Socialist' candidate for a by-election in the Abbey Division of Westminster. The official local Conservative association put up their own candidate, and a very significant event occurred. Churchill appealed to Baldwin to intervene to persuade the association to withdraw their candidate, alleging that improprieties had occurred in his selection. Baldwin could not go along – the independence of local associations from the central office is jealously guarded in the Conservative party – but he could at least remain neutral. He persuaded Balfour not to send a public letter of support for Churchill, but, when Amery publicly supported the official candidate (on the grounds that Churchill was a Free Trader) on the eve of the poll, Baldwin released Balfour's letter.*

In this campaign Churchill had declared that the Conservative party 'must now become the main rallying-ground for the opponents of the Socialist Party', and he was supported by a number of Conservative M.P.s and the newspaper magnate Lord Rothermere. (Other assistance was supplied by a red-haired young schoolmaster, Brendan Bracken, and by the chorus girls of Daly's Theatre; the Churchill children were drawn into the fray, progressing in a vehicle marked with the message 'Vote for My Daddy'.) In the event, he just failed – by forty-three votes – to defeat the official candidate. It was another lucky escape. If he had won, or had put the Socialist (Fenner Brockway, who canvassed the staff of Buckingham Palace) in, the official Conservative party might have had much difficulty in extending forgiveness to him, and his reputation as a 'wrecker' would have been augmented. As it was, he had given dramatic evidence of his electioneering vigour and ability, and of his political bona fides. His campaign was, to put the matter mildly, alarmist in tone.

On 7 May 1924, at Liverpool, Churchill stepped on to a

* The complete correspondence may be found in the Baldwin Papers at the University Library, Cambridge.

Conservative platform for the first time in twenty years, the occasion being organized by Sir Archibald Salvidge, the unattractive but powerful Tory boss in the city, who had organized his first major political meeting for Lord Randolph – then in melancholy decline – in 1893. Churchill spoke on the topic of 'The present dangers of the Socialist Movement' with characteristic vigour, describing the Labour Government as being 'driven forward by obscure, sinister, and in part extraneous forces', a recurrent theme of his speeches at this time. On the next day he addressed the Liverpool Conservative Club, and later spoke to a Scottish Unionist gathering in Edinburgh, presided over by Arthur Balfour.

Shortly afterwards, Churchill found political sanctuary at Epping; he stood as a 'Constitutionalist', but his attitudes were indistinguishable from those of the Conservatives. His political stock-in-trade was vigorous anti-Socialism, and when the Liberal–Labour alliance collapsed in the autumn of 1924 and another general election took place, this was virtually the only theme in his speeches. Shortly before the polling, the Foreign Office issued the text of a letter allegedly written by Zinoviev, president of the International, to British Communists. It is now definitely known that it was a forgery, and that the Conservative central office was involved in the use made of it. The effect of the Zinoviev letter on the 1924 election result is problematical, but it is of interest to see what Churchill's reactions were. Writing in the *Weekly Dispatch* of 2 November, he stated:

From the earliest moment of its birth the Russian Bolshevist Government has declared its intention of using all the power of the Russian Empire to promote a world revolution. Their agents have penetrated into every country. Everywhere they have endeavoured to bring into being the 'germ cells' from which the cancer of Communism should grow. Great assemblies have been held in Russia of conspirators and revolutionaries of every race under the sun for the purpose of concerting world revolution. From the beginning, Britain, the British Empire, and, above all, India, have been openly proclaimed as the first and chief objectives. . . . There was, therefore, nothing new and nothing particularly violent in the letter of Zinoviev, alias Apfelbaum, to the British Communists.

Churchill was elected with a large majority. A year later he resumed his membership in the Carlton Club, in abeyance since 1904. The prodigal had returned.

Churchill's return to the Conservatives was a natural event. 'I have always felt,' Ian Hamilton wrote, 'that Winston's coat of many colours was originally dipped into a vat of blue; a good fast Tory background, none of your synthetic or aniline dyes. The bedrock of this singular being is Conservatism.' It may be argued that it was not he who had changed, but others, and that he was holding the same views and urging similar solutions as he had in his early years. There is force in this argument, but the more his career after 1918 is studied, the more the observer is struck by a very perceptible and positive movement to the Right. There was some truth in the *mot* of Sir Robert Horne that 'Churchill is a Tory by prejudice, whereas I am one by conviction'.

The supreme irony of the situation was that by the time Churchill reached the Conservative party, its centre of gravity had moved to the Left. His failure from 1929 to 1939 does not make any sense unless this fact is fully appreciated. 'I have always said,' Amery wrote in August 1929, 'that the key to Winston is to realise that he is mid-Victorian, steeped in the politics of his father's period, and unable ever to get the modern point of view. It is only his verbal exuberance and abounding vitality that conceal this elementary fact about him.'

The Conservative leader was the genial and under-rated Stanley Baldwin. The gulf between his attitudes towards Labour and those of Churchill can be well illustrated. Thus, Churchill, 4 May 1923:

We see developing a great, vehement, deliberate attack upon the foundations of society. . . . We see not only Liberals of the Left but Conservatives of the Right assuring the country that there is no danger of Socialism or a Socialist Government, that it is a mere bogey or bugbear not worthy of serious attention. . . . Thus all resistance to violent change is paralysed or reduced to feebleness and futility.

And Baldwin, 1 January 1925:

There is only one thing which I feel is worth giving one's strength to, and that is the binding together of all classes of our people in an effort to make life in this country better in every sense of the word. That is the main end and object of my life in politics.

Baldwin was not only the leader of the Conservative party. His conciliatory attitudes and belief in the future of co-operation between classes were highly attractive to the younger, progressive Conservatives now entering public life. His style and attitudes were in welcome contrast to those of the so-called 'industrials' and Right-wing Conservatives. On the other hand, Baldwin was always subjected to a running fire from those Conservatives who considered that his approach to political questions was indistinguishable from that of Labour. Another new M.P., Clement Attlee, was struck by the fact that Baldwin always seemed more at ease in the company of Labour M.P.s than with Conservatives. Baldwin, believing emphatically that the Conservative party could only survive if it continued to recruit from the Left, had more positive effect on Conservative thinking than any leader since Disraeli; but, throughout, his leadership was in peril.

In 1924, after the election victory, he gave high office to the former Coalition Conservatives and to Churchill. Austen Chamberlain became Foreign Secretary; Birkenhead became Secretary of State for India; Churchill, astonishingly, became Chancellor of the Exchequer. It had been expected that Baldwin would give some office to Churchill – as he told Neville Chamberlain, 'he would be more under control inside than out' – but to select this wholehearted Free Trader dumbfounded the party, and particularly the Protectionist wing.

It is now considered that Churchill's tenure of the Treasury from 1924 to 1929 was an unmitigated disaster. In particular, the decision to return to the gold standard in 1925 at the pre-war parity has received no defenders, although at the time it had few critics.

Churchill's period at the Treasury has not yet received detailed study, and for the purposes of this essay the economic arguments need not concern us. But Churchill's critics have tended to put inadequate emphasis upon the virtual unanimity of the expert advice he received on the matter of the return to the gold standard and upon the fact that it had been the policy of all governments – including Labour – to work for this since the end of the war.* Perhaps the most fair judgement is that of Robert Boothby, Churchill's Parliamentary Private Secretary, although a strong critic of certain aspects of Churchill's policies:

The essence of genius is vitality, fecundity and versatility. These were the most impressive things about him. His output was colossal. He was basically uninterested in the problems of high finance. But his Budgets were skilfully contrived and superbly presented. And given the conditions under which he was obliged to work ... he could hardly have done better, or other, than he did.[15]

Inadequate attention has been given to perhaps the most serious error that Churchill committed at the Treasury. Since the end of the war he had been a vigorous proponent of economy in the armed services, and it had been he who had originally proposed, in 1919, the formula whereby the service estimates would be prepared on the assumption that there would be no war for ten years. In 1928 he succeeded in having this 'ten-year rule' formally established by the Cabinet. Of course there was no Hitler in sight in 1928, but there was strong justification for what the First Sea Lord, Admiral Beatty, wrote on 14 October 1926:

The politician says there are no external dangers. That may be true, but if so, it is due to the fact that we are strong; directly we become weak, external dangers will grow up like mushrooms.[16]

Churchill had already been directly responsible for the run-down of the Royal Air Force after the war, and he now attempted to lay strong hands on the Navy. This precipitated a major crisis in the Government, and it was only resolved after the entire Board of Admiralty had threatened to resign and Baldwin had intervened on their side. The cruisers for which the Navy fought became an issue of principle between the service

* See P. J. Grigg, *Prejudice and Judgment*, pp. 181–2, for a good defence of Churchill.

departments and the Chancellor. The Navy won on this occasion, but the service departments lost the war. The baleful long-term consequences can hardly be over-emphasized. As Sir Warren Fisher, the Permanent Under-Secretary of the Treasury at the time, wrote many years later:

We converted ourselves to military impotence. To have disarmed so drastically in the two or three years after the war was not unnatural, though possibly not wise. But the Government of 1924 to 1929 had no excuse for further reducing our armed forces to a skeleton, as by then it was known that the Weimar Republic (so called) was in process of reconstructing a disguised army on a truly formidable scale. This British Government's tragic action formed unfortunately a model for subsequent governments.[17]

This episode at first sight seems amazingly out of character. In fact, it confirms the essential truth of Esher's comment quoted before about his obsession with the matter in hand and failure to take genuinely wide views. There was substantial truth in Beatty's angry comment that 'That extraordinary fellow Winston has gone mad. Economically mad, and no sacrifice is too great to achieve what in his short-sightedness is the panacea for all evils – to take 1 shilling off the Income Tax.'[18]

At the time, Churchill's well-publicized campaign for economy in government expenditure and the return to the gold standard did him no harm at all politically. Keynes's trenchant articles in the *Evening Standard*, subsequently published under the title of *The Economic Consequences of Mr Churchill*, had much less impact at the time than they had subsequently, when it became fashionable – particularly among Labour economists – to heap all the blame for the economic troubles of the 1920s upon Churchill personally. But Keynes had nevertheless been right when he wrote of his policies that 'the whole object is to link *rigidly* the City and Wall Street. The movement of gold or of short credits either way between London and New York, which is only a ripple for them, will be an Atlantic roller for us.'

The basic contrast in attitudes between Baldwin and Churchill was graphically demonstrated in the general strike of

1926. There was no fundamental divergence in policy between the two; Baldwin was as determined as Churchill that the Government should not negotiate under duress. But the gulf in attitudes was profound. Baldwin sent Churchill off to manage a government newspaper, the *British Gazette*, having taken certain steps to ensure that he would not have a completely free hand. Churchill was accordingly neatly removed from the day-to-day control of the strike, and, to judge from what appeared in the *British Gazette*, it was just as well. The *British Gazette* was inflammatory enough as it was; if Churchill had been given his head it would have been infinitely worse. Churchill cheerfully accepted the accusations of gross partiality levelled against the *British Gazette*, but his conduct in this colourful episode did nothing to endear him further to Labour. Once again, his warmest support came from the Conservatives' Right wing.

*

When the Baldwin Government was defeated in the general election held in the early summer of 1929, Churchill's position in the Conservative party was apparently quite secure. He could – and did – take credit for the important measures of social reform pushed through by Neville Chamberlain (Minister of Health) and himself, and criticism of his performance as Chancellor was not as widespread as it was later. Asquith described him as 'a Chimborazo or Everest among the sand-hills of the Baldwin Cabinet', and of his presentation of his budgets, Macmillan has written that 'none of us had ever heard anything of the kind – such mastery of language, such careful deployment of the arguments, such dexterous covering of any weak point'. The second Baldwin Government had achieved much, but had not been greatly loved. It was, as Churchill commented, 'a capable, sedate Government'. The *Annual Register* commented that 'The fall of the Baldwin Ministry, while hailed with exultation by the progressive parties, was not deeply regretted by the bulk of its own supporters, who found much to criticize in its leading personages. Mr Baldwin had been more amiable than forceful, and had shown himself too much inclined to wait on events instead of trying to direct them. Mr Churchill had proved himself the most able debater in the party, if not in the House, but as a financier his success had been questionable.'

But in spite of appearances, Churchill's position in the party was not a strong one. The dank tides of mistrust still swirled ominously about his combative and self-confident personality. All might have been well, however, had he not immediately plunged himself into a prolonged controversy which was to imperil his career, cast a heavy shadow over his reputation, and to deprive him not only of office but any influence in the events of the 1930s.

Churchill's Imperialism was essentially nationalistic. The Empire was an instrument that gave to Britain a world position that she would not otherwise have had. For Churchill, as Amery once noted, 'England [is] still the starting-point and the ultimate object of policy.' He never visited India or South-east Asia after he left the Army at the age of twenty-four; he never returned to South Africa after the Boer War, although in 1907 he travelled in Africa on an official visit; he never visited Australia or New Zealand. Wilfrid Blunt considered in 1909 that Churchill was 'championing an optimistic Liberal Imperialism whereby the British Empire was to be maintained, in part by concession, in part by force'. He was a strong opponent of Imperial Preference in the 1900s, unenthusiastic over the 'new Commonwealth' concept of the 1920s that had its formal culmination in the Statute of Westminster in 1931, and had no zest for the campaign for 'Empire Free Trade' that caused severe strains in the Conservative ranks between 1929 and 1931.

It is difficult to detect in Churchill's Imperialism any difference of substance throughout his career. As in the case of Rosebery, there was no dichotomy between his early attitudes towards foreign entanglements and British Imperial responsibilities; indeed, far from clashing, these attitudes were complementary. Blunt's phrase – which may have been Churchill's, for Blunt was recording a long conversation with Churchill – 'an optimistic Liberal Imperialism', describes Churchill's attitudes very well, particularly in the events leading up to the creation of the Union of South Africa and the immediate prelude to the Irish Treaty.

In the case of India, there had been a slow but steady increase in the degree of Indian consultation without affecting in any way the reality of British rule at every level. The Morley–Minto Reforms of 1908 and the Montagu–Chelmsford Reforms of 1917 (established in the Government of India Act of 1919) had been further cautious steps in the policy of 'gradualness'.

By the mid-twenties it was becoming apparent that this was not going to be enough. The emergence of Gandhi, the drastic increase in racial and communal violence, and the revival of the Congress party presented an entirely new situation.

It was deeply unfortunate that Churchill's close friend Birkenhead was Secretary of State at this crucial time. In public he discounted the possibility of Indian self-government in 'any foreseeable future'; in private he wrote that 'it is frankly inconceivable that India will ever be fit for Dominion self-government'.[19] Under the 1919 act, a royal commission had to be appointed to review the situation; in order to forestall its being appointed by a Labour Government, Birkenhead set it up in 1927 under the chairmanship of Sir John Simon, and the careful choice of its membership ensured that it was not likely to make any drastic recommendations for alteration in the basic structure of British rule in India. (One of the members was Clement Attlee. His contribution was far from revolutionary.) The Simon Commission was several years too late, and its work was, in the essentials, wholly irrelevant. Nevertheless, the fact that its report – published in 1930 – made no reference whatever to Dominion status was to be an important weapon in the armoury of those who were strenuously opposed to any further extension of autonomy to Indians.

Churchill had been, to all appearances,* a loyal member of the Baldwin Government, but his impatience with what he regarded as Baldwin's unheroic attitudes became apparent shortly

---

* This was not the opinion of some of Baldwin's associates, notably Lord Bridgeman and J. C. C. Davidson, the party chairman. No evidence has yet emerged to confirm their private suspicions of Churchill's loyalty in the 1924–9 Government.

after the 1929 general election. He himself has expressed this difference in attitude clearly enough, and in characteristic terms, in a revealing passage in *The Gathering Storm*:

My idea was that the Conservative Opposition should strongly confront the Labour Government on all great Imperial and national issues, should identify itself with the majesty of Britain as under Lord Beaconsfield and Lord Salisbury, and should not hesitate to face controversy, even though that might not immediately evoke a response from the nation. So far as I could see, Mr Baldwin felt that the times were too far gone for any robust assertion of British Imperial greatness, and that the hopes of the Conservative Party lay in accommodation with Liberal and Labour forces and in adroit, well-timed manoeuvres to detach powerful moods of public opinion and large blocks of votes from them. He certainly was very successful. He was the greatest party manager the Conservatives had ever had.[20]

This is an illuminating comment. What exactly 'the majesty of Britain as under Lord Beaconsfield and Lord Salisbury' meant is not clear; and the last thrust against Baldwin is unfair to Baldwin in the context of 1929–31; it may also be remarked upon that 'the greatest party manager the Conservatives had ever had' lost two general elections (1923 and 1929) and won two (1924 and 1935) on his own account, a ratio of success and failure exactly equalled by Churchill himself as party leader.

Baldwin's position was made particularly difficult by the fact that the Viceroy of India was Lord Irwin (later Lord Halifax), a former Conservative minister who had come to the conclusion that the Indian situation required more drastic steps than the programme of provincial administration reform approved by the Simon Commission. The 'Irwin Declaration' of 31 October, to the effect that the granting of Dominion status was implicit in the 1919 act, was a thunderbolt to the Conservative party. By identifying himself with Irwin and the Government, Baldwin put his leadership in hazard and divided his party. It is difficult to portray this conduct as that of a man obsessed by party considerations.

The effects of the Irwin Declaration were quickly seen. Birkenhead, supported by a former Viceroy, Lord Reading, delivered a violent attack in the Lords against the suggestion that

India should receive Dominion status. Churchill fired an ominous warning shot in a fierce article in the *Daily Mail* early in November. The style of this article was a portent of what was to come:

Against the perpetration of such a crime as the immediate granting of Dominion Status it is necessary without delay to marshal the sober and resolute forces of the British Empire, and thus preserve the life and welfare of all the people of Hindustan.

The rupture grew nearer in 1930. Baldwin's leadership was threatened from several quarters. Beaverbrook and Rothermere – sometimes acting in concert, sometimes not – sponsored and vigorously supported anti-Baldwin candidates at by-elections. As Baldwin's attitude of support towards Irwin and the Government hardened, his critics on the Right became more outspoken. The sacrifice of the party chairman, Davidson, and votes of confidence from party meetings could not restore the leader's position.

Churchill's speeches on India became markedly more violent by the end of 1930. There is no doubt that he was passionately sincere in his opposition to a policy that would end in the granting of Dominion status; but the removal of Baldwin can hardly have escaped his expectations.

In January 1931, Irwin released Gandhi and his principal colleagues from prison and removed the proscription on Congress; the Government – again with Baldwin's approval – called for further consultations with Indian representatives. On 26 January, Churchill angrily attacked these decisions in a long speech; two days later he resigned from the Opposition 'business committee', which was the approximate equivalent of the modern 'shadow Cabinet', removed himself from the Opposition front bench and established himself as a declared rebel in the corner seat below the gangway.

Churchill was now the leading spirit of the India Defence League. His speeches were alarmist to a degree. 'Gandhi-ism and all it stands for will, sooner or later, have to be grappled with and finally crushed. It is no use trying to satisfy a tiger by feeding it on cat's meat'; he painted a dark picture of India if

Congress took over, 'when the British will be no more to them than any other European nation, when white people will be in India only on sufferance, when debts and obligations of all kinds will be repudiated, and when an army of white janissaries, officered if necessary from Germany, will be hired to secure the armed ascendancy of the Hindu'; Congress should be broken up forthwith and its leaders deported.[21] This was a relatively early speech; later ones were more violent and alarmist:

We have 45 millions in this island, a very large proportion of whom are in existence because of our world position – economic, political, imperial. If, guided by counsels of madness and cowardice disguised as false benevolence, you troop home from India, you will leave behind you what John Morley called 'a bloody chaos'; and you will find Famine to greet you on the horizon on your return.[22]

This was to be a frequent theme. As late as February 1935, in the course of a national broadcast, he warned that 'two million bread-winners in this country would be tramping the streets and queuing up at the Labour Exchanges' in the event of Indian Home Rule, and he prophesied that one third of the population of Britain 'would have to go down, out, or under, if we ceased to be a great Empire'.

Gandhi was a particular object of Churchill's scorn. He was depicted as 'this malignant and subversive fanatic', and on 23 February 1931, Churchill told the Council of the West Essex Unionist Association – which passed a vote of confidence in him – that it was 'alarming and also nauseating to see Mr Gandhi, a seditious Middle Temple lawyer, now posing as a fakir of a type well known in the East, striding half-naked up the steps of the Viceregal Palace, while he is still organizing and conducting a defiant campaign of civil disobedience, to parley on equal terms with the representative of the King-Emperor'. It was in this speech that Churchill made the personally disastrous statement that he would not join any government 'about whose Indian policy I was not reassured'.

Baldwin, like Gladstone, was 'terrible on the rebound', or, as one commentator once put it, 'his spiritual home is the last ditch.' On 13 March, he turned on the critics within the party

in the Commons; the scene has been vividly described by one
who was there:

The late Premier and his Chancellor, both evidently moved by strong
emotion, were within a few yards of one another. Churchill, seated,
with flushed features and twitching hands, looked as though about
to spring; Baldwin, on his feet, gave that impression of a passion
frozen with obedience which is his trump card.[23]

Having temporarily routed his opponents in the Commons,
Baldwin turned on Beaverbrook and Rothermere in a crucial by-
election at St George's, Westminster. Shortly before this he had
resolved to resign; fortified by his closest friends, he resolved to
fight. He won. His leadership was never again in peril. Within
six months the Labour Government had fallen, and Baldwin
was in effect co-Premier of a National Government. His critics
either hastened to demonstrate their loyalty and allegiance, or
relapsed into a sullen, sulky silence.

The India dispute, however, dragged on for another four
years. It would be wearisome to resurrect the lengthy speeches,
the public letters, the newspaper articles, the debates in Parliament, the succession of conferences, commissions, white papers,
and blue books which constitute the record of the prolonged
history of the Government of India Act, 1935. This act gave
India the title of Dominion status without the reality. It was
not enough for India; it was too much for Churchill and his
allies.

This lengthy episode had many consequences for Churchill.
It debarred him from consideration for office in the National
Government of 1931–5, but this was in some respects the least
serious of the effects on his career. His only consistent support
came from the Right wing of the party, who were to prove to be
his supporters only on this issue. This in itself alienated the
sympathies of younger and progressive Conservatives. Certain
performances – notably the attempt to indict the Secretary of
State for India, Sir Samuel Hoare, and Lord Derby on a charge
of breach of Parliamentary privilege in April 1934 – did his reputation particular harm. The careful and well-prepared campaign
that lasted throughout 1933 to repudiate the party leadership

was not likely to boost his reputation for party loyalty.* His refusal to serve on the Select Committee of both Houses of Parliament to consider the proposals of the Government gave the
strong impression that he was hostile to *any* proposals for reform
in India. Throughout, his attitudes were negative and critical.
By the summer of 1935, when his long battle ended in defeat,
ministers and back-benchers alike had had enough.

Most serious of all, he had grievously debased the language
of alarmism. The portrayal of men like Gandhi and Nehru as
'evil and malignant Brahmins', with 'itching fingers stretching
and scratching at the vast pillage of a derelict Empire', became
increasingly difficult to take seriously, and the oft-repeated
theme of 'Wake up, England!' became less and less effective by
sheer repetition. 'We are suffering from a disease of the will.
We are the victims of a nervous collapse' (5 March 1931). 'On
we go, moving slowly, in a leisurely manner, jerkily onwards,
towards an unworkable conclusion, crawling methodically
towards the abyss' (July 1931). He used such phrases in a
different context between 1934 and 1939. But men had heard it
all before, and took no heed. This was the real tragedy of the
now long-forgotten struggle over the Government of India Act,
1935.

By 1935, Lloyd George's entire political following in the House
of Commons consisted of his son, his daughter, and his son-in-
law. Churchill's consisted of two young men derided by Baldwin
on one occasion as 'the faithful chelas', Brendan Bracken and
Robert Boothby, subsequently joined by Churchill's son-in-
law, Duncan Sandys. Lloyd George – now ageing noticeably –
was no longer a political figure to be feared. Churchill's fortunes
had reached a very low ebb. He seems to have believed that,

* Another episode in this vein occurred in January 1935. Churchill's
son, Mr Randolph Churchill, presented himself as Independent candidate at the Wavertree (Liverpool) by-election. Churchill had no prior
knowledge of his son's venture, but he spoke at his eve-of-poll rally,
declaring that 'this is not an election, it is a national uprising'. Randolph
Churchill, after a whirlwind campaign, got over ten thousand votes,
and his intervention gave the seat to Labour. The wrath of the party
faithful was intense.

with the end of the India controversy, he could return to the Government, and he appears to have been genuinely surprised when his overtures had no success. Churchill, although very sensitive to criticism against himself, often quickly forgot his jibes against others. Men who had been compared as late as June 1935 to pygmies were hardly likely to look upon him with favour. Yet Churchill was surprised at his continuing exclusion, and for the next three years castigated ministers in public and made overtures in private. Baldwin appointed him to the important Air Research Defence Committee in the teeth of opposition from other members of the Cabinet; since 1932 he had been supplied with important official information on rearmament abroad; after 1936 the Admiralty told him a great deal. These links with officialdom were of great significance, but they marked the limits of his penetration into the Government.

His prolonged campaign over India had emphasized his by now very pronounced Conservatism. In his enchanting *My Early Life*, published in 1930, he described Joseph Chamberlain addressing a meeting in Oldham in 1900 in significant terms (italics mine):

I must explain that in those days we had *a real political democracy led by a hierarchy of statesmen*, and not a fluid mass distracted by newspapers. There was a structure in which statesmen, electors and the Press all played their part. . . . All this was *before the liquefaction of the British political system had set in*.[24]

In October 1932, at the height of the India struggle, Churchill declared in a public letter that:

Elections, even in the most educated democracies, are regarded as a misfortune and as a disturbance of social, moral, and economic progress; even as a danger to international peace. Why at this moment should we force upon the untutored races of India that very system, the inconveniences of which are now felt even in the most highly developed nations, the United States, Germany, France and in England itself?

By 1934 he was in effect advocating a retreat from the principle of 'one man, one vote', and was saying that 'a universal suffrage electorate with a majority of women voters will have shown themselves incapable of preserving those forms of government under which our country has grown great and from which all the dignity and tolerance of our present life arise.' His proposed solution to 'a timid Caesarism refreshing itself by occasional plebiscites' was to give a second vote to every householder – 'by which I mean the man or woman who pays the rent and the rates of any dwelling in which more than two persons habitually reside'* – and proportional representation for the great cities.

Churchill was genuinely concerned about the decline in British public life, but his proposals to return to the pre-1914 privileged system were symptomatic of what appeared to be a considerable dislike of the new political conditions. 'All experience goes to show that once the vote has been given to everyone, and what is called full democracy has been achieved, the whole [political] system is very speedily broken up and swept away.' In holding such views and in advocating such solutions, Churchill's remoteness from the movement of progressive political views was vividly demonstrated. No doubt, things had been more convenient before 1914. But a great deal had happened since 1914.

By 1933, when Churchill began his warnings over the menace of Nazi Germany, he was politically isolated and to a large extent discredited. Many Conservatives who agreed with him on India did not share his apprehensions over the rise of Germany, and the younger Conservatives, who had backed Baldwin in the India dispute, did not turn to Churchill's leadership when they began to agree with his alarming analysis of what was happening in Europe. Even when Labour began to awake from its feckless euphoria, fundamental differences of outlook and experience prevented any close sympathy. 'Throughout the 1930s,' as George Isaacs has written, 'suspicion of Churchill was one factor in preventing any attempt by the trade unions to make a closer alliance with him in opposition to the foreign policy of the Baldwin and Chamberlain Governments.'

---

* This would have been rather rough on property-owning bachelors and spinsters, not to mention property-owning childless couples! Churchill's arguments were set out in the *Listener*, 17 January 1934, and the *Evening Standard*, 24 January.

Churchill accordingly delivered the speeches on defence between 1933 and the end of 1936 in a hostile environment. He had fallen so low in the estimation of all that these speeches – some of which are the greatest that he ever made – were made to an audience that was weary of his rhetoric, bored by his incessant alarmism, and deeply distrustful of his judgement. The fact that he made the impact that he did was an immense tribute to the skill and persistence with which he brought the question before the House of Commons and the public, but that impact was far less than would have been the case had he not so grievously compromised his reputation.

Nevertheless, the facts of the situation were such that, by the middle of 1936, Churchill was beginning to make real progress. The fact that the Government publicly accepted Churchill's extremely exaggerated claims of German air power had shaken confidence in Baldwin; the volte-face of the Hoare–Laval pact immediately after the clear declaration of support for the League of Nations over Italian aggression in Abyssinia had produced an unparalleled storm of protest and had caused the resignation of the Foreign Secretary, Hoare, in December 1935; Baldwin was ageing, and in the summer of 1936 suffered what was in fact a nervous breakdown. Britain may not have been prepared to fight over the remilitarization of the Rhineland in March 1936, but public concern had been aroused.

The divergent streams of opposition to the Baldwin Government's attitudes – whereby the Covenant of the League was to be preserved and rearmament maintained – were canalized into the 'Arms and the Covenant' movement which had considerable political potentiality. On 3 December 1936, it held its first public meeting at the Albert Hall, with Walter Citrine – General Secretary of the T.U.C. – in the chair. But 3 December was the day on which the British press broke its long silence over the relationship of King Edward VIII with Mrs Simpson.

The abdication crisis that now engrossed the nation showed Churchill at his best as an individual and his worst as a politician. His romantic and loyal instincts made him rally to the King's side at this very late stage. He blundered into a very difficult and delicate situation heedless of the warnings of his wife and his friends, too late to save the King but not too late to destroy himself. A very lengthy and somewhat tendentious public statement on 5 December accused the Government of ignoring the House of Commons and attempting to 'extort' abdication from the King. In taking this stand he had fatally misjudged the situation and the mood of the hour. Rightly or wrongly, Mrs Simpson was unacceptable to the Royal Family, the Government, the Labour and Liberal parties, and the Dominion Prime Ministers. Baldwin, as Churchill subsequently wrote, 'undoubtedly perceived and expressed the profound will of the nation'. In these circumstances, an apparent attempt to create a 'King's party' aroused intense anger in all parties. On 7 December, when Churchill rose to plead for delay in the House of Commons, he was literally shouted down.

The effect of this characteristic performance was severe. 'All the effect of the Albert Hall meeting was destroyed,' Macmillan has recorded, '– first by the Abdication and secondly by the catastrophic fall in Churchill's prestige. It was not possible to restore the situation.' Churchill himself has written that 'all the forces I had gathered together in Arms and the Covenant . . . were estranged or dissolved'. Lady Asquith has recorded that several strong sympathizers within the movement 'expressed to me (and no doubt to others) the view that if he continued to lead us our cause would be hopelessly compromised'. The abdication crisis had succeeded in exactly reversing the political fortunes of Baldwin and Churchill.

Disastrous though this sad episode was, in a sense one would not have had it otherwise. What was folly in the politician was to the credit of the man. His motives seem to have been entirely directed towards saving the King and not destroying the Government (the motives of others, notably Beaverbrook, were very different). But appearances were against him, and a reading of the statement of 5 December makes it plain why his actions were misinterpreted. One is reminded of what he had written of his father in *My Early Life*: 'He never sat down to play a cold, calculated game. He said what he thought. It was better so.'

*

The collapse of the Arms and the Covenant movement was followed by a lull in foreign affairs that lasted until March 1938. Churchill continued to urge accelerated rearmament, but throughout 1937 he – like so many others – did not see the way ahead clearly. He had always had a high opinion of Mussolini, and in October 1937 he wrote that 'it would be a dangerous folly for the British people to underrate the enduring position in world history which Mussolini will hold; or the amazing qualities of courage, comprehension, self-control and persever-ance which he exemplifies'. In the Spanish Civil War, although a convinced believer in British neutrality, he definitely favoured the Franco cause up to the spring of 1938. In 1937 he repub-lished a 1935 article on Hitler which was by no means condem-natory, and on 17 September he wrote that 'one may dislike Hitler's system and yet admire his patriotic achievement. If our country were defeated, I hope we should find a champion as in-domitable to restore our courage and lead us back to our place among the nations'. In another newspaper article he admitted that he had been 'a loud alarmist' but that he now considered that war would not come.

These hesitations and doubts must not be permitted to con-travert Churchill's record in these years, but they do demon-strate the fact that his warnings were not as clear as he made them appear to have been in *The Gathering Storm*. In particular, his pro-Franco feelings were not likely to endear him to those people who saw in the Spanish Civil War the great cause of their lives.

By 1938, when the storm broke over Europe, Churchill's position was very low. His personal following was so small as to be disregarded for practical political purposes. Some of his greatest speeches on defence matters were made to a half-empty or inattentive House of Commons; even when he did make an impact, it was a temporary one. He never gave up, and he main-tained an exemplary self-control and determination. But those fine speeches, which read so powerfully in retrospect, were largely failures at the time. Mistrust of him was not confined to his opponents. Sir Alan Herbert, Independent Member for Oxford University, and an old friend and deep admirer of

Churchill, has written of his feelings towards him in 1937 and 1938:

I did not think, as so many thought in those days, that he was brilliant, resourceful, brave, but nearly always wrong. I thought that he was nearly always right. . . . But I did think that he rather enjoyed a war: and, after three years in the infantry, in Gallipoli and France, I did not.[25]

This feeling – which was very strong in the Labour party – played a very important part in explaining why so many of his warnings went unheeded. Furthermore, in his attempt to arouse his countrymen to their peril, he painted a picture of the war to come in colours so lurid and appalling that the effect was often exactly the reverse of what he had intended. The feeling that Churchill 'rather enjoyed a war' was not likely to be diminished by the evident relish with which he related military matters in *Marlborough*; and his terrible warnings of the horror of another war were not likely to diminish the national apprehension and eagerness for a negotiated settlement.

The true extent of Churchill's isolation was eloquently illustrated by the fact that those Conservatives who opposed the Government's policies did not gather under his leadership. Indeed, they went to some trouble to avoid doing so. After Anthony Eden's resignation from the Foreign Office in March 1938, a distinct 'Eden Group' was formed. Its purpose was to influence the Chamberlain Government (Neville Chamberlain had succeeded Baldwin as Prime Minister in May 1937) rather than to assail it, and it attracted a relatively small but talented following in the Conservative party, known to the irritated Whips and loyal supporters of the Government as 'the glamour boys'. The Eden Group held itself deliberately aloof from Churchill, and rebuffed any attempts at joint action; when Duncan Sandys asked if he could attend a meeting of the Group it was made very plain to him that his presence would not be welcomed. Any co-operation was fortuitous and pragmatic. This attitude did not offend Churchill as much as it infuriated some members of his very small personal entourage.

Munich, and its dismal aftermath, awoke the nation at last to the reality of Nazi intentions, and the Chamberlain Government was propelled unhappily towards more belligerent attitudes. By the early summer of 1939, two very different newspapers – the *Daily Telegraph* and the *Daily Mirror* – began to agitate for Churchill's inclusion in the Government. But in hard political terms this did not amount to a great deal. His personal following in the Commons was still miniscule; he narrowly survived a motion of no-confidence in him in his own constituency; the Eden Group still acted – no doubt with good cause – as if association with him were the political kiss of death. But it was becoming more and more evident that, as Neville Chamberlain wrote in his diary, 'Churchill's chances [of office] improve as war becomes possible, and *vice versa.*' Halifax, who was a good barometer, had startled Chamberlain immediately after Munich by advising a coalition with Labour and the recall of Churchill and Eden, but Chamberlain, who believed in the possibility of averting war up to the last moment, regarded such action as being provocative to the dictators. But by midsummer 1939, appeasement had become discredited, and an ever-increasing element in the House of Commons and the country was becoming actively eager to provoke Hitler. The one thing that had acted against Churchill for so long, his belligerence, now suddenly became his most attractive quality. In 1935, Herbert Morrison – who subsequently served in the wartime coalition under Churchill – described him as 'a fire-eater and a militarist'. This was now exactly what people were looking for.

Thus, when war came, Churchill returned with it. Reluctantly bowing to pressures in the press and Parliament, Chamberlain reconstructed his government to include Eden and Churchill. Churchill returned to the Admiralty, and at once ordered that his 1915 map be restored to its old position in his office.

It has become almost a historical cliché to say that Churchill would never have become Prime Minister had it not been for the Second World War. Unlike most historical clichés, it is essentially true. By 1939, for reasons which I have endeavoured to describe, he was politically *déconsidéré*, largely ignored even by those who agreed with his attitudes on foreign affairs. His career since 1915 had been, in the main, a story of failure. Now,

in his sixty-fifth year, after some forty years in active political
life, he was at last given his opportunity.

Throughout the winter of 1939–40, the period immortalized
by an American reporter as 'the phoney war', the one gleam
of achievement was provided by the Royal Navy – an interesting
contrast with the reaction to the performance of the Navy in the
first months of the First World War. Churchill considerably exaggerated these achievements, and his claims of submarine sink-
ings in particular were very greatly – and deliberately – dis-
torted. But his vigour and spirit were in refreshing contrast with
the attitudes of the majority of his colleagues in the Government. It was this, above all else, that made him look more and
more like the war leader that men increasingly craved for.

Nevertheless, it was significant that when the Chamberlain
Government had plainly lost the confidence of the nation and
the House of Commons by May 1940, Churchill was not regarded as the inevitable successor. The Labour party made it
clear that it would be prepared to serve under Halifax or, indeed, almost any Conservative except Chamberlain. It was when
Halifax considered that it was impossible for a peer to be Prime
Minister, particularly in the desperate situation facing the nation at that time, that Churchill's succession became certain.
Looking back, it seems astonishing that there was any hesitation about the matter; but, even in May 1940, pre-war political
memories remained strong. The Conservatives accepted the
situation without enthusiasm; it was only after the first of the
great speeches in the Commons that the mood changed. It is
often said that speeches do not affect votes in the House of
Commons; this is almost, although not quite, true; but it is
true that speeches can affect reputations. What will always be
remembered as the 'blood, sweat, and tears' speech was a real
turning point. It stirred the Commons to its depths. It came to
the British people as a call to service and sacrifice. It rang
round the world, and thrilled the many friends of Western
civilization with the realization that Britain was going to fight.
There were those in 1940 who believed that Britain should seek
a negotiated settlement with Hitler; perhaps it was, technically,
the wisest thing to do. But, after that first, unforgettable speech,

such arguments lost whatever appeal they might have had.* Here was the authentic voice of leadership and defiance. It was Churchill's outstanding quality as a war leader that he made the struggle seem not merely essential for national survival, but worthwhile and noble. No one – not even a child, as I was – who was in England in the summer of 1940 will ever forget the *cheerfulness* of the people. It was not even a gallows-humour mood. One caught Churchill's infectious spirit that this was a great time to be alive in; that Destiny had conferred a wonderful benefit upon us; and that these were thrilling days to live through. Of course, this mood could not be permanent, and the reality of sacrifice was a very different thing to the prospect. But the horror of war was to a remarkable extent exorcized by the exhilaration of the struggle, and I have no doubt that it was this that brought the British people through their ordeal.

Churchill's entire career – his experience of war and high office, and his experience of disappointment, of failure – reached its culmination in the war. He did not repeat Lloyd George's mistake of neglecting the House of Commons, though he borrowed many of Lloyd George's methods. Nor did he repeat Lloyd George's fatal failure to have a party behind him; his insistence upon securing the leadership of the Conservative party after the death of Neville Chamberlain in November 1940 was extremely significant. Leading a wartime coalition and retaining a tight control on the strategy of the war, he could not devote much attention to the future post-war Conservative programme, but he could at least ensure that he would be the Conservative post-war leader.

As the war approached its conclusion it was evident that a substantial change of attitude towards Churchill had taken place in Britain. The brief, glorious period of reconciliation was over. Men were less concerned about how the war had been won than what was to be done with the victory. This is not entirely

---

* A little-known story of this speech must not be omitted. As Churchill left the chamber after an emotional ovation, considerably moved himself, he caught the eye of an old friend. With a sudden impish grin Churchill said to him: 'That got the sods, didn't it?'

wisdom after the event; to anyone returning to Britain in 1944, as I did, it was evident at once. What was not evident was that the British were to turn so decisively to other men for the solution of these problems; it seemed that the Lloyd George victory of 1918 was to be repeated, and for the same reason: the man who won the war would win the peace.

The subsequent fiasco – from the Conservative point of view – of the 1945 general election had many causes. The Conservative campaign had at least one major flaw. Churchill was starred as the great national leader, but – urged on by Beaverbrook – he conducted a campaign of such old-style vigour and partisanship that all the advantages of his great prestige were thrown away. The insensitiveness of his performance was characteristic, but disastrous. What was most disconcerting of all was to hear the familiar voice now being used for such purposes. It was as if David had started catapulting the Hebrews!

No doubt the election was lost to the Conservatives before the campaign began. While Churchill's audiences were large and enthusiastic, his performance did succeed in reviving old suspicions and antipathies. The fact that an unknown Independent polled over ten thousand votes against him in his own constituency renders the oft-stated assumption that the British wanted Churchill but not the Conservatives open to some doubt. Nevertheless, the crash of Churchill's fall astonished the British no less than foreigners, and the new Labour ministers did not succeed in adequately concealing their own amazement.

Thus, Churchill became Leader of the Opposition for the first time in his career. There were those who urged him to retire from active politics, who still regret that he did not, and who consider that his influence between 1945 and 1950 would have been far greater if he had been outside the day-to-day political battles. Certainly he was not a very effective Leader of the Opposition in the Commons,* and his stature abroad often seemed greater than in his own country. The ugly use of the 'warmonger' allegations in the 1951 general election – in

* For two contrasting views, see Winterton, *Orders of the Day*, p. 317; and Lord Kilmuir, *Political Adventure*, pp. 148–9.

which, although Labour lost in terms of seats won, it won a majority of the popular vote over the Conservatives – was a reminder of old, not-forgotten suspicions.

Thus, even in the glowing evening of his career, substantial reservations remained. Gratitude for his war leadership was not transformed into confidence in his abilities in calmer times (or what were thought to be calmer times). Only when he reached his eightieth birthday did these reservations seem to evaporate like one of those interminable sea mists which seem so permanent and yet which blow away in an instant. The end of the story was as it had been in *Savrola*:

Those who care to further follow the annals of the Republic of Laurania may read how, after the tumults had subsided, the hearts of the people turned again to the illustrious exile who had won them freedom and whom they had deserted in the hour of victory. They may, scoffing at the fickleness of men, read of the return of Savrola and his beautiful escort to the city he had loved so well.

Churchill's political career is bound to be the subject of prolonged and detailed interest and controversy. In length and complexity it is only matched by that of Gladstone in modern British political history. No career since that of Chatham has ended in such triumph and glory. Perhaps the time has not yet arrived when that career can be seen as a whole. The unsuccessful politician for forty years is overshadowed by the lustre of the war leadership and the post-war statesman. Yet, confronted by this astonishing career, one must seek some tentative conclusions.

It would be simple to say, as his admirers do, that he was always regarded with the suspicion that mediocrity reserves for genius. But this explanation is too facile. It ignores, above all else, the fact that many of the suspicions that haunted Churchill were, *prima facie*, well justified, and, in politics, *prima facie* is perfectly sufficient.

It is impossible to divorce Churchill the politician from Churchill the man. His great qualities were courage, integrity and – not far behind – immense application. His persistence was perhaps the greatest personal and political quality of all, and never seen to greater advantage than in the 1930s. On three occasions – 1915, 1922, and the mid-1930s – it seemed that his reputation was irretrievably stricken, yet, by determination and persistence, he survived. If he was lucky, he worked for his luck. Then he was a firm friend and a blessedly bad intriguer. If his moods were variable – as they were – he made no attempt to conceal them. Although he fought hard, he rarely left any deep wounds in his opponents. His essential humanity and generosity of spirit gave him few real enemies, although he always had many critics. His magnanimity has perhaps been rather over-stressed. He had a habit of taking criticism personally, and his magnanimity could be highly selective; but, when one considers the vigour of his political life and his total absorption in it, the absence of rancour in his character must be accounted a remarkable quality.

His failings were closely allied to his qualities. He was ego-centric to a remarkable degree, and possessed a strong sense of destiny. Without these, it is difficult to see how he could have survived the exceptional vicissitudes of his career; nevertheless, they removed him from a full comprehension of the problems and feelings of great masses of people. Egocentricity had other defects. As Boothby has written: ' "Thou shalt have none other gods but me" has always been the first, and the most significant, of his Commandments. And woe betide him who is suspected of any deviation from this straight and narrow path. So be it. These defects, which made some mistrust and others fear him in time of peace, turned into the qualities which led us to victory in the war.' Churchill's eye for character was often deficient, and his enjoyment of buccaneers sometimes led him into unfortunate relationships. It is difficult to think that the influence of Birkenhead, particularly in the 1920s, was a good one, for example. As Lady Asquith has written:

I think that for him human beings fell, roughly, into three categories; the great figures whom he weighed, measured and assessed in a historical perspective and about whom his judgement rarely erred; the (so-called) average man and woman who often made no impact on his attention, let alone his mind; and lastly his friends – those who had found their way into his heart.[26]

Churchill's principal failing as a politician was one of communication. To quote Lady Asquith again: 'Armies are just as necessary in politics as in war. And they can only be recruited by persuasion.' Churchill's essentially rhetorical approach, and the fixity with which he adhered to a point when he had carefully considered it, gave neither his public speaking nor his private conversation the impression of a dialogue. As Morley once commented: 'Whereas Winston knows his own mind, Lloyd George is always more concerned to know the minds of other people.' It is sometimes difficult to decide whether this was Churchill's outstanding virtue or one of his major deficiencies; but it certainly gave him a remoteness from his audience which was often unfortunate.

Churchill always lived on a different plane to the vast bulk of mankind. He, and others, have emphasized the fact that he was never, until his last years, a rich man, and that he worked for everything he earned. Churchill's poverty was, however, somewhat relative. He demanded a high standard of living, and he worked for it.

But his real remoteness was of a more subtle kind. Isaiah Berlin has written:

As much as any king conceived by a Renaissance dramatist or by a nineteenth-century historian or moralist he thinks it a brave thing to ride in triumph through Persepolis; he knows with an unshakeable certainty what he considers to be big, handsome, noble, worthy of pursuit by someone in high station and what on the contrary he abhors being dim, grey, thin, likely to lower or destroy the play of colour and movement in the universe.[27]

The Romantic sense is most attractive when regarded from a distance of time. It is less engaging when contemplated at closer range by those cast in the role of supporting players in a drama over which they have no control and in which they have little interest.

Churchill's imperious attitude towards Party has already been emphasized. It ensured his political survival and advantage, but did not win him the loyalty and following that he might otherwise have had. His independence was the independence of the adventurer and the opportunist. Until the 1930s it is difficult indeed to see in him the pursuit of any identifiable cause. But he was not one for making long-term calculations. Ardent in the pursuit of the immediate, he often neglected the future. In view of his warnings of 1912–14, 1934–9, and 1946–8, this may appear an unfair comment. But in all these cases he was drawing public attention to actual rather than hypothetical situations; his achievement – not to be disparaged by any means – was in diagnosis rather than in prognosis. It is in no way to belittle his formidable intellect to state that it was principally applied to the meeting of immediate situations rather than to anticipating future ones. What was often ascribed to reckless-ness was in fact the consequence of this aspect of his character. In domestic politics, this failure to illuminate the future or to en-visage a new and changed society was not an advantage; it also goes far to explain why he leaves no message and no vision for the new rising generation today. He is regarded by them as a fascinating historical personality but essentially a man of his time. To an older generation for whom the war was the most vivid experience of their lives, this cold-blooded attitude ap-pears incomprehensible and even blasphemous. But they forget that, for some forty years, Churchill was to his contemporaries as unreal, as remote, and as irrelevant a personality as he now ap-pears to the young men and women who were unborn when the war ended. But although he may have no message for them, it is to be hoped that they will realize that here was one of the most astonishing men of modern times; that, if the British Empire were to die, it was right that it should have had a final blaze of glory; be commanded by a man who would not realize that its great days were past, and who, by this belief, made others be-lieve it as well. In 1931, when Churchill was in eclipse, Harold Nicolson had written of him that: 'He is a man who leads for-lorn hopes, and when the hopes of England become forlorn, he will once again be summoned to leadership.' Thus it came to pass. There are times when dreams are better than facts.

NOTES

1. Lord Winterton, 'Churchill the Parliamentarian', *Churchill By His Contemporaries*, edited by Charles Eade, pp. 86–7.
2. Beatrice Webb, *Our Partnership*, pp. 269–70.
3. William George, *My Brother and I*, p. 211.
4. R. Boothby, *I Fight to Live*, p. 45.
5. T. Jones, *Lloyd George*, p. 91.
6. Randolph S. Churchill, *Winston S. Churchill*, companion vol. I, part 2, pp. 816–21.
7. Sir Isaiah Berlin, *Mr Churchill in 1940*, pp. 25–6.
8. Edward Marsh, *A Number of People*, pp. 151–2.
9. William Beveridge, *Power and Influence*, p. 87.
10. Lord Beaverbrook, *Politicians and the War*, p. 98.
11. Beaverbrook, op. cit., pp. 125–6.
12. V. W. Germains, *The Tragedy of Winston Churchill*, p. 278.
13. C. Hassall, *Edward Marsh*, p. 565.
14. Minutes of the War Council, 3 March 1915.
15. Boothby, op. cit., p. 44.
16. Chalmers, *Beatty*, p. 411.
17. Sir Warren Fisher, 'The Beginnings of Civil Defence', *Public Administration*, vol. XXVI, Winter, 1948.
18. Chalmers, op. cit., pp. 403–4.
19. Birkenhead, *Halifax*, p. 206.
20. Churchill, *The Gathering Storm*, p. 26.
21. Speech to the Indian Empire Society, 12 December 1930.
22. Speech at the Free Trade Hall, Manchester, 30 January 1931.
23. Hugh Martin, *Battle*, p. 229.
24. Churchill, *My Early Life*, pp. 352–3.
25. A. P. Herbert, *Independent Member*, p. 109.
26. Violet Bonham Carter, *Winston Churchill As I Knew Him*, pp. 145–6.
27. Berlin, op. cit., p. 17.

J. H. Plumb THE
HISTORIAN

1

The Baroque chimney stacks of Blenheim flaunt their grandeur against the sky, the final dramatic gesture of a palace that was always a monument and rarely a home. Achievements riotously carved in stone, obelisks of victory, sweeping columns, vista piled on vista create a sense of drama, of battle, of victory. There is no house like it in the Western world; and certainly not one in England that is dedicated so emphatically to one man – John Churchill, Duke of Marlborough, who decisively defeated the French armies of Louis XIV with a motley crew of Dutch, Germans, Danes, Scots, and a few regiments of the English. This great palace lies, therefore, at the heart of the Whig legend of that past which the English had manufactured in order to underpin their Imperial ambitions and in which Winston Churchill had implicit belief. Born at Blenheim, educated amongst the descendants of the great Whig aristocracy of Stuart and Georgian England, his life was spent as a politician, strategist, and historian in the service of that curious ideology of the Whigs, half truth, half fiction; half noble, half base. Many of its principles possessed for Churchill the quality of absolute truth, indeed as absolute as any religious dogma. Somewhat sceptical in religion, towards which at times he could permit himself a caustic yet felicitous epigram, he was totally unhumorous and solemnly reverent when it came to the great institutions of government – monarchy and parliament – or even to 'freedom' and 'liberty' as interpreted by the English governing class. Such unthinking acceptance of the traditional beliefs of his class was to temper his strength as a statesman and, indeed, was to enable him to lead his country through its darkest and most desperate hours, but it fissured his history and rendered much of it obsolete as soon as it was written. This is particularly true of his formal historical works, although, perhaps, less so with his autobiographical works of contemporary history, whether it be the *Malakand Field Force* or the massive volumes on the two World Wars. To understand Churchill the historian, one must look closer at his inheritance; particularly the historical assumptions of his class. .

For Churchill, English history was a progression, a development of inherent national characteristics, a process whereby the Englishman's love of liberty, freedom, and justice gradually, by trial and error, discovered those institutions of government which were apt to his nature. Churchill, like all good Whigs before him, discovered the seed of this momentous historical process in the dark Saxon days.

After the shapeless confusion of darker centuries, obscure to history and meaningless to almost all who lived through them, we now see a purpose steadily forming. England, with an independent character and personality, might scarcely yet be a part of a world civilization as in Roman times, but there was a new England, closer than ever before to national unity, and with a native genius of her own. Henceforward an immortal spirit stood forth for all to see.

This genius absorbed the Danes and the Normans, triumphed over the ravages of the former and the conquest of the latter. The barons, the great landowners, checked the tyrant kings, particularly John, calling in the people of substance to help them keep a balance in the Constitution. And so Parliament, sometimes weak, sometimes strong, rooted itself in English life, becoming the bulwark of freedom and liberty. Justice, from time to time corrupt and perverse, grew in stature and in independence as century followed century. The break with Rome, followed as it quickly was by England's first victories overseas, underlined England's special destiny and confirmed her powerful individuality. England, at last, found her full identity in the reign of Elizabeth I. All was put in peril by the Stuarts, and England was unhappily plunged in fratricidal strife. But again this proved providential. The taste of republicanism proved too bitter and Englishmen returned to their natural allegiance, monarchy. True, at first there were faltering steps and a peculiarly stupid monarch in James II. But the Glorious Revolution of 1688 – the most venerable of all events in Whig mythology – brought the perfect relationship: a permanent parliament and a docile monarchy. Under the aegis of the great Whig magnates, the freedom-loving English battled against the tyrant French, first Louis XIV, then Napoleon, and defeated both. And, of course, marched forward to her Imperial Destiny. Difficulties there were and faults. The loss of America could be, and was, blamed on George III and his sycophantic friends. Industrialization threatened the cherished institutions, yet brought such wealth that it had to be fostered. Both Empire and the people were problems which taxed English genius to its utmost, but it solved both. The British Empire was the most just the world had seen, and its people enjoyed the richest and freest democracy history had ever known. The English and their institutions were the result of time working on natural genius. And the centuries-old leaders of this miraculous historical development were those 'great Oaks', as Edmund Burke called them – the great landed aristocratic families who were the guardians of England's destiny and its natural rulers.

This, of course, was not history; it was a past which genera- tions of Englishmen – workers, politicians, poets, even novelists – had created to give a sense of meaning and purpose to the events in which they were involved. It was a past which always confirmed the present. It was intensely usable and Churchill used it constantly. It helped him formulate his political ideas. It governed his attitude to India, to Ireland, to Europe. It invaded his strategy and his tactics. It inflamed his rhetoric with a mea- sured and unforgettable passion. It regulated his political deci- sions. It imbued everything that he wrote. One of his motives as a historian was to demonstrate the truth of these beliefs which he had inherited.

Time and time again these sentiments crop up in his books and speeches like a favourite chord in music. His very first book, *The Story of the Malakand Field Force*, ends with these sen- tences:

The year 1897, in the annals of the British people, was marked by a declaration to the whole world of their faith in the higher destinies of their race. If a strong man, when the wine sparkles at the feast and the lights are bright, boasts of his prowess, it is well he should have an opportunity of showing in the cold and grey of the morning that he is no idle braggart. And unborn arbiters, with a wider knowledge, and more developed brains, may trace in recent events the influence of that mysterious Power which, directing the progress of our species and regulating the rise and fall of empires, has afforded that opportunity to a people of whom at least it may be said that they have added to the happiness, the learning and the liberties of mankind.

Forty years later, in his *Marlborough, His Life and Times*, the same theme was being played but with more mature and complex variations.

No dreamer, however romantic, however remote his dreams from reason, could have foreseen a surely approaching day when, by the formation of mighty coalitions and across the struggles of a generation, the noble colossus of France would lie prostrate in the dust, while the small island, beginning to gather to itself the empires of India and America, stripping France and Holland of their colonial possessions, would emerge victorious, mistress of the Mediterranean, the Narrow Seas, and the oceans. Aye, and carry forward with her, intact and enshrined, all that peculiar structure of law and liberty, all her own inheritance of learning and letters, which are to-day the treasure of the most powerful family in the human race.

This prodigy was achieved by conflicting yet contributory forces and by a succession of great islanders and their noble foreign comrades or guides. We owe our salvation to the sturdy independence of the House of Commons and to its creators, the aristocracy and country gentlemen. We owe it to our hardy tars and bold sea-captains, and to the quality of a British Army as yet unborn. We owe it to the inherent sanity and vigour of the political conceptions sprung from the genius of the English race.

For Churchill, the past confirmed the peculiar genius of the English race and proved its right to be rich, Imperial, and the guardian of human freedoms. He was not alone. He imbibed this attitude from all that he read or saw. His views were the commonplace of the classroom and the themes of the historical best-sellers throughout his long life – J. R. Green, G. M. Trevelyan, Sir Arthur Bryant. And this mythology, basically aristocratic, or at least landed and genteel, had been accepted unthinkingly by the industrial middle class and by vast sections of the literate labouring population too. They needed no further proof than a map of the world splashed all over with red. Churchill and the governing classes of the English nation shared a common sense of the past. To grasp this is most important, for history was not, for Churchill, like painting, something one turned to for relaxation or merely to turn an honest guinea to meet his mountainous expenses. History was the heart of his faith; it permeated everything which he touched, and it was the mainspring of his politics and the secret of his immense mastery. Just as in a sense De Gaulle has been engaged in a historical dialogue with his nation, so Churchill was with his. His violent disagreement with Neville Chamberlain did not spring solely from thwarted ambition or personal dislike. Such motives may have sharpened the phrases and honed his epigrams, but the long policy of appeasement, the weakening of Britain's world role, the acceptance of oppression and racialism were to Churchill a denial of England's historical destiny and, because a denial, bound to end in disaster. And, on the verge of war, he advised Hitler to study English history so that he might ponder what would very likely be his fate. And when the final challenge came, it was the strength of the past to which Churchill turned again and again. For he well realized that he was leading a nation more deeply conscious of, and committed to, its sense of the past than any the world has known since Imperial China. Churchill the historian is far more than Churchill the writer of history books. He is, perhaps, the last great practitioner of the historic theme of England's providential destiny. The past in which he intensely believed has been shattered by the fifties and sixties. It no longer holds credence either for the governing élite or the nation at large. There are pockets of believers who comfort themselves with the works of Sir Arthur Bryant, but they know in their bones that their past is dead. What gave Churchill his confidence, his courage, his burning faith in the rightness of his cause – his deep sense of the miraculous English past – has been lost. It no longer explains our role or our purpose. The role of history is vanishing from politics, but because it is, it is so very necessary to stress how deep the roots of history penetrated Churchill's world and how in tune this attitude was with the feelings of the nation he served. In consequence, therefore, it is not surprising that when he composed his historical works they should enjoy from first to last the most exemplary success.

Yet before turning to their consideration, there remains a further strand to be explored in the making of Churchill the historian.

2

Historians are formed not only by the age in which they live and the class into which they are born, but also by their own personal characters and the interplay of them with their environment and education. And in this Churchill was no exception. Professional historians are forced by their training to develop an acute sense of awareness of their conditioning and of the response of their own personalities to the subjects which they may be investigating. Churchill, however, had no professional training as a historian at all. To him, historical criticism was an almost unknown art, hence the effect of his personality, of his prejudices, and of his enthusiasms on his historical writing was very direct.

Churchill had a difficult childhood in the ordinary circumstances of his class. His father, Lord Randolph, was gifted, flamboyant, reckless, an orator who could hold the Victorian House of Commons spellbound and yet behave with outstanding pettiness and pomposity towards his own sons. Unpredictable, he seized the young Winston's imagination in a vice-like grip and at the same time totally over-awed him. Lord Randolph died early, a failure: crushed and defeated by the inexorable men of small mind who are the bone and sinew of politics. And his father's fate bit deeply into Churchill's heart, drawing him to the odd, the flamboyant, the reckless, and nurturing a bud of hatred for the complacent, the controlled, the cautious men of self-confirmed moral rectitude. One has only to turn to *Great Contemporaries*, one of Churchill's most valuable contributions to the understanding of English political personalities of the twentieth century, to see how deep was his attachment to his image of Lord Randolph, and how the bitterness that he felt in regard to his father worked itself out in his relationship with other men. His delight in Birkenhead, in Rosebery, in Joseph Chamberlain, in Lloyd George and, above all, in Charles Parnell had its origins in his father's character. And it is not surprising that the first formal piece of historical writing which Churchill attempted was the life of his father. Churchill's mother – gay, pleasure-loving, self-preoccupied, affectionate and indifferent by fits and starts – played a less important emotional role in Churchill's life. Her effects were more practical. She encouraged an extravagant husband to expenses they could not afford. Accustomed, as the daughter of an American millionaire, to riches, she squandered her inheritance with insouciant eagerness. In personal relations, much as she loved social life, she always remained a little apart. She created no warm home life for her sons. And although they enjoyed the solid trappings of aristocratic life – governesses, expensive preparatory and public schools, houses in Grosvenor Square and weekends at Blenheim or Althorp – Churchill early realized that he was poor. He was poor at Sandhurst, and poorer as a subaltern in the 4th Hussars. Yet the only life that he knew was aristocratic and rich. His education was as fissured as his social background. Backward at Harrow, he learned little. He struggled with Latin prose, plodded dutifully through the abridgement of Hume's *History of England*, and enjoyed odd bits and pieces of literature, Macaulay's *Lays of Ancient Rome*, and Robert Louis Stevenson's tales. At Sandhurst, he did better. He loved the military life – strategy and tactics fascinated him: he rode and shot with pleasure. He got into scrapes. His cheques bounced, and he became a leader of a clique of high-spirited, horseplay-addicted subalterns. And then the change came. His father's death, the loss of his old nurse whom he loved like a mother, a turn of duty in India – suddenly the springs of his creative nature were released. He wanted fame, he wanted power: to acquire both required knowledge. So, during the long, hot Indian afternoons at Bangalore he lay on his bed and read Gibbon, Macaulay, Adam Smith, and Hallam. He had a score of volumes of the *Annual Register* sent out to him, and he carefully worked his way through the Parliamentary debates, reliving the issues which had streaked his father's life with controversy, making elaborate notes as he went. Both Gibbon and Macaulay entranced him. Here he found history entirely to his liking –

forceful, decisive, Olympian in the grandeur of its prose. Afterwards, when he learned more of the age of William III and Queen Anne, he came to detest Macaulay, whom he considered to be something of an intellectual fraud, yet Macaulay's influence and that of Gibbon remained paramount. They caught his imagination at the moment of his intellectual adolescence, and they left an indelible mark on all that he wrote. They were in harmony with his own nature, which was rich but not complex, decisive rather than devious; basically happy, eupeptic, outward-going, even though furrowed by shadows, by intimations of the tragedy of human life. At the roots of his personality Churchill was a simple man as, I suspect, most great statesmen are likely to be, no matter how subtle and complex they may appear on the surface. Churchill's private life was always straightforward and easy. He married late and very happily. There was no complexity, no unmentionable passionate drives as in Lloyd George. Yet friendship did not come easily to him. Most men, particularly the safe and the mediocre, distrusted him. They were disturbed by his burning thirst for power, his vivid imagination, and his natural assertiveness. He was drawn to colourful, unusual men like himself – Birkenhead, Beaverbrook, Brendan Bracken, and even the weird Cherwell: his relationships with these men were marked by an obstinate loyalty. Many thought Churchill rash because he made decisions easily – not only about actions, but about people and about principles. Once made they were difficult to change. He enjoyed being obstinate, being demonstrably right, even though he alone did the demonstration. And it was this compulsive desire for decisive action which led him to prefer military and political history, to delight in the forceful delineation of character, and to make lively, almost immoderately pungent historical judgements. Although simple and somewhat inflexible, Churchill's character bubbled with passion. He obviously enjoyed anger and ferocity, yet he was also warm-hearted, quickly moved to tears, and could indulge in generosity that is rare in political life. He responded directly to a sense of occasion with something of the unawareness of a child. This is as true of his histories as of his life. And here again one is reminded of Macaulay, another man of straightforward feeling and judgement, quick to praise, quick to condemn, resolute, forthright, blinkered to subtlety: ebullient, self-centred, yet magnanimous. Certainty, warm feeling, a restless love of action – these are all qualities which, when transformed into the language of literature, make for a mastery of narrative, a clarity of exposition which most historians can never hope to possess. And, like Macaulay too, Churchill possessed one other inestimable virtue as a writer – elephantine stamina, an essential necessity for a narrative historian who must go on and on without losing zest, without checking his pace, through hundreds of thousands of words. And Churchill's histories are immensely long, far, far longer than most professional historians': probably among these only Ranke rivals him in output. These advantageous gifts, however, had their corollary of weakness. Unlike Macaulay, Churchill was not technically a clever man: his intellectual machinery was adequate rather than distinguished. This, of course, saved him from self-criticism, from that gnawing intellectual doubt which may haunt the creative faculties of gifted men. In Churchill the historian, however, it created serious limitation. A self-indulgent man, he could not drive himself where he did not wish to go; hence, the history of ideas, of science, of complex intellectual issues remained an almost closed book to him. He never mastered the giant intellectual figures of his youth and early middle age – Marx and Freud. He never turned hungrily to the works of philosophers, economists, social scientists. His intellectual tastes were as simple as his taste for literature. The devious subtleties of human nature, as explored by Proust or Dostoyevsky, possessed no charm for him. There was and is, in his work, a touch of the philistine. His culture, such as it was, was the simple culture of his class – the Bible, Shakespeare, Milton, Scott, Dickens, and a little Trollope, topped off with Rudyard Kipling.

Social background and temperament mould the historian, and so does experience. Churchill first became ebulliently, passionately, creatively alive when he experienced the frontier skirmish which he described in *The Story of the Malakand Field Force*. Indeed, the taste was so heady that he plunged into a welter of military activity – Egypt and the Boer War. No one can read any of the accounts of these adventures without realizing that through them Churchill fulfilled his nature in an exceptionally deep sense. So, too, did his first essays in politics. His success at Oldham intoxicated him. He spoke night after night for hours on end to audiences ranging from hundreds to thousands. The wonder and power of rhetoric gripped him in a thrall from which he was never to escape. War and politics, these were the grand themes of his life, the springs of his creative imagination, and the muscle of his immense stamina. They led him to greatness, to world stature, to immortality. But, and this should be remembered, he was a writer first, an apprentice historian even before he was first defeated at Oldham. Hence he was a rare and singular hybrid: a writer-statesman and a statesman-writer.

Few historians have experienced the drama of history so closely, so intimately as Churchill; among English historians only Clarendon, to whom he must be compared – and, alas, to his disadvantage. They had much in common: both their careers were outstandingly successful yet marked by defeat and rejection, although Clarendon's was personally the more tragic experience. Both in their political worlds were rather lonely men, somewhat out of tune with the less sensitive, politically committed men of their times. Both changed their parties early in their political careers and were never, in consequence, uncritically accepted by the party which they joined. Clarendon, however, was a sadder man, sadder in his temperament as well as in consequence of his experience (after all, he died in exile). He was less ebulliently creative than Churchill, but he penetrated further. He sensed the deeper tides in men and affairs: the forces that would break long-established institutions, those which might topple the most securely held power. Many a Marxist historian had gone to the old royalist to condemn only to be amazed by Clarendon's grasp of economic and social issues. Clarendon stood a little aside from life, somewhat suspicious of men and events. He lacked the deeper convictions and certainties which were as natural a part of Churchill as his red hair and pink skin. Churchill never saw so far nor so deeply into human character as Clarendon. In perception, the balance tips towards Clarendon, and for me still tilts that way when their styles are compared. Churchill could write magnificently about the events of his time: no statesman, other than Clarendon, can compare with him for splendid and majestic set pieces; but, good as Churchill's prose is, it remains all too frequently rhetoric, oral rather than written literature, and his style is something of a confection, a hybrid by Macaulay out of Gibbon, a style which by the nineteen-forties, let alone the fifties, was curiously old-fashioned and somewhat out of place, like St Patrick's Cathedral on Fifth Avenue: a building perfect in its faithfulness to the Gothic and splendidly designed and built, but distinctly odd in the context of Rockefeller Center. Clarendon, however, was the natural master of the prose of his age. His sentences unfurl their coils with the smoothness of an arabesque by Inigo Jones, yet carry the weight, the richness, the fruitfulness of a Grinling Gibbons carving. Clarendon never achieved the brutal and pungent epigram which Churchill could produce with explosive effect, but he achieved dignity and precision and sensitivity in page after satisfying page. Intellect and style both subtly make Clarendon the more satisfying a historian – at least to me.

In narrative, the balance tips slightly Churchill's way. His forceful, impatient character bullies the narrative along and the reader with it – an admirable quality in a historian who writes works in six volumes. Whereas Clarendon was leisurely – given to quite gigantic asides – even though he never lost his grasp on the overall structure of his history. And finally, what gives merit to both their works, shared by few other historians, English or foreign, is the wonderful sense of reality and truth which they create when writing of their contemporaries in *political action*. And this, of course, derived from their involvement in the great events of their age. The fact that they were both figures of the greatest significance in their time adds a dimension to their histories which is denied to other historians. Their histories are also the living material of history. And how rare this is!

3

Churchill's histories fall into two categories – those in a formal, professional sense and those which deal with contemporary events in which he himself was involved. The second type evolved from the quasi-autobiographical *The Story of the Mala-kand Field Force* to the multi-volume *History of the Second World War*, in which Churchill attempted not an autobiography, nor quite a general history, but a mixture of both. Churchill's contemporary histories are more numerous and much more interesting than his formal histories, which consist of two acts of piety and a bid, wildly successful, to make a heap of money. As they throw light on his character as a statesman and contemporary historian, it is easier to deal with them first of all. The acts of piety were his life of his father, Lord Randolph Churchill, whom he felt to have been wronged by the Conservative party, above all by Lord Salisbury (the Prime Minister), and his vast biography of his ancestor John, Duke of Marlborough, the greatest of English generals, whose reputation he felt had been blackened by Macaulay. The bid for cash was his four-volume *History of the English-Speaking Peoples*, conceived when his career was in the doldrums during the thirties, completed but not proofread by 1939 when, naturally, it had to be laid aside for many years: much revised it began to appear in 1956, by which time Churchill himself was almost too tired to appreciate its staggering success with the general public. In many ways the most satisfying of these works is the life of his father.

Churchill published this biography in 1906. His experience of politics, although not profound, was already sufficiently deep not only to weigh professionally the decisive moments of his father's career, but also to sense the changes in the national life which made that career possible. Furthermore, he had come to know many of Lord Randolph's allies and a few of his enemies. He knew them both as men and as politicians. He had also become acquainted with Lord Salisbury, Arthur Balfour, Lord Rosebery, and Joseph Chamberlain, and several of Lord Randolph's great Liberal opponents – particularly Lord Morley. He was as familiar with the political issues as his father's enemies, for in India Churchill had steadily worked through the Parliamentary debates of his father's lifetime, including the petty, as well as the major, matters of state. And, of course, he possessed his father's papers. He was also able to draw very considerably on Lord Rosebery's archives; a generous gesture, since Rosebery was himself writing an essay about Lord Randolph. Even so, much was denied Churchill. He does not, however, seem to have made very strenuous efforts to get at documents in the possession of others which would have helped him. Some papers, among those which he had, he quietly suppressed – not only the Duchess of Marlborough's outburst to Salisbury on Lord Randolph's death, which is understandable, but much of the sharp and savage invective which Lord Randolph showered on his contemporaries. Where he could, he smoothed Lord Randolph's prose, adding a little in stateliness and dignity even though he could not, and probably did not wish to, eradicate entirely the ferocity, the arrogance, the vituperation embedded in Lord Randolph's character and reflected in all that he wrote. The detachment of the professional historian is not present in this book. It was a justification of a life, an act of piety, not a historical assessment. The major characters were polished for presentation. Yet Churchill grasped forcibly enough the central success of Lord Randolph's life – the rallying of the newly enfranchised working class to the Tory standard. And he stresses, very rightly, how miraculous this seemed to men of that time. The incredulity of the Tory leaders led them to indifference, and it took all the determined energy of Lord Randolph and a few friends to make them realize the extraordinary future which was opened for them, but which they scarcely deserved. Churchill makes us realize that what often seems so obvious, so inevitable, was almost unbelievable in 1880. Only a man of the political genius of his father was able to perceive the opportunities offered for the slogan of 'Tory democracy' among the newly enfranchised masses. Here we see at work Churchill's strong grasp of political realities, and his description of Lord Randolph's dialogue with the electorate and its effects on the leadership of the party is, in many ways, the best part of this book, the liveliest and the most convincing. And yet, even here, he asks no questions that a natural or a trained historian would ask. What was the reason for this paradox? Why did millions of men, working-class men on the edge of poverty, vote for a party of aristocrats, landowners, and bankers? Why was it that Toryism steadily grew in radical Birmingham? Here is a suggestive problem calling for the conceptual powers of a historian and his knowledge of social processes. But into these matters Churchill does not delve. Lord Randolph won the labouring classes for Toryism by his own efforts and those of a few supporters. 'To rally the people round the Throne,' cried Lord Randolph. 'To unite the Throne with the people, a loyal Throne and a patriotic people – that is our policy and that is our faith.' According to Churchill, Lord Randolph did just that by convincing them of the rightness of his ideas, but why the sense of the past of the upper classes or their traditional institutions appealed to a new industrial proletariat is a historical problem of the greatest significance, but one upon which Churchill throws no light.

His life of Lord Randolph was acclaimed as one of the great political biographies of the age, which is a gross over-assessment. It is highly readable: it gives a good, if biased and doctored, account of Lord Randolph's life. It evokes some of the clash of personalities and ideas, and that is all. Had it been written by a man of less significance, it would have long since grown dusty on the library shelves. It lacks historical penetration into the nature of the society which made Lord Randolph's political career possible, but a greater deficiency is a lack of psychological insight into his father's character which, even when the history had become dated, might have kept the book alive. Lord Randolph, as a human being and a politician, still awaits his biographer, his character was so very complex, and his capacity for self-destructive action so curiously compulsive; his bitterness went down to the very roots of his character, and his relations with even his friends were so very spiky that the man remains an enigma. The difficulties of his character Churchill describes, but the causes for them he discovers in the superficial events of his life, explaining that Randolph's quarrel with the Prince of Wales drove him into Tory Radicalism. What eludes Churchill is that in the bitter invective, in the outrageous violence of language, and in the wild response this evoked, Lord Randolph found his own nature.

As with Lord Randolph, so with John, Duke of Marlborough. The main motive for Winston's huge biography of his ancestor, apart from turning an honest penny, which he never despised, and of which in the thirties he was always in need, was to repolish and render refulgent the image of his ancestor which he felt Macaulay had tarnished. Macaulay's Marlborough loved power and loved money: in his youth he exploited his handsome good looks amid the courtesans of Charles II's court; in his middle age he laid his hands on whatever gold was going; fearful of a fall from power, he was quite prepared to correspond with James II at St Germains while he served William III at Kensington. He went, according to Macaulay, even as far as jeopardizing an English expedition sent to attack France in the famous case of Camaret Bay. That this last accusation was false was well known, for it had been exposed by John Paget as early as 1874. The other charges proved more difficult for Churchill to refute, but he tried hard enough.

For his life of Marlborough Churchill had inestimable advantages, some of which he exploited and some of which he ignored. He was rich enough to be able to employ first-class research students to do many of the grinding chores of historical research – the long tedious hours copying and searching in muniment rooms. And he had the disposal of the vast archives at Blenheim. These were closed for many years to other scholars, even to G.M.Trevelyan, so that whatever they might reveal could be reserved for Churchill's benefit. This last advantage, however, was useful rather than great. The indefatigable Archdeacon Coxe, whose monumental *Memoirs of the Duke of Marlborough* (1820) provides not only the foundations but much of the structure of Churchill's biography, had printed fully, and reasonably accurately, the core of the Blenheim archives.* And so the new material that emerged when the volumes were published did not add up to much. Nevertheless, Churchill's

* And what he had not published was largely to be found in his voluminous transcripts in the British Museum. These Trevelyan used.

transcripts are far more accurate in detail than Coxe's and some-what fuller in extent, and the most valuable part of Churchill's volumes lies in these extensive quotations. They are the one aspect of the book that a professional historian might still consult. Churchill also sent his assistants to the obvious sources – the diplomatic correspondence and state papers at the Hague, Vienna, Paris, and, of course, London. These were the obvious sources. Churchill used few others; and those that he did were dealt with most superficially.

Every country house in England would have opened its archives at Churchill's request. But the request was rarely made. Apart from Blenheim and Althorp, the Duke of Portland's archive at Welbeck was the only substantial private archive in England that is listed in Churchill's bibliography. But the use was superficial. This archive contains huge quantities of letters and memoranda which belonged to Robert Harley, a major figure in Marlborough's career in Queen Anne's reign. Virtually no use is made of any of these papers. Further correspondence of Harley, and well known to scholars, is to be found at Longleat, a short drive from Blenheim. Not a paper was looked at. This was typical, and one could list a score of houses that Churchill should have ransacked and did not. The Brydges papers, which belonged to Marlborough's paymaster, were over in America at the Huntington Library. They presented difficulties because they were scarcely catalogued. In consequence, their surface was skimmed in the lightest possible way. The archival research for these volumes was superficial, exceptionally superficial. Valuable material was missed even in the Blenheim archives – a large block of the Cabinet memoranda of Marlborough's son-in-law, Sunderland, remained unopened: indeed, the treatment of Sunderland's papers as against Marlborough's was somewhat cavalier. The consequence is that the political side of this biography adds next to nothing to our knowledge of the period, which has since been vastly enriched by the archives which Sir Winston skimmed or ignored. The opportunity was there; it was not taken. The biography, huge as it is, remains deficient in sources.

The best parts of the book are the set battle pieces. Almost equally well handled are the complicated diplomatic manoeuvres which secured the grand alliance against Louis XIV, but even here there are many errors of detail and emphasis.

And the book is also splendidly constructed. The problem which confronted Churchill was a difficult one, the type of problem, indeed, which a professional historian tends to shy away from. There were many distant battles and several wars – and these were always far from the centre of control, which, in London at least, depended on the fortunes of an intricate political structure and violent party warfare: in Holland the problem was almost as involved: in Paris, Turin, Vienna, and the German states it was less so, but even in these places Churchill faced the necessity of dealing with internal pressures as well as foreign policy and military activity. Hence the narrative problem was very complicated, with the distant theatres of war having repercussions on Marlborough's strategy. Furthermore, there was the struggle at sea, or rather on the Seven Seas. In addition, England and France were also fighting each other in Canada, in America, in the West Indies, and in the Far East. Add to this the richness of personalities and their conflicts in all armies, navies and governments. To orchestrate so many instruments and to develop so many themes required Wagnerian genius, but Churchill achieved it. His long book is eminently readable and so pellucid that the complexity of so many interlocking themes is very easy to grasp. The qualities which gave Churchill his massive mastery of detail in time of war are present in the biography of Marlborough. Although open to criticism as history, it remains a splendid work of literary art.

Does it succeed as biography? The answer is no. There is far too much piety in the treatment of Marlborough and his virago duchess, that impossible termagant. Marlborough loved money, loved fame, and loved Sarah. These sentiments might be shuffled into a different sequence, but their truth persists. The Marlboroughs became immensely rich, as rich as a sovereign prince of Germany, which Marlborough longed to be, and for this honour he intrigued with relentless assiduity. And the riches were acquired by all the dubious methods of this age. But Churchill did not bother to probe. That Marlborough loved money Churchill could not deny, but he used all his oratorical skill to gloss the fact, writing 'this though was not without a certain grandeur' etc., etc., even maintaining that in William's reign Marlborough was the most impecunious earl in England, a ridiculous statement that a trivial amount of research would have quickly destroyed. Marlborough was a large-scale investor in the Bank of England, in the East India Company, and, probably, other companies. This may be trivial, but it is typical; Marlborough, a complex, arrogant, princely character, who cultivated his personality with the care of a skilled stage director, emerges from Churchill's biography glowing with virtue, skill, and grandeur, a paragon among men *sans peur et sans reproche*.

The book's faults, therefore, were the lack of archival work, a generous sprinkling of historical errors of fact and interpretation, and a gross misjudgement of the major characters; its strengths lie in the splendid clarity of a complex narrative and the brilliant descriptions of battle.

A graver fault remains. Churchill was unable to disentangle himself from his belief in the traditional interpretations of the English past: this is all implicit in the book – the freedom-loving English, Parliament the watchdog of liberty, the tyranny of France – the old Whig claptrap echoes in chapter after chapter. The confusion of purpose, the haphazard nature of men's intentions, the totally different nature of institutions in Queen Anne's reign to those which bore the same name in Queen Victoria's – these were never perceived. What dominated Churchill's writing was a sense of the past that was interlocked with history only to distort it.

This was even more obvious in the *History of the English-Speaking Peoples*. Although Churchill, under the general guidance of Alan Hodge, the editor of *History Today*, employed a small army of professional scholars to vet his proofs, the effect on the book was very small. Errors of fact were changed with courteous alacrity; subject to strong pressure, an adjective might or might not be pruned, but the grand design proved immutable. Likewise the interpretation. By 1950 Churchill was too old, too tired to undertake the detailed work necessary to bring himself up to date with the previous forty years of

English historical scholarship, even had he had the inclination. And it is doubtful whether he ever enjoyed professional historical work or read much of it. Judging from Lord Moran's invaluable diaries, it is obvious that he still read a great deal, but the books which he chose were largely the old biographical authorities of his youth and early manhood, Moneypenny and Buckle on Disraeli, Morley on Gladstone, the giants of his father's day. His greatest pleasure, which Lord Moran also reveals, as he worked over his proofs, was to savour the sentences, to change an epithet here and there, or reverse the order of phrases, break up sentences and sharpen them, to enjoy indeed the creative delights of writing. But, as with his statesmanship at that time, detailed application was too burdensome for him. He was too tired, too old. So when the *History of the English-Speaking Peoples* appeared, it was like an apparition from the nineteenth or early twentieth century, as if Henry Hallam, Bishop Stubbs, J. R. Green, or the young G. M. Trevelyan were still the accepted authorities in English historical scholarship. Yet it was a remarkable book and its publication a remarkable event, remarkable, very largely, because Churchill had written it. (What would we not give for Roosevelt's *History of America*, or Stalin's *History of Russia*, or, for that matter, Mao's *History of China*?) In it he laid bare the core of his national faith, displaying on what foundations his beliefs in the singular destiny of the English peoples were based. To comprehend fully Churchill's statesmanship, or even his strategy, let alone his relations with the working class, or India, or the monarchy, one must study this book. It contains his secular faith. As history, it fails, hopelessly fails; as a monument to a great Englishman's sense of the past, it is a brilliant success.

As might be expected, the military and political history is well told: the narrative rattles along, the comments are pungent, and human achievements in war, especially endurance and courage, are expressed in eloquent and moving prose. But it is descriptive history: the motives, the reasons for conflicts largely those which contemporaries themselves felt to be the causes of their actions. And the judgements of men and events are conventional and Victorian – one has only to read the section on the

Civil War and the Commonwealth to see the banality of
Churchill's interpretation, beautifully phrased as it often is.
There is no real grasp either of Charles I's or Cromwell's character or intentions. Every opportunity of mockery of the Puritans
is eagerly seized – their destructions of maypoles, the savage
laws against adultery, their opposition to racing and cock-
fighting; sneer follows well-directed sneer. No understanding
whatsoever is shown of the Commonwealth Government's
remarkable attempts to reorganize on a far more rational basis
the institutional machinery of law and of government. Churchill's aristocratic blinkers are right down. Vigorous and lively as
the prose is, sharp and strong as the delineation of men and
events may be, there is an absence of historical imagination and
also of human warmth, not for individuals – there is pity for
Charles I, even compassion for James II – but for the mass of
mankind. Take even the military history – it is the glory, the
courage, the triumph, the valour of British arms which draw
forth the majestic phrases, not the terrible horrors of the
soldiers' and sailors' lot – we are never regaled with the broken
heads, the spilled entrails, the burning and reeking flesh, the
wild hysterical cries of men shattered to death, driven to their
desperate trade by poverty, by social injustice, and the curse of
fate. As with war, so with society – this is a gentleman's history
and, therefore, contains little or no discussion of the labouring
masses, or even of the reaction of the governing classes to them.
It is politics and men seen through the eyes of generals, admirals, and statesmen.

One looks in vain for so much that has conferred distinction
on the English-speaking peoples – their literature, their science,
their philosophy, and their industrial technology. There is
scarcely a word on Shakespeare or Hobbes or Locke, hardly anything on Newton, Boyle, Davy, Faraday, Clerk Maxwell, or
Rutherford. The Industrial Revolution and all the political and
social changes which it produced are brushed aside in a few
pages. In fact the major part of England's contribution to world
civilization is blankly ignored. And these serious omissions are
indicative of Churchill's major fault both as a historian and as
a statesman: he lacked a sense of the deeper motives that con-

trol human society and make it change, just as he lacked an
interest in the deeper human motives. The past is only compre-
hensible in the terms of its future, but Churchill's mind was
immersed in tradition. This made him a splendid symbol for a
nation in torment, but inhibited his vision when he came to
survey the broad sweep of English history. The influence of
England's exceptionally intricate class structure and the
problems created by an even more remarkable tenacity of its
feudal continuum in an industrial society eluded him. The
pageantry of a coronation superimposed on the steelworks of
Sheffield or the sprawling suburbia of Manchester never struck
him as odd; for him the right things were in the right places;
embattled they might be, threatened perhaps by the future, but
so long as the Island people rallied round their monarch and
their Parliament, the world might be defied. In spite of his
generosity and the warmth of his devotion to the British soil
and its people, he could not see its future; so his vision of the
past was clouded, limited to the past of his ancestors, of Lord
Randolph, of Marlborough, of Blenheim. Here was the true
heart of England. For Churchill, the core of English history lay
in the struggle of its gentlemen against the Crown for their
liberties, and then, when these had been won, in the harmony
with it on their forward march to wealth and Empire. Churchill's
old-fashioned, deeply patriotic book is the elegy for the generous
view of English history and institutions, but one which lay at
the core of the beliefs of the class in which he was nurtured.
Faulted and criticized it may easily be, but this tradition is not
all nonsense: it possesses some grains of truth. The English
acquired and maintained political liberty, not for the reasons
Churchill would have given, but acquire it and maintain it they
did. And the history of Europe, or the world for that matter,
shows that this is no easy thing even for an affluent and
dominant society. And the Whig aristocracy played some part
in England's unique achievement. It should not be forgotten.
As we shall see, when Churchill combined his historical beliefs
with statecraft, his dream acquired reality.

In those fields where his work challenges comparison with
professional history, Churchill remains, at the most generous

assessment, a gifted amateur. His abilities are clear – narrative power, grasp of structure, and a rich, full-blown style. His weaknesses are equally glaring – paucity of historical knowledge, lack of analytical power, and an ignorance of economic, social, and intellectual history of staggering proportions. The major significance of these works will lie in the fact that Churchill was the author. They illuminate his mind far more than they do the subjects about which he wrote.

4

The formal historical works are, however, only a part, and a lesser part, of Churchill's output of historical writing. From the earliest days in India to 1950, Churchill was actively engaged in writing accounts of the great historical events in which he himself was involved. They range from the slight but exciting *The Story of the Malakand Field Force* and *The River War* to the vast, multi-volumed accounts of World Wars I and II. Yet among these books a further distinction can be made between the tales of adventure of Churchill's youth and the great war books, or the assessment of his friends and colleagues in *Great Contemporaries*. The early adventure books provided Churchill's apprenticeship in narrative history, for which he possessed a natural gift that he exercised, pruned, and sharpened. And, indeed, this application was necessary, for his capacity was overlaid with glaring faults. Fortunately for Churchill, his personality and social position gave his books a flying start which would have been denied to an unknown writer. Even though his temperament disturbed many of the leaders of opinion, he was a member of the Establishment, and the Establishment worked for him. The Prince of Wales wrote him a letter of congratulation on his first book, society talked about his book, even read it and pushed it. The space given in reviews was generous in the extreme. The book is verbose, uncertain in style, plummeting from Gibbonian phrases to the crooked complexities of a schoolboy in search of a style, and yet throughout shines a most definite personality – decisive, pungent, generous, alive. Even now, when subject and style are as outdated as Kipling's *If*, it retains a curious vitality – that vitality in writing which can only come from a deeply creative writer whose personality has been absorbed, totally absorbed, in his task. And Churchill's own response to his first book was typical of the committed writer's: despair at the proofs, fury at the obvious errors and misprints, a sinking sense of opportunity missed. He need not have worried, for the book sold and the fame came. And Churchill realized what he could do. With his connexions, with the success of this first book, he could launch himself into the world that he wanted. And that emphatically was not Bangalore and the Indian Army. Wherever great events were taking place, there he wanted to be – both participating in them and writing about them. Journalism, politics, books – the life of action, decision, and creation. These beckoned. But he was, for his social rank, poor and extravagant, with a younger brother, and a mother whose self-indulgence soared beyond his own; indeed she raped his inheritance and reduced his own slender resources. So although the future beckoned, and in his heart of hearts the decision was taken, he hesitated and tried to make the best of both worlds, retaining his commission as a soldier but seeking material for his pen. And he got it. By sheer persistence and by tugging every wire persistently, he got himself seconded to Kitchener's army in the Sudan. The result was *The River War*, which confirmed his qualities as a writer and plunged him into the controversies that he enjoyed. But before that book was published, he had quitted the army. A juicy contract with the *Morning Post* and the prospect of financial success with *The River War* confirmed a decision already half made. Furthermore, even though he toned down his criticisms of Kitchener, he well realized that his military career was bound to be frustrated by his journalism, especially as his temperament was frank, critical, and not easily controlled. His hopes of his book were very high, and he was assiduous in collecting information from Lord Cromer in Egypt as well as from Kitchener's staff officers; he attempted far more in this book than in his first. He wanted to see *The River War* in its historical context, to trace England's involvement in Egypt, the rise of the Dervishes, the failure of Gordon, and then on to his climax at Omdurman. The result is a long, uneven book: the professional historical part poor, the personal experience vivid and absorbing. Churchill simply did not know enough, and had not read enough, to give an adequately balanced account of the complex Egyptian problem. He felt a lack of mastery, and, as is usual in such cases, his style labours and verbosity echoed the uncertainty of touch. But when Churchill reached the dramatic events – the Battle of Omdurman, in which he himself took part – the book flares into life. The sentences are short, economic, sparse in adjective, and the Gibbonian echoes are used only to give an occasional solemnity. And in handling this battle, Churchill shows great advance on his first book, not only in control and narrative power, but also in rendering with extreme clarity the battle's complexity. The tactics, the terrain, the deployment of forces, the effects of gun-power are all made obvious *within* the excitement of the story. And any reader can feel the confidence of Churchill in these pages, the confidence that derived from the mastery of creative powers. That he possessed this confidence and was aware of it is further borne out by the type of books which he was considering writing at this time – either a life of Garibaldi or a history of the American Civil War. *The River War* obtained excellent reviews but far fewer sales than Churchill's first book; and yet it was a finer one, more ambitious, more important in theme, better written, and it has secured a permanent niche in historical literature. There is no better, no more vivid account of Kitchener's final campaign against the Dervishes, for what that may be worth.

Fortunately for Churchill, no sooner was *The River War* at the printers than the thunder clouds loomed up in South Africa. Churchill scented war, did a splendid deal with the *Morning Post*, packed six dozen bottles and collected field glasses and telescope, and careered off to the Veldt. The upshot was two more books, and the most dramatic material for his most satisfactory book of all, his autobiography *My Early Life*. The two South African books, *From London to Ladysmith* and *Ian Hamilton's March*, both sold splendidly, 14,000 and 8,000, even though they were largely the *Morning Post* articles refurbished. They have never been republished, partly because their ma-

terials are used again in *My Early Life*. They are not of great
importance in Churchill's development as a historian – they
exercised further the powers of which he was already aware:
his capacity to tell a story well, his direct and shrewd observa-
tion, his growing capacity for a phrase that stabbed the reader.
There is, however, no development.

These early books of adventure would, probably, have fallen
into oblivion had they not been written by a man who became
a world statesman. Perhaps they would have been discovered
by a historian of India, Egypt, or the Boer War and plundered
for a phrase or two, or used to illuminate a historical setting
with first-hand experience. As it is, they are of enormous
biographical value, historical documents within the context of
Churchill's life, and because they are so vividly alive they will
continue to present the image of the young politician at the
outset of his career. As he was to continue to do throughout his
life, Churchill began his career writing his own history.

Read alongside his vast works on the First and Second World
Wars, they cast a curious and revealing light. These great
dramas are approached in the same way that Churchill ap-
proached Omdurman or the attack on Chakdara. The story is
Churchill's major concern: and it is the surface drama upon
which he lavishes his rich prose which now has a strong rhetorical cast and, even if one did not know, one would have suspected
that these books were dictated rather than written. *The World
Crisis*, together with *The Unknown War: Eastern Front* and
The Aftermath, make up a six-volume study of the First World
War, and are far patchier books than his great effort on the
Second World War. For one thing, he commanded, in his own
possession, far fewer archives. After all, he was out of power
after the failure of his Dardanelles campaign, and the offices
which he held did not give him the same comprehensive sweep
which was naturally his as Prime Minister. Hence, for much of
his account he had to rely on external, published sources, and
he was further constricted by the need to maintain a certain
secrecy. Naturally all statesmen-writers are generous to themselves and to each other in the interpretation of the Official
Secrets Act; nevertheless it constrains them, and in these books

Churchill glides over matters of paramount importance not only in diplomacy, but also in subjects such as Intelligence, which had a direct bearing on strategy. Often the books give the appearance of overwhelming documentation, when in fact the amount used is, from a professional historian's point of view, quite slight. Churchill prints fully his own memoranda and letters and, naturally enough, those from others which he received or which had been officially received, but always this material is within the context drawn by Churchill himself. The documents never, as they so often do in professional history, create the context because they are drawn from diverse sources and not used merely to substantiate or enrich an argument.

Other archives, of course, existed, and some have since appeared, but at the time Churchill wrote, either they were not available, or Churchill did not make serious efforts to get at them. Hence these books, constructed in the methods of formal history, are really personal accounts, based on personal papers of a uniquely placed observer. And none of these works can ever be regarded as a reliable account either of the war or its direction; this is more particularly true of *The World Crisis*, which now wears a dated air. The major virtue of this book lies in its sharp perception of the statesmen, admirals, and generals at work: Churchill's vignette of Lloyd George in 1917 summarizes brilliantly the Prime Minister's achievement, and underlines his effectiveness and mastery better than anything that I know.

Mr Lloyd George possessed two characteristics which were in harmony with this period of convulsion. First, a power of living in the present, without taking short views. Every day for him was filled with the hope and the impulse of a fresh beginning. He surveyed the problems of each morning with an eye unobstructed by preconceived opinions, past utterances, or previous disappointments and defeats. In times of peace such a mood is not always admirable, nor often successful for long. But in the intense crisis when the world was a kaleidoscope, when every month all the values and relations were changed by some prodigious event and its measureless reactions, this inexhaustible mental agility, guided by the main purpose of Victory, was a rare advantage. His intuition fitted the crisis better than the logical reasoning of more rigid minds.

The quality of living in the present and starting afresh each day led directly to a second and invaluable aptitude. Mr Lloyd George in this period seemed to have a peculiar power of drawing from misfortune itself the means of future success. From the U-boat depredations he obtained the convoy system: out of the disaster of Caporetto he extracted the Supreme War Council: from the catastrophe of 21 March (1918) he drew the Unified Command and the immense American reinforcement.

His ascendancy in the high circles of British Government and in the councils of the Allies grew in the teeth of calamities. He did not sit waiting upon events to give a wiseacre judgement. He grappled with the giant events and strove to compel them, undismayed by mistakes and their consequences. Tradition and convention troubled him little. He never sought to erect some military or naval figure into a fetish behind whose reputation he could take refuge. The military and naval hierarchies were roughly handled and forced to adjust themselves to the imperious need. Men of vigour and capacity from outside the Parliamentary sphere became the ministerial heads of great departments. He neglected nothing that he perceived. All parts of the task of government claimed his attention and interest. He lived solely for his work and was never oppressed by it. He gave every decision when it was required. He scarcely ever seemed to bend under the burden. To his native adroitness in managing men and committees he now added a high sense of proportion in war policy and a power of delving to the root of unfamiliar things. Under his Administration both the Island and the Empire were effectually organised for war. He formed the Imperial War Cabinet which centred in a single executive the world-spread resources of the British Monarchy. The convoy system, which broke the U-boat attack at sea: the forward impulsion in Palestine, which overwhelmed the Turks, and the unified command which inaugurated the victories in France, belonged in their main stress and resolve as acts of policy to no one so much as to the First Minister of the Crown.

This is a fascinating passage displaying Churchill's strength and weaknesses as a contemporary historian. Firstly it summarizes the creativity and effectiveness of Lloyd George as a statesman: one can immediately sense why he dominated those years and why it was right that power was given to him. Churchill carries conviction; a true professional assessing generously another professional and analysing his success. But it stops there.

We know from Beaverbrook and a host of other writers that
Lloyd George's methods were as devious as they were subtle,
that he was vindictive, that he personally relished power. To the
darker side of motive Churchill shuts his eye; perhaps he could
never open it. And this is responsible for a certain naïveté in
the total picture. It is a vivid summary of action, not a portrait.
Similarly, the style is a compound of good and bad. Obviously
this passage was dictated: the cadences are those of speech, and
echo with Churchill's mature and measured rhetoric, yet, from
time to time it is repetitious, some phrases are clumsy, and the
whole passage is mildly verbose. It could do with more Tacitus
and less Gibbon. Whatever its shortcomings, it illustrates
Churchill at his best and most valuable. In *The World Crisis*,
his dramatic battles may be more brilliant set pieces (Jutland is
a fine example), but they do not add much to history, even
though they are great contributions to entertainment. But this
passage expresses effectively what we might easily miss: the
technique of Lloyd George's statesmanship in action. If, however, we wish to see Churchill at his rhetorical worst, one has
only to turn, in the same book, to his chapter on the Russian
Revolution and, in particular, to his paragraphs on the abdication of the Tsar. Here is overblown rhetorical prose combined
with a naïveté of insight that borders on the ridiculous, especially in one who, for a short time, controlled so effectively
the destiny of the British people. *The World Crisis*, therefore,
is a very uneven book: much of it is naïve, dated, and opaque.
It is largely story-telling, eschewing analysis in depth and devoid
of penetrating studies of personality, but it handles the
executive capacities of men with rare and masterly skill. It deals
convincingly, as few books do, with men operating power –
ignoring why they sought it and, very largely, even the means
by which they gained it. The same excellent quality runs
through his book *Great Contemporaries*. When he writes of men
with whom he had sat in the Cabinet or mixed with in active
politics, as with Birkenhead, Joseph Chamberlain, or even
Philip Snowden, he has always something penetrating to say;
he always, as it were, adds a dimension which other historians
rarely perceive – the quality of men as rulers. When he tries to

assess great men whom he scarcely knew or actively disliked, such as Lenin or George Bernard Shaw, the lack of insight and imagination, the dominance of simple but vice-like prejudice is quite depressing in so great a man. Both these books, *The World Crisis* and *Great Contemporaries*, need to be handled with care, but they will remain an invaluable source for that age.

The Second World War 1939–45 is in a different category. Churchill was the only statesman, caught up in the huge complexity of a world war fought on a scale that man had never endured before, who realized, even as he toiled, that he might one day write the history of the events in which he was involved. Knowing this, he took the necessary measures not only to acquire the materials but to arrange them. Events and their planned history marched hand in hand. Hence, these six huge volumes on the Second World War require the most careful assessment, and one not yet made: soon, however, the scholars must get to work, and what a task they will have! By 1940, Churchill had been writing and living history for well over forty years, and no one was more anxious than he that all that he did and all that he said would be judged by the historians of the future. This must have influenced him, both consciously and unconsciously, particularly when he set out his arguments in memoranda which he knew would become historical documents. All this not only led to a certain inflation, but also to an emphasis on what Churchill himself thought to be of major significance for the future. To assess the effects of this interplay of forces, character, and sense of future time will require an exceptionally sensitive scholar. But the historian in Churchill was responsible for deeper issues than this, which is a problem of intricacy rather than depth. He came to the Second World War with the memory and knowledge, not only of the First World War, but also of the whole panorama of European military history stretching back over a thousand years. To him, Germany was not only the Germany of Hitler but of Bismarck and of Frederick the Great; Russia was not Stalin's Russia but also the Russia of Nicholas II and Alexander I and of Peter the Great. Above all, France was not merely the France of Pétain, but of Clemenceau, of Napoleon, of Louis XIV. His sense of the European past was as acute as that of General De Gaulle, and it informed and, at times, moulded his strategy and his forward-thinking of the European future. A less historically based statesman might easily have been unnerved by the collapse of France and the deep penetration of the German armies into Russia; but Churchill well knew that an encircling alliance had only temporarily failed in the previous three hundred years of European history and, short of a qualitative change in the balance of weapons, was unlikely to fail in 1941 or 1942. At times his sense of historical strategy may have clouded his judgement – it is arguable that he placed too strong an emphasis on the Mediterranean and the Balkans, too little on a frontal assault on Europe. In this book, such strategic concepts as the projected thrust of Alexander's forces into the Danubian basin are argued historically as well as justified by the subsequent course of events. Yet one cannot fail to realize how deeply his sense of history enriched his strategic thinking if one turns from Europe to the East. There his knowledge of history helped him not at all, and he constantly played with dangerous ideas such as landing in Sumatra or Java. He knew the historical geography and military history of Europe supremely well; of the Orient and the Pacific he was as innocent as Roosevelt was of Europe. A fruitful comparison could be made between the great leaders as to the effect history had upon their concepts both of war and peace. Certainly Roosevelt would emerge as the booby. But to analyse all these matters with the care that they deserve would prolong this essay into a book.

When Churchill came to write his history of the Second World War, he had the materials organized, the concepts at hand, the structure ready. Backed up by a massive organization, he was the first in the field (a fact of which he realized the importance). With his huge resources he was able to cast his work into an almost official mould, and often it rises to a degree of objectivity rare in the memoirs of great statesmen. Nevertheless it is Churchill's book, in which he himself looms larger than life and his role in the drama, great as it was, magnified. More important is the fact that the war, its narrative and its structure, is organized in a deliberate way by Churchill. The phases of the war are the phases into which he divided it. And this will deeply influence, indeed has already deeply influenced, subsequent historians. They move down the broad avenues which he drove through war's confusion and complexity. Hence, Churchill the historian lies at the very heart of all historiography of the Second World War, and will always remain there. And the book itself will continue to be read. It is too verbose, at times it is too heavy with self-justification, and, quite understandably, its orientation is often too British. Nor is Churchill always fair to those, such as Wavell, who fell foul of him during the course of the war: of others, especially the Navy, he is too uncritical. The work has the faults that one expects, but it also possesses majestic passages, and throughout it is pervaded by a generous and magnanimous spirit. Furthermore, Churchill's sense of the past brought him a modest measure of hope for the future of mankind. It is, in spite of its theme – war and destruction – a heartening book.

History served Churchill best in his dialogue with his nation. He of all the leaders could give a sense of hopeful destiny even in the hours of darkest trial, and he was able to do this because he had faith in what history taught him about men and women. He was aware of evil, of corruption, of self-seeking and self-indulgence, but when he looked at the great panorama of the past from Blenheim, he saw not only the dark valleys but the broad uplands which he felt humanity might reach. And this hope, this faith, call it what you will, was historically based, and nationally based. England's history was a long struggle for liberty, for freedom and the decencies of human life. In spite of poverty, of greed, of exploitation, the movement had been towards greater civility, towards a greater and more general prosperity. The economic side, of course, was much less significant to him than the political liberties, of which he felt his nation to be the proud guardian – this gave Britain the right to act as a moral bulwark of mankind's decencies. There is, of course, immense simplicity in this attitude. Its historical justification lies in the power of a manufactured past. Yet it is not entire nonsense. The British people have been freer to speak their minds, to dissent from their governments, to go their own wayward way in politics and religion than almost any other community in the Western world; and certainly none so powerful, with so vast an empire, has had so long a history of political and intellectual freedom for its governing classes or made the transition to full democracy with such ease. And this was not only Churchill's source of strength, his constant refreshment in times of tribulation and disaster, but also the nation's which he led. They, too, were historically oriented in a way which few other nations were in 1939. Their national symbols were all historically based. Historical memories were cultivated with extravagant care. Their historical heritage – in cathedrals, castles, manor houses – littered the land but spoke not, as in France or Russia, of revolution; nor, as in Germany, of fragmentation, but of a continuous past, a continuous growth in liberty and in power. And so, throughout the war years, particularly in his great speeches to the people, there was a constant dialogue between Churchill and the nation, in which the past was constantly invoked to fortify the present. And I venture to think that only a statesman steeped in history could have roused and strengthened the nation in the way in which Churchill did during those years. And yet he was using a past which died with the war: indeed, the remarkable thing about Churchill was that this past which he used was still so living, so dynamic a reality for him.

His attitude to the past had been shared by most of his class, and by the historians who belonged to it. G. M. Trevelyan, particularly, thought and felt about the past in much the same way that Churchill did. He, too, was concerned with the story of freedom, of liberty, of the right to dissent, of the decencies between men and classes of men that marked English history over the last two hundred years or more. But in his works there is a strong elegiac note, a sense of despair that is not purely personal, a deep regret for a world that is fading – the world of manor houses, country pursuits, the rule of liberal and tolerant gentlemen – these things, Trevelyan knew, were being destroyed by the accelerating Industrial Revolution. And he realized, too, that the Empire had gone as well as the old values. His view of the past brought nostalgia, a surge of love, but also hopelessness; above all, he wished to turn away from the future.

And Trevelyan's mood was, I suspect, much more in tune with that of the governing class than Churchill's. In 1939, the ruling circles in Britain did not give the impression of being full of eupeptic optimism, but the mood of the upper classes was not necessarily the mood of those who had to fight the war. Their lives, in spite of depression and unemployment, had become decisively better in the twenties and thirties. They were enjoying leisure and mild affluence and a liberty that their grandparents had never known, and they possessed just enough sense of the past for Churchill to draw from them the response that was needed. He painted for them a sense of heroic destiny, and for a time, stimulated by the Blitz, they accepted it. And so Churchill imposed on his nation an essentially aristocratic sense of the past, and so effectively, that the nation responded to his rhetoric.

Once the dangers were over, that sense of the past, so close to myth, did not last: reality broke in. The past which held Churchill in so powerful a grip can no longer move men and women in the way that it did: some of the middle classes may be nostalgically moved, but to the emerging world of scientists, technologists, or affluent suburbia, it is a pasteboard pageantry that indicates nothing and certainly does not signpost the future. Above all, it dictates neither action nor belief.

The past which Churchill served died with him. In many ways he is the last historic symbol of the Whig tradition – a tradition that was dying and only sprang into renewed vitality through the stress of war. And yet, no one can deny that Churchill was deeply conditioned by his ideological inheritance; that history was not an activity to which he turned for solace or for profit, but a living reality which imbued all that he did or said. History for Churchill provided the dogmas of his faith, the dynamic force which kept him going through the long years of waste and the frightful burdens of power.

Basil Liddell Hart   # THE MILITARY STRATEGIST

More than sixty years ago, a very small boy, of Anglo-American origin, was playing at soldiers. He was not what grown-up people are apt to class as an attractive child. No pretty sayings or winning ways are recorded of him. He was snub-nosed, sandy-haired, and regarded by everyone who knew him as an out-and-out young Turk, the naughtiest little boy ever seen, a generating focus of aggressive energies.

That was the opening paragraph of a most perspicacious study entitled *Churchill – the Making of a Hero* by Dr Esmé Wingfield-Stratford which was published in 1942, covering Churchill's life up to the time he became Britain's Prime Minister in the crisis of May 1940.

Almost as significant was the opening paragraph of the book's third section:

Not the least of Lord Randolph's brilliant achievements, and one that was never to be clouded by subsequent failure, was his marriage to the daughter of a Wall Street broker, Leonard Jerome. For it cannot be too clearly realized, or firmly borne in mind, that their son Winston, as far as blood can make him so, is as much American as he is British, and derives no less from the fighting stock of the Jeromes than that of the Churchills.

That second theme was brought out, and emphasized still more, in R. W. Thompson's 1963 book, *The Yankee Marlborough*, and I would agree with its view that Winston Churchill showed more Jerome than Churchill influence, and derived more from the tougher Jerome stock.

But the opening sentence of Wingfield-Stratford's book was the most illuminating and penetrating of all.

As a boy, Winston Churchill had a large collection of toy soldiers – 'model soldiers', as adult collectors now call them – and he went on playing with them at an age long after most other boys give them up. They had a lasting influence on his mind, and on his life.

Soon after he had scraped into Harrow he 'succeeded in

passing the preliminary examination for the Army while still almost at the bottom of the school'. He mentions this himself in his interim memoirs, *My Early Life* – published in 1930 when he was fifty-five – while going on to say: 'This orientation was entirely due to my collection of soldiers. I had ultimately nearly fifteen hundred.' They were 'all British, and organized as an infantry division with a cavalry brigade'. He fought battles with his brother Jack, five years younger, who 'was only allowed to have coloured troops; and they were not allowed to have artillery'.

The day came when my father himself paid a formal visit of inspection. All the troops were arranged in the correct formation of attack. He spent twenty minutes studying the scene – which was really impressive – with a keen eye and captivating smile. At the end he asked me if I would like to go into the Army. I thought it would be splendid to command an Army, so I said 'Yes' at once: and immediately I was taken at my word. For years I thought my father with his experience and flair had discerned in me the qualities of military genius. But I was told later that he had only come to the conclusion that I was not clever enough to go to the Bar.

These remarks, particularly the asides, are endearingly characteristic of Churchill's sense of humour. But they also tend to show how his lowly place at Harrow, and his father's low opinion of his ability, left a lasting scar. It may help to explain why he later tended to surround himself, unlike Lloyd George, with colleagues and assistants whose minds moved more slowly than his own and whom he could thus more easily dominate.

From the moment Churchill left Sandhurst, and got a commission in the 4th Hussars in 1895, he did his utmost to get into a fight, wherever a war was going on. To attain his desire he used his mother's influence and that of many friends in high circles. Within a few years he had seen fighting in Cuba, the north-west frontier of India, the Sudan, and South Africa – going to the battlefields as a war correspondent when he could not get a regular appointment.

Winston Churchill felt intense exhilaration in the sense of battle, and the sounds of battle – more, indeed, than most professional soldiers. General Sir Frederick Pile, the Commander-in-Chief of Anti-aircraft Command, who conducted him round the anti-aircraft defences in the Second World War, related how, when the bombing started, he found it difficult to get him under cover and away from the guns – to protests, Churchill gleefully exclaimed: 'I love the bangs.'

His account of the war games he played in youth, and of the campaigns in which he so eagerly played a part later, has strangely little comment about strategy or even tactics. It was the thrill of fighting that enthralled him, as becomes very clear in reading *My Early Life*; and the vividly descriptive accounts of fighting in his early books – *The Story of the Malakand Field Force* (about the suppression of the Pathan revolt of 1897), *The River War* (about the advance on Khartoum and Battle of Omdurman in 1898), and his subsequent books on the South African War of 1899–1902, *London to Ladysmith* and *Ian Hamilton's March*.

It does not seem to have been until later that he developed a growing interest in the technical side of warfare.

His activities as a war correspondent had made his name widely known and given him an early celebrity such as no other young officer could hope to have if he stuck to the military profession. That fame had been heightened, first, by his participation in the charge of the 21st Lancers at Omdurman – a charge so vividly written up by him that it had come to appear a greater episode than it was – and second, barely a year later, by his escape from a Boer prison camp after being captured in an armoured train.

Instead of being merely 'the son of Lord Randolph', he had become a personality in his own right. The father, after becoming Chancellor of the Exchequer at thirty-six, had wrecked his future by a misjudged resignation, and died at forty-six, early in 1895, from a tragic mental form of paralysis. He remained a figure of devout admiration and emulation to the son, while no longer on the scene to deter or discourage the son from taking up a political career. Returning to England immediately after Omdurman, Winston applied to the Conservative party to be supplied with a constituency, and he soon obtained an offer to

stand for election at Oldham. He and his fellow candidate, however, lost this double seat at a by-election that shortly followed.
But on returning from South Africa a year later, with the increased glamour he had gained there, he stood again for Oldham
at the 'khaki' election of 1900 – a general election launched by
the Conservatives to reap the benefit of war fever and the illu-
sory capture of Pretoria – and this time regained the seat for
that party, although by a narrow majority. He had achieved
election at the early age of twenty-five, the same age as his
father had done.

At his third speech in the House, he came out with strong
criticism of the Army proposals set forth by his own party's
Secretary of State for War, Mr Brodrick, arguing against increased expenditure on the Army – the same issue on which his
father had resigned as Chancellor of the Exchequer – and
preference for the Navy. His speech caused a sensation, and *The
Times* recalled, as a warning, the fate of his father. From this
time onward he swung increasingly towards the Left, on one
issue after another, and still more strongly when the Conservative party committed itself to Joseph Chamberlain's policy of
Tariff Reform, and against Free Trade. Eventually, in 1904,
after his views were repudiated by the Oldham Conservative
party, he accepted an invitation from North-West Manchester,
the core of Free Trade, to stand as a Liberal at the next
election. At the end of May he walked across the House and
seated himself next to Lloyd George, in the corner seat below
the gangway that Lord Randolph had occupied when,
after leaving the Government, he had launched his Fourth
party.

The Conservative party had never been sagacious enough to
offer Churchill ministerial office. By contrast, he was shrewd in
quitting it when the popular tide was, clearly, running against it.
In the general election of 1906, the Conservatives were swept
out of office, and the Liberals swept in with a large majority,
almost a landslide. Winston Churchill was elected for North-
West Manchester, as a Liberal, and was immediately offered
office, as Under-Secretary of State for the Colonies – at the age
of thirty-one.

Early in 1908, the Liberal Prime Minister, Sir Henry Campbell Bannerman, was forced to retire through mortal illness, and handed over the reins of government to his Chancellor of the Exchequer, Herbert Asquith. In the reconstruction of the Government, Asquith chose Lloyd George to succeed him at the Exchequer, and promoted Churchill to replace Lloyd George as President of the Board of Trade, a post with Cabinet rank. He might have had the Admiralty, but for the time being had lost interest in the defence sphere. That year was still more happily marked by his marriage to Clementine Hozier – to whose combination of great charm and cool common sense he owed much throughout his life. In the reshuffle that followed the general election of 1910, Churchill was again moved up, to be Home Secretary. During a year and a half in that office he helped to introduce a number of social reforms, particularly prison reforms.

In general, however, he became prominent during these years of office as an opponent of military expenditure, and the chief supporter of Lloyd George's opposition to any increase of the battleship programme. The admirals urged the need for building six new Dreadnoughts. Lloyd George and Churchill refused to agree to more than four. The First Lord of the Admiralty, Reginald McKenna, threatened to resign, and was supported by the Foreign Secretary, Sir Edward Grey. In the outcome, the Cabinet agreed to the building of *eight* such battleships, over a somewhat extended period! The compromise was helped by Asquith's shrewd idea of arranging an exchange of offices between McKenna and Churchill, at the end of October 1911. Growing tension with Germany had revived the possibility of war, and Churchill showed no hesitation in accepting the proffered exchange, although it meant implementing a policy he had vigorously opposed.

His devoted friend and admirer, Lady Violet Bonham Carter, now Lady Asquith, has a significant passage in her illuminating book *Winston Churchill As I Knew Him*, when quoting from her diary record of a Mediterranean voyage she made the following spring with her father, then the Prime Minister, as guests of Churchill in the Admiralty yacht *Enchantress*:

W. in glorious form though slightly over-concentrated on instruments of destruction. Blasting and shattering are now his *idées fixes*. As we leaned side by side against the taffrail, gliding past the lovely, smiling coastline of the Adriatic, bathed in sun, I remarked: 'How perfect!' he startled me by his reply: 'Yes – range perfect – visibility perfect – If we had got some six-inch guns on board how easily we could bombard . . .' etc. etc. – and details followed showing how effectively we could lay waste the landscape and blow the nestling towns sky-high. He was enthralled by the technology of naval warfare and his sense of its results in human terms was for the time being in abeyance.

It seemed an astonishing change in a man who, after moving from the Conservative side of the House to the Liberal, had made his mark there and reached Cabinet rank by supporting social reforms while urging successive cuts in the battleship programme, and discounting possible danger from Germany – until he himself was invited by Asquith to become First Lord of the Admiralty, and thus the political head of the Navy. The poacher had been turned into the gamekeeper.

The change in his attitude was characteristic of his tendency to become obsessively concentrated on promoting the interests of any role he assumed, or department of which he was put in charge. Lloyd George, whose programme of social reform he had previously supported so strongly, soon complained that Churchill was 'taking less and less interest in home politics', and that when he himself wanted to discuss the new National Insurance Act, Churchill 'declaimed about his blasted ships' for a whole morning.

The tendency was also influenced by Churchill's close friendship with Admiral Lord Fisher, the former First Sea Lord – with whose ebullient spirit and reforming zeal he had a natural kinship. On taking office as First Lord, Churchill had been on the verge of recalling Fisher to be First Sea Lord, although Fisher was then seventy-one, and he eventually did so soon after the outbreak of war in 1914, three years later. With constant contact in the interval, friendship had ripened into affection, on both their parts.

Here we are brought to a very important factor in Winston

Churchill's make-up – and one on which Violet Bonham Carter's book has some significant and revealing passages:

When we were ardently aligned on public issues he liked to share his thoughts with me. He poured them out in a molten torrent and we burned and glowed together in passionate agreement. But when we differed our disagreement was all the more distasteful to him because I was his friend. He reproached me with his glowering look: 'You are not on my side' – and took scant interest in the reasons which had brought me to this pass. Disagreement was, in any form, obnoxious to him, but when combined with personal affection it became a kind of treachery. He demanded partisanship from a friend, or (at the worst) acquiescence.

His friendship was a stronghold against which the gates of Hell could not prevail. There was an absolute quality in his loyalty, known only to those safe within its walls. Their battle was his own. He would concede no inch of ground, no smallest point against them. In a friend he would defend the indefensible, explain away the inexplicable – even forgive the unforgivable.

This inner citadel of the heart held first and foremost his relations, in their widest sense. . . . His blood relations were accepted without question and en bloc. Next came his friends, strangely diverse in character.

During these pre-war years in the Admiralty, Churchill received a continual stream of letters full of advice and guidance from Fisher, and as he remarks: 'From the very beginning his letters were couched in an affectionate and paternal style. "My beloved Winston", they began, ending usually with a variation of "Yours to a cinder", "Yours till Hell freezes", or "till charcoal sprouts", followed by a P.S. and two or three more pages of pregnant and brilliant matter.' They kindled a reciprocal warmth that made the recipient the more responsive.

Within a month of his appointment Churchill had changed the whole Board of Admiralty with one exception, finding that the First Sea Lord and other naval members were opposed to his aim of creating a Naval War Staff similar to the Army's General Staff. Prince Louis of Battenberg was made Second Sea Lord (and the following year became First Sea Lord) – 'I find myself in cordial agreement with him on nearly every important question of naval policy. . . .' At Fisher's urging, he appointed Sir

John Jellicoe over the heads of several senior admirals to be
Second in Command of the Home Fleet, so that he would automatically succeed to this supreme command before the end of
1913. Fisher was exultant that 'My two private visits to
Winston were fruitful'.

The crucial strategic switch of strength from the Mediterranean to the North Sea had already been made in Fisher's time
as First Sea Lord, before Churchill went to the Admiralty, and
so had the great tactical switch to the 'all big gun' battleship –
the Dreadnought type – as well as the 1909 advance from the
12-inch to the 13·5-inch gun, with its shell of nearly double the
weight. But Churchill helped to secure the development and
production of the still more powerful 15-inch gun. He also
backed the creation of a fast division of battleships in place of
the lightly armoured battle-cruisers – another wise move, as the
battle-cruisers were to prove all too vulnerable under the test of
war. That idea in turn led him to back the full conversion of the
Navy from coal fuel to oil fuel, a tremendously important
development. Even if it carried some long-term strategic disadvantages, because of Britain's consequent dependence on
distant, overseas supplies, its tactical advantages were great.
Another feature of Churchill's period at the Admiralty was the
impetus given, in accord with Fisher, to submarines and naval
aircraft. He also did much to improve, and accelerate, the
arrangements for the mobilization of the fleet to meet a war
emergency.

In sum, there was remarkably little ground for criticism in
any of the steps he took during these momentous years before
the First World War. The best tribute to it that he ever
received, or could have desired, came in May 1915 – from the
man he had removed from the office of First Sea Lord in 1911,
Admiral Sir Arthur Wilson. In October 1914, Prince Louis of
Battenberg had felt compelled to resign that office in view of
ignorant and scurrilous public attacks on his German birth and
parentage. Churchill had then brought Fisher back to the
Admiralty, as First Sea Lord, although he was then seventy-
four, with 'Tug' Wilson, likewise recalled to service, as 'his
principal coadjutor'. When Fisher resigned the following May

in a moment of exasperation – thereby precipitating a political crisis – Wilson agreed to take over the post. But when he saw in the newspapers three days later that a reconstruction of the Government was probable, he wrote to the Prime Minister saying that he was 'not prepared to undertake the duties under any new First Lord'.

Churchill in the First World War

When the war crisis came in July 1914, Churchill responded characteristically. He was 'very bellicose', Asquith records in his *Memories and Reflections*, 'and demanding instant mobilization'. Moreover on 2 August, when news came that Germany had declared war on Russia, Churchill ordered that the Naval Reserves should be called out, a step for which he had no authority, and for which the Government had on the previous day refused to give him permission.

Asquith's daughter, Lady Violet, once again supplements this with a fuller picture of Churchill's attitude when war came:

Next morning (August 4th) the news came that the Germans had invaded Belgium. An ultimatum to Germany, to expire at midnight, was drafted by my father and Sir Edward Grey and dispatched. In his daily notes my father wrote: 'The whole thing fills me with sadness.'

No one could have described Winston as 'filled with sadness'. He rose to this greatest of all adventures with glowing zest. (And who can blame him? – though some did.) For three years he had devoted all his powers to preparing the Navy to meet the challenge of this hour, and he knew that he had done it well. The hour had come. He hailed it with a cheer. . . . It is true that the dark and tragic certainties to which Grey and my father were alive were hidden from Winston's eyes. Against this he was alive to things which others did not see. His power of concentrating on one aim to the exclusion of all else was at once his weakness and his strength.

Churchill's instinctive reaction turned out to be of far-reaching effect. The history of the naval struggle must be dated from 26 July 1914, when Prince Louis of Battenberg, in telephone accord with Churchill, sent orders from the Admiralty to the fleet, assembled for review at Portland, not to disperse in view of the clouded international situation. If the review was a happy chance, the use made of it was one of the decisive acts of the war, for while free from any of the provocation of an army mobilization, it placed Britain in automatic control of the situation at sea. It was followed, on 29 July, by the unnoticed sailing of the fleet for its war stations in the North Sea, and warning telegrams to all squadrons abroad. Churchill concealed that move, and order, from the Cabinet – which might have objected to it as provocative – and only informed the Prime Minister, who agreed to it.

At seven o'clock that morning, the Grand Fleet sailed from Portland for its war station at Scapa Flow. Few eyes saw its passage, fewer minds knew its destination in those northerly Orkney Isles controlling the passage between North Britain and Norway, but from that moment Germany's arteries were subjected to an invisible pressure which never relaxed until, on 21 November 1918, the German fleet arrived in those same northern waters to hand itself into the custody of a force of which it had had no more than a few fleeting glimpses during four and a half years of intangible struggle.

Thus Britain was able to exert her traditional weapon – sea power. Its effect on the war was akin not to a lightning flash, striking down an opponent suddenly, but to a steady radiation of heat, invigorating to those it was used in aid of, and drying up the resources of the enemy.

In the First World War the Navy was to win no Trafalgar, but it was to do more than anything else towards winning the war for the Allies. For it was the instrument of the blockade, and as the fog of war dispersed in the clearer light of the post-war years, that blockade was seen to assume larger and larger proportions, to be more and more clearly the decisive agency in the struggle. Helplessness induces hopelessness, and history attests that loss of hope and not loss of lives is what decides the issue of war. No historian would underrate the direct effect of the semi-starvation of the German people in causing the final collapse of the 'home front'. But leaving aside the question of how far the revolution caused the military defeat, instead of vice versa, the intangible, all-pervading factor of the blockade intrudes into every consideration.of the military situation.

There is, however, little sign in Churchill's papers that he visualized its vital, and decisive, importance beforehand – his mind, characteristically, was filled with thoughts of 'battle'. And he left the Admiralty in the spring of 1915, before blockade became a predominant factor.

Churchill made two other strategically important contributions to the Allied cause in the early stages of the war, and in them his personal part is easier to trace. Both were outside what might be considered his 'proper' sphere – and none the less significant for that. The first of these initiatives had a crucial influence on the land-battle of the Marne, although taken prior to it.

No battle has caused more controversy, or given rise to more popular interest and legend, than that of the Marne. This crisis of September 1914 wrought the downfall of the German war plan, and thereby changed the course of history. The Marne was a psychological rather than a physical victory – as have been most of the great victories of history, with the actual fighting a secondary influence. For the issue of battles is usually decided in the minds of the opposing commanders, not in the bodies of their men.

Before and during the crisis, the German commanders were constantly looking backward apprehensively over their right shoulders, fearful of an Allied stroke against their ever-lengthening communications in Belgium and northern France. Actually, there was small warrant for this nervousness. The earlier idea of landing the British expeditionary force on the Belgian coast had been overruled in favour of the policy of dispatching it, and attaching it, to the French left wing. But the Belgian field army, though under German guard at Antwerp, had at least caused a serious detachment of German strength to this guard, and was a chronic irritation to German nerves. The fertile brain of Churchill was also at work. Resources were scanty, but he dispatched a brigade of marines to Ostend, with orders to give their presence the fullest publicity. They landed on 27 August, and stayed ashore until the 31st.

On 5 September, the very day when the French troops from Paris were moving forward to strike at Kluck's First Army – the flank army of the great German circling sweep into France – and inaugurate the counter-offensive, Colonel Hentsch, the representative of the German supreme command, came to that threatened army with this ominous and despairing warning: 'The news is bad. The VII and VI Armies are blocked. The IV and V are meeting with strong resistance. . . . The English are disembarking fresh troops continuously on the Belgian coast. There are reports of a Russian expeditionary force in the same parts. A withdrawal is becoming inevitable.' We know from other sources that the three thousand marines had grown in the German Command's imagination to forty thousand, and that the Russians were said to be eighty thousand.

Hence the German flank army was left to face the ordeal with the belief that its rear was seriously menaced, and that, in any case, the supreme command was contemplating a withdrawal. At the least such knowledge must have been insidiously enervating during a period of strain. If the supreme command came to have doubts of the Belgian news, it also became imbued with the idea of a retirement, and when Hentsch came again on 9 September with full powers to co-ordinate it, 'should rearward movements have begun', not only had these begun, but they also coincided with fresh disturbing news from Belgium. For although the Belgian sortie from Antwerp that day was short-lived, it had all the incalculable psychological effect of menacing news at a moment of crisis. The German retreat gathered momentum and spread. With it turned the tide of the war.

Historians who explore the causal factors in great decisions should recognize the effect of Churchill's inspiration and handful of 'marine promenaders'. Equally helpful was that amazing 'Russian' myth, which originated and spread so mysteriously. Churchill, we know, had actually proposed to bring a Russian expeditionary force in such a way. The proposal seems to have leaked out and become exaggerated into realization in the process.

Churchill's next initiative is better known, and has been more contentious. The so-called 'Battle of the Marne' was followed by the successive attempts of either side to overlap and envelop the other's western flank, a phase known popularly, but inaccurately, as the 'race to the sea'. Before it could reach its logical, lateral conclusion, a new factor intervened. Antwerp, with the Belgian field army, was still a thorn in the German side, and Falkenhayn, who had succeeded Moltke on 14 September as director of German strategy, determined to reduce it, while a German cavalry force swept across to the Belgian coast as an extension of the enveloping wing in France.

The menace to Britain, if the Channel ports fell into German hands, was clear. It is a strange reflection that, inverting the German mistake, the British Army command should hitherto have neglected to guard against the danger, although Churchill, the First Lord of the Admiralty, had urged the necessity even before the battle of the Marne. When the German guns began the bombardment of Antwerp on 28 September, he was allowed to send a brigade of marines and two newly formed brigades of naval volunteers to reinforce the defenders, while the Regular 7th Division and 3rd Cavalry Division, under Rawlinson, were landed at Ostend and Zeebrugge for an overland move to raise the siege. The meagre reinforcement delayed, but could not prevent, the capitulation of Antwerp, 10 October, and Rawlinson's relieving force was too late to do more than cover the escape of the Belgian field army down the Flanders coast.

Yet, viewed in the perspective of history, this first and last effort in the West to make use of Britain's amphibious power, inspired by Churchill, applied a brake to the German advance down the coast that just stopped their second attempt to gain a decision in the West. It gained time for the arrival of the main British force, transferred from the Aisne to the new left of the Allied line. While the heroic defence at Ypres, aided by the French and Belgians along the Yser to the sea, was the human barrier to the Germans, it succeeded by so narrow a margin that the Antwerp expedition must be adjudged the saving factor.

The expedition also produced a proposal that, although of no effect itself, is a key to the understanding of the proposer. Churchill himself had gone to Antwerp at an early stage, and his fighting instinct was shown, characteristically, in a reaction that is best related in Violet Bonham Carter's words:

I prided myself on an intimate understanding of Winston and had usually been able to explain his actions to myself – though not always to others. But he now took a step which staggered me. On October 5th he telegraphed to my father offering 'to resign his office and undertake the command of the relieving and defensive forces assigned to Antwerp. . . .'

What amazed and shook me was the sense of proportion (or lack of it) revealed by Winston's choice. His desire to exchange the Admiralty, in which for years he had invested all his treasure and which was now faced with its first test and greatest opportunity, for the command of a mere major-general, one of many, in the field seemed to me to be hardly adult. It was the choice of a romantic child. In terms of scope and power the two jobs were not comparable. He would be abdicating his part in the grand strategy of the war, which he had always seen in world-wide terms, in order to play a personal part in a small patch of it. On the great issues of war aims and peace-terms he would have no say. He would be exiled from the inner councils of the nation in the greatest crisis of its history. Had he imagined life without his telegrams and boxes? – his access to the heart of things? He had always found action at close range irresistible and at a lesser moment in a narrower sphere I could imagine his preferring action in a limited and visible field to greater power at a desk. But *now* . . . ? I could not reconcile his wish with his dramatic sense or his imaginative range.

Asquith himself had evidently come to understand Churchill better. For he promptly and briefly quashed the suggestion: 'Of course without consulting anybody I at once telegraphed to him warm appreciation of his mission and his offer, with a most decided negative saying we could not spare him at the Admiralty.'

On the side of the Western Allies, the reality of the trench deadlock produced diverse reactions. While the desire to hold on to territorial gains swayed German strategy, the desire to recover their lost territory dominated the strategy of the French. Their concentration on the Western front, where lay the main armed force of the enemy, was justified by military tenets, but without any key to unlock the barrier they were merely knocking themselves to pieces. Their winter and spring campaigns provided costly proof that General Joffre's 'attrition' policy became attrition on the wrong side of the balance sheet. As for any new key, the French were lacking in fertility of idea.

Britain's trouble was rather an excess of fertility – or, in effect, an inability to decide in choosing a course. In large measure this failing was due to the obscurantism of professional opinion, whose attitude was that of blank opposition rather than expert guidance.

British-inspired solutions to the deadlock crystallized into two main groups, one tactical, the other strategical. Churchill played a foremost part in both.

The prime tactical solution was to unlock the trench barrier by producing a machine invulnerable to machine guns and capable of crossing trenches, which would restore the tactical balance upset by the new preponderance of defensive over offensive power. The idea of developing a machine for this purpose was conceived by a number of minds in the early months of the war, but principally by Colonel Swinton, in the Army, and Winston Churchill, outside. Their ideas were conceived separately, and independently. Swinton's proposals, after a promising start, were soon annulled, although only for a time, by the scepticism of higher circles at general headquarters and in the War Office. Churchill's ideas were less practicable, but he was more powerful. It was through his interest, and the experiments he started, that the basic concept was kept alive until, in the following summer, the heads of the Army itself came round to see the need of a new tactical solution, and took the lead in reviving Swinton's ideas, which eventually came to maturity in 'the tank'.

The connexion between Churchill, the head of the Navy, and the Army's most important weapon development is such a strange and complex story that fuller examination of it is best deferred until later, as it did not become of key importance until after the strategical alternative that Churchill espoused had been tried, and resulted in a failure that came near to ending his political career.

The strategical solution was to go round the trench barrier. Its advocates – who became known as the 'eastern' in contrast to the 'western' school – argued that the enemy alliance should be viewed as a whole, and that modern developments had so changed conceptions of distance and powers of mobility, that a blow in some other theatre of war would correspond to the historic attack on an enemy's strategic flank. Further, such an operation would be in accordance with the traditional amphibious strategy of Britain, and would enable it to exploit the advantage of sea power – as Churchill saw, and emphasized.

The fault was not in the conception, but in the execution. If the British had used at the outset even a fair proportion of the forces they ultimately expended in driblets, it is clear from Turkish accounts that victory would have crowned their undertaking.

The basic cause of this piecemeal application of force, and dissipation of opportunity, lay in the opposition of Joffre and the French general staff, supported by Sir John French. Despite the evidence of the sequel to the Marne, of the German failure at Ypres, and of his own ambitious yet utterly ineffectual offensive in December, Joffre remained confident of his power to achieve an early and decisive victory in France. Study of the documents conveys the impression that there has rarely been such a trinity of optimists in whom faith was divorced from reason as Joffre, Foch, his deputy in Flanders, and French – albeit the latter's outlook oscillated violently.

In contrast, the British Government considered that the trench-front in France was impregnable to frontal attacks, had strong objection to wasting the manpower of the new armies in a vain effort, and at the same time felt increasing concern over the danger of a Russian collapse.

These views were common alike to Churchill, Lloyd George, and Kitchener, who, on 2 January 1915, wrote to Sir John French – 'The German lines in France may be looked upon as a fortress that cannot be carried by assault and also that cannot be completely invested, with the result that the lines may be held by an investing force while operations proceed elsewhere.'

Lloyd George advocated the transfer of the bulk of the British forces to the Balkans, both to succour Serbia and to develop an attack on the rear of the hostile alliance. This view was shared by a section of French opinion, and, in particular, by General Galliéni, who proposed a landing at Salonika as a starting point for a march on Constantinople with an army strong enough to encourage Greece and Bulgaria to combine with the Entente. The capture of Constantinople was to be followed by an advance up the Danube into Austria–Hungary in conjunction with the Rumanians.

But the commanders on the Western front, obsessed with the dream of an early breakthrough, argued vehemently against any alternative strategy, stressing the difficulties of transport and supply, and insisting on the ease with which Germany could switch troops to meet the threat. (The Germans, in contrast, pointed out in their staff calculations that it was far easier for the Allies to move troops by sea to the Balkans than for them to move troops by rail!)

The weight of military opinion bore down all these counter-proposals, and the Balkan projects were relinquished in favour of a concentration of effort on the Western front. But misgivings were not silenced, and at this juncture a situation arose which revived the Near Eastern scheme in a new, if attenuated, form.

On 2 January 1915, Kitchener received an appeal from the Grand Duke Nicholas for a diversion which would relieve the Turkish pressure on Russia's army in the Caucasus. Kitchener felt unable to provide troops and suggested a naval demonstration against the Dardanelles, which Churchill, appreciating the wider strategic and economic issues, proposed to convert into an attempt to force the passage.

His naval advisers, though not enthusiastic, did not oppose the proposal, and, in response to a telegram, the admiral on the spot, Carden, submitted a plan for a methodical reduction of the forts and clearance of the minefields. A naval force, mainly of obsolete vessels, was got together, and after a preliminary bombardment, entered the Straits on 18 March. An unsuspected row of mines, however, caused the sinking of several ships, and the attempt was abandoned.

A prompt renewal of the advance might possibly have succeeded, for most of the Turkish ammunition in the forts was exhausted, and in such conditions the mine obstacle might have been overcome – if the Turks' mobile howitzers could also have been silenced. But the new naval commander, Admiral de Robeck, decided against it, unless military aid was forthcoming.

Already, a month before, the War Council had rather vaguely agreed to land support, initially to garrison Constantinople, and begun the dispatch of a military force under Sir Ian Hamilton. But as the authorities had drifted into the new scheme, so were they tardy in releasing the necessary troops, and even when sent, in inadequate numbers, several more weeks' delay had to be incurred – at Alexandria – in order to redistribute the force in its transports suitably for tactical action. Worst of all, this fumbling policy had thrown away the chance of surprise.

When the preliminary bombardment took place in February, only two Turkish divisions were at the Straits; this was increased by four by the date of the naval attack, and to six when Ian Hamilton was at last able to attempt his landing, on 25 April. For this he had only four British divisions and one French division.

Owing to the Turks' uncertainty, the British were able to gain a lodgement on several beaches of the Gallipoli Peninsula, which dominated the Straits. But the momentary asset of tactical surprise was forfeited, and the difficulties of supply were immense, while the Turks held the commanding heights and were able to bring up their reserves. The invaders managed to hold on to their two precarious footholds, but they could not expand them appreciably, and the stagnation of trench warfare set in.

Eventually, in July, the British Government decided to send a further five divisions to reinforce the seven now on the peninsula. But by the time they arrived, the Turkish strength in the region had also risen, to fifteen divisions. Thus success, and the retrieval of opportunity, had become basically improbable even before the fumblings of Ian Hamilton's subordinate commanders annulled the surprising initial surprise that his new landings momentarily gained.

The Government lost faith in the venture and became anxious to withdraw, although fear of the moral effect delayed the decision. Kitchener at first refused to sanction a withdrawal, but his influence was on the wane, and the Conservative members of the new Coalition Government that had been formed in May were almost as eager to get rid of him as to get rid of Churchill, who had been pushed out of the Admiralty as a condition of their entry into a Coalition. Asquith, who had remained as Prime Minister, feared a public outcry over Kitchener's removal only less than he feared the Conservatives' withdrawal, and so temporized that autumn by giving way to the demand for the evacuation made by their leader, Mr Bonar Law, and by excluding Churchill from the War Committee of the Cabinet. The evacuation was carried out in two stages, on the nights of 18 December and 8 January – and, to most people's surprise, without loss.

This outcome of the Dardanelles expedition was the more regrettable in view of the verdict of General Falkenhayn himself: 'If the straits between the Mediterranean and the Black Sea were not permanently closed to Entente traffic, all hopes of a successful course of the war would be very considerably diminished. Russia would have been freed from her significant isolation ... which offered a safer guarantee than military successes ... that sooner or later a crippling of the forces of this Titan must take place ... automatically.'

The immediate cause of the formation of a Coalition Government in mid-May, and of Churchill's ejection from the Admiralty then, was the resignation of Lord Fisher as First Sea Lord, after a violent emotional storm, on the ground that Churchill was continually overriding him. Moreover, he asserted that he had been against the Dardanelles operation from the beginning – an assertion that was far from true. But it provided the Conservative leaders with a good excuse for presenting a formidable challenge to the Government, and demanding Churchill's head on a charger.

Far more extraordinary was Churchill's own reaction to the events of May, and here again the most significant comment is to be found in Violet Asquith's book. She was on her way to Egypt, to visit her wounded brother Arthur, when she got some further news about the political crisis in a letter from Asquith's private secretary, Sir Maurice Bonham Carter, whom she later married:

I was surprised to hear that Winston was still clinging to the hope of keeping the Admiralty and struggling to remain there. I found it even more difficult to understand that he should have addressed his appeals to the leader of the Tory party.... His letter to Mr Bonar Law, written as late as Friday, May 21 (of which I knew nothing until its publication many years later), in which he asks to be 'judged justly, deliberately and with knowledge', reveals a curious imperviousness to the Tory party's inveterate dislike of him and all his ways. That he could have brought himself to plead for mercy from his bitterest enemies would have seemed to me a lapse from pride – and realism – wholly out of character, had I known it at the time.

On the retrospective view of history it seems shocking, and historically ironical, that Churchill should have been shelved and his career nearly wrecked after he had made such signal contributions to Britain's war effort. His only consolation, and a poor one from his point of view, was that the Secretary of State for War, Haldane – who had done so much to reorganize the Army and to create the well-organized British expeditionary force of 1914 – had suffered a similar fate, and been sacrificed still earlier to appease his virulent political opponents among the Conservative party and its leaders – in Haldane's case on the flimsy pretext of having expressed admiration for German philosophy and for describing Germany as his 'spiritual home' because of his early studies at the University of Göttingen. That was a sad and striking illustration of how the flimsiest excuse has been exploited in the world of politics.

During these war years of flaring conflict Britain, like Rome of old, went far to fulfil the bitter saying that 'ingratitude towards their great men is the mark of strong peoples'. To none of her leaders did she owe more for weathering the onset of the storm in 1914 than Haldane and Churchill; none did she repay worse. But the latter was too buoyant, or too unphilosophical, to sink.

In examining Churchill's contributions it can be seen that his influence on the turn of the war tide on the Marne, by intervention at Ostend, was too indirect for its effect to be realized until post-war years when the facts and documents of the campaign on 'the other side of the hill' were available for study. It was likewise with his intervention at Antwerp, while there it was all too obvious on the surface that his action had culminated in a rather costly fiasco which looked all the worse for his romantic behaviour and impetuosity. Over the Dardanelles, his tendency to 'rush his fences' became still more evident, and the vision apparent in his conception was marred partly by his own fault in overlooking practical difficulties and logistical needs. But nothing can detract from the value of his contribution towards getting the Navy ready and at its war stations in the nick of time. Nor from the part he played as foster-parent of the tank, the tactical key to victory that was at last fitted to the Western front lock at Cambrai in November 1917, and after that triumphal trial used with more consistent success from August 1918 onward.

In analysis, it becomes evident that Churchill claimed too much for his part in the development of the tank in the first two volumes of his book *The World Crisis*, especially when he said in volume I: 'The first design of the Tank, made at my request by Admiral Bacon in September 1914, carried a bridge in front, which, on arriving at a trench, it dropped, passed over, and automatically raised behind it.' Bacon's machine, designed as a means of haulage for heavy howitzers, was not in any real sense the prototype of the tank, even in the more developed form that Churchill had in mind. It was not a 'caterpillar tractor', as Churchill wrongly stated in the second (1915) volume of *The World Crisis*, but had eight-foot driving wheels – looking like an elongated version of the familiar steamroller used for road construction. Unfortunately, the experiments with a trench-crossing machine that Churchill ordered to be carried out, in the autumn of 1914, by the armoured car force of the Royal Naval Air Service, were at first concentrated on a machine with large driving wheels and rollers in front, to crush down barbed-wire entanglements and crush in trenches; and then, after it was found that the rollers would not climb slopes, turned into plans for a 'landship' with giant forty-foot wheels to transport infantry forward – a grandiose idea that fired Churchill's imagination, but would have resulted in machines all too easily vulnerable to enemy gunfire. It was not until the spring of 1915 that attention was brought back – by the failure of these experiments coupled with Swinton's persuasive missionary efforts – to the tractor line of development, and to the tactical purpose of producing a machine that should be primarily for destroying the defender's machine guns.

But without Churchill's impulsion, and the naval experiments he initiated, however misguided, the new idea might never have survived the chill of that first winter in official Army quarters. Churchill, indeed, might have had better justification for claiming that the activities of Royal Naval Air Service armoured cars in the autumn of 1914, and his endeavour to provide them with off-the-road mobility, foreshadowed the future development of armoured warfare that was to be fulfilled in the Second World War. But even on the very different First World War concept of the tank, as a revival of the ancient siege-warfare battering ram, his efforts had a valuable effect.

Moreover, in regard to the first use, and misuse, of the tanks in September 1916, in the futile hope that a mere handful might resuscitate the chances of success on the Somme, Churchill could show that he had warned the Government, as Swinton had warned the War Office and Haig, that this surprise weapon must be kept in hand, like a trump card, until it could be launched in decisive mass. On this and other points, Churchill could justly claim in *The World Crisis* that 'I pass no important criticisms on the conduct of commanders unless there exists documentary proof that substantially the same criticisms were put on record before or during the event, and while every point was disputed and unknowable'.

After his enforced departure from the Admiralty, Churchill was given a sinecure post as Chancellor of the Duchy of Lancaster, although it still left him nominally a member of the Cabinet and of the War Council. In November 1915, the War Council was reconstituted, and he was dropped. Following that palpable rebuff, he decided to return to the Army, with his Yeomanry rank of major, and after a probationary period was given command of the 6th Royal Scots Fusiliers, a 'new army' unit. But when in the spring of 1916 he heard that his battalion was to be merged with another, and knowing that under Haig as C-in-C he was unlikely to be given command of a brigade, as earlier promised by Haig's predecessor, Sir John French, he left France and returned to the back benches of Parliament.

Then, after twenty months 'in the wilderness' – or, more truly, twenty-six months – Lloyd George brought him back into the Government, as Minister of Munitions – although only in face of strong and widespread Conservative opposition, and thus at serious risk to Lloyd George's own situation. Churchill's new post did not carry with it a seat in the Cabinet, but did give him important influence on an essential sphere. He soon showed, however, that his years in the wilderness had left a deep mark, making him far more careful in his behaviour and chary of opposing official opinion.

I had a long account of this later from Sir Albert Stern, a banker in civil life and a forceful personality, who took a very active part in the development of tanks from the earliest days onward, and became head of the Mechanical Warfare Supply Department in the Ministry of Munitions. 'Winston, despite the great part he had played in promoting the development of the tank up to the spring of 1915, when he was First Lord of the Admiralty, had shown little interest in it in 1917–1918 when he returned to office as Minister of Munitions. He had never even gone to see any of the tank trials, although other Ministers less concerned, did so.' (Stern mentions in his memoirs that on 19 September he wrote to Churchill saying: 'Lack of action and lack of decision will most assuredly ruin the chances of Mechanical Warfare in 1918. . . . Every day and hour that passes renders Mechanical Warfare on a large scale for 1918 more improbable. On July 23rd you informed me that after a preliminary study of the Ministry you would investigate the position of Mechanical Warfare. It is now two months since that date. Immediate action must be taken.')

Early in October, Stern was told that his recommendation of a programme for building at least 4,000 tanks for 1918 had been overruled by the War Office and reduced to one for 1,350 tanks. He promptly asked for an interview with Churchill, to get him to take action in the matter. Churchill showed reluctance to do so, saying that he could not go against professional opinion, and that he had been out 'in the wilderness' for over two years as the price of opposing professional opinion, and was not inclined to court such a risk again. Stern argued with him that as the foster-parent of the tank, he surely could not stand aside while the infant was being suffocated, and that, if such was his attitude, he was a 'dishonest politician'. 'Winston flared up', and they 'had a row in the office'. Churchill insisted that Stern should withdraw the insulting remark. Stern refused, and 'demanded of Winston that he should put in writing the order for my dismissal. Winston did so' – and Stern kept the paper.

But when Stern saw the Prime Minister, Lloyd George appealed to him 'not to break with Winston', and brought about a reconciliation. Lloyd George told him that he must go on working with Churchill, as neither of them 'could be spared', but that he could deal with the question, if he wanted to, when he came to write his memoirs after the war.

Soon after the Armistice, Stern wrote his memoirs 'in justice to the men who had worked under me', and they dealt critically with Churchill's negative part. But Lloyd George sent for him and said that he understood that the book 'was damaging to Winston, and that he, Lloyd George, could not afford to see such an effect, since Winston was one of the few strong members of his Government and the situation of the country was very difficult'. At Lloyd George's behest, Stern then went to see Churchill with the manuscript of his book and offered to let him censor it. Churchill handed it over to Masterton-Smith, who cut out pages which reflected badly on Churchill.

Churchill was evidently more in sympathy with Stern than appeared at the time of this row, for although he bowed to the War Office generals' opposition and removed Stern from his post – appointing in his place an admiral who had no prior experience of tanks – he contrived a way of getting round the military obstacle by creating a new department and putting Stern in charge of it, as 'Commissioner for Mechanical Warfare (Overseas and Allies)'. This 'indirect approach' had the aim of gaining American aid in the expansion of the tank programme that the War Office opposed. Stern soon reached agreement with the Americans for the joint production of an additional 1,500 tanks. Although approval of the plan was delayed several weeks, it was given a few days after the Battle of Cambrai, in November 1917, had triumphantly demonstrated the value of tanks. From that time onward, the climate of opinion changed, and although interdepartmental discussions still consumed time, a decision was reached by the beginning of March that the 1918 programme should be expanded to a total of nearly 5,000 tanks.

Churchill Between the Wars

In the first volume of his Second World War memoirs, Churchill vividly told the story of how Britain's National Government, under the leadership of Ramsay MacDonald and Stanley Baldwin, tragically failed to grasp the obvious threat created by Hitler's accession to power in 1933, and was fatally dilatory in developing Britain's own rearmament even when they did see the red light. His account was a severe indictment. But it was not the whole story. There was no mention, or confession, of the fact that Britain's rearmament was handicapped from the start by the extent to which its foundations had been recklessly impaired at an earlier date.

Churchill himself was War Minister and Air Minister combined from 1918 to 1921, the crucial period for the reconstruction of the forces. The Air Staff had evolved a plan under which the post-war R.A.F. was to consist of 154 squadrons, of which forty were for home defence. Under Mr Churchill's aegis, this was whittled down to a mere twenty-four squadrons, with only two for home defence, and the plan for state-aided airways covering the Empire was also discarded. When he moved to a fresh office in 1921, *The Times* had this comment on the fruits of his régime at the Air Ministry: 'He leaves the body of British flying wellnigh at that last gasp when a military funeral would be all that would be left for it.'

In the War Office, too, he sadly disappointed all the progressive younger soldiers who had built their hopes on his vision and activity as foster-parent of the tank early in the war. To their dismay, he allowed the older school to refashion the Army on 'back to 1914' lines – thus missing the best opportunity of reconstructing it on a modern basis. Then from 1924 to 1929 he was Chancellor of the Exchequer, and each year the Army Estimates were pared down, with particular detriment to the development of Britain's diminutive but highly promising tank corps, which then led the world in ideas and design.

How can these remarkable changes of attitude on his part be explained? Like most other people during the first decade after the First World War, Churchill did not foresee the recurrence of a threat from Germany; in so far as he visualized a renewal of war, the possibility of long-term danger outside the colonial sphere was from Communist Russia. But he was eager to make a fresh mark in current political affairs, and the best chance lay in the post-war retrenchment of expenditure. That naturally became a still more dominant impulse, and intensified preoccupation, when after losing his seat at Dundee and suffering two further electoral defeats, he rejoined the Conservative party, won election for Epping as a Conservative in the general election of 1924, and was promptly invited by Baldwin to become Chancellor of the Exchequer in the new Conservative Government. That unexpected fulfilment of his dream of following in his father's footsteps made him all the more desirous of making a similar but more effective mark himself as a tax-cutting Chancellor.

In 1927, the first 'Experimental Mechanized Force' was formed as a result of years of argument and effort by Fuller and myself. In the speech on the Army Estimates that year, the project had been announced with a big flourish by the then War Minister, Sir Laming Worthington-Evans. Adverse influences in the War Office, however, reduced it to a mere shadow, with the result that Fuller, who had been appointed to command it, resigned in despair. I then came out in the *Daily Telegraph* with a pungent article entitled 'Is There a Mechanized Force?' This created a sensation. By writing it, I sacrificed my privileged position with the War Office, of which I had been given the free run. Nevertheless, the effect was a compensation – there were questions in Parliament; the War

Minister bluntly told his military advisers that they had made a fool of him; and the force was hastily formed (although the value of having Fuller to direct it had been lost). Shortly after this, Churchill, who was then Chancellor of the Exchequer, asked me to lunch with him and Worthington-Evans at Number 11, and there I expounded my ideas about the mechanization of the Army – which had a good reception – and for a time things looked promising. Churchill had paid a visit to the exercises of the Mechanized Force and seemed much impressed. He went so far as to confront the War Office with something approaching an ultimatum for the abolition of horsed cavalry regiments, or their conversion into a mechanized form. But the forces of tradition rallied from the shock, and he yielded to their objections. His traditionalist instincts were always in conflict with his progressive impulses.

With better justification, Churchill recounts his efforts from 1934 onward to spur Britain's laggard rearmament and check Hitler's ominously purposeful steps. On rearmament Churchill was always emphatic, and over Munich defiant, but on other issues he was not so clear in mind or speech about the right course as he appeared later. At the time he did not seem to see the ultimate risks of permitting Japan's and Fascist Italy's initial steps in aggression and in flouting the League of Nations, while in the Spanish Civil War his own sympathy with the Francoists tended to blind him to the purpose and dangers of Hitler's and Mussolini's support of that side.

One had expected that he of all people would be quick to realize the strategic danger to us of a Fascist victory promoted and achieved by German and Italian help. Instead, his class instincts and fear of the Communist element on the Republican side obscured his strategic vision, and led him to throw his influence against any effort on the part of Britain and France to check the German-Italian moves in Spain. It was not until April 1938, after the war had been in progress nearly two years, and the doom of the Republicans was virtually sealed, that he reversed his line of argument and pointed out the dangers to us of a Nazi-made victory for Franco in Spain.

Even in regard to Britain's defence preparations, his influence was less effective than it could have been owing to his traditionalism and the way it confused his vision. He admits that he 'accepted too readily when out of office the Admiralty view of the extent to which the submarine had been mastered', and also 'did not sufficiently measure the dangers to, or the consequent deterrent upon, British warships from air attacks'. Unfortunately, his confident assertions reinforced the Admiralty's obscurantism, and weighed the scales against more progressive views. He definitely aligned himself with the 'battleship school', as powerfully represented by Admiral Chatfield (First Sea Lord 1933–8), and tended to discount what seemed to me the almost certain threat that air power, as well as the submarine, would bring to our naval supremacy. I have a clear recollection of his attitude on these questions in various discussions – and that recollection is confirmed by reference to a record of his pronouncements at the time. In January 1938, he declared that: 'The air menace against properly armed and protected ships of war will not be of a decisive character.' Eight months later he reiterated this opinion, and went on to say: 'This, added to the undoubted obsolescence of the submarine as a decisive war weapon, should give a feeling of confidence and security so far as the seas and oceans are concerned, to the Western democracies.'

He also discounted, though he does not mention it, the effect of air power on armies. For in 1938, his verdict was: 'It may be said with some assurance that the whole course of the war in Spain has seemed to show the limitations rather than the strength of the air weapon. . . . It would seem, therefore, that so far as the fighting troops are concerned, aircraft are an additional complication rather than a decisive weapon.' Many observers drew the opposite deduction from analysis of these operations – a deduction that was to be confirmed in the Polish and Western front campaigns of 1939–40, where the German dive-bombers in combination with tanks proved the decisive factor.

As for tanks, he still thought of them in the slow-motion terms of 1918, so that he failed to understand the new *Blitz-*

krieg technique of swift and deep mechanized thrusts to cut the arteries of supply. This he admits in his account of the 1940 campaign, where he says:

I did not comprehend the violence of the revolution effected since the last war by the incursion of a mass of fast-moving heavy armour. I knew about it, but it had not altered my inward convictions as it should have done.

That frank admission puzzled me, since he had often heard, and also read, the views of Fuller and myself about the potentialities of mechanized warfare. Perhaps the clue was provided in a significant remark made by his close friend and associate Brendan Bracken in explanation of Churchill's perplexingly ambivalent attitude towards tanks: 'Bear in mind that Winston always remains the 4th Hussar.'

In the autumn of 1937, I was surprised to find that he no longer took the German danger as seriously as he had earlier, and in October he remarked publicly: 'Three or four years ago I was myself a loud alarmist. . . . In spite of the risks which wait on prophecy, I declare my belief that a major war is not imminent, and I still believe that there is a good chance of no major war taking place in our lifetime.' Significantly, too, he had said in the spring: 'I will not pretend that, if I had to choose between Communism and Nazism, I would choose Communism.'

Once Austria was violated, however, he saw the danger to Czechoslovakia. Swallowing his distrust of Soviet Russia, he was quick to respond to her government's proposals for a Franco-British-Russian alliance to check Hitler's designs. He did all he could to combat Chamberlain's course of appeasement towards Hitler and cold-shouldering of Stalin.

Churchill was at his best and clearest in that crucial year. His instinct coincided then with the basic facts of the situation.

The following spring, after Hitler's next transgression, Neville Chamberlain abruptly reversed his course and gave the impracticable guarantee to Poland, without even securing Russia's support. Churchill endorsed it, whereas Lloyd George sagely pointed out its folly. Churchill's impulse overrode his judgement. In retrospect, he seems less certain about his choice:

Here was decision at last, taken at the worst possible moment and on the least satisfactory ground, which must surely lead to the slaughter of tens of millions of people.

Yet at the time he, along with almost all Britain's political leaders except Lloyd George, supported this irrational guarantee in the fond belief that it would check Hitler. Never has there been a more astonishing case of collective self-delusion under the influence of righteous indignation.

Churchill in the Second World War

The outbreak of war brought Churchill back into the Government – initially in his old, 1914, office of First Lord of the Admiralty (i.e., the political head of the Navy). His memoirs record his manifold activity towards accelerating military steps both inside and outside his own department. But they are also a self-revelation of his tendency 'to miss the wood for the trees' in his absorption with the exciting detail points of the 'war game'. That tendency was increased through the way he became fascinated by striking phrases, as I had found in my own experience of him. When the 'Munich crisis' arose, and during the year that followed, he asked me to come as military adviser to private meetings of his 'Focus', a small group of people who shared his views about the German danger; it included a number of subsequent members of his wartime government. At these meetings he used to call on me to deal with the strategic aspects of the situation. In the discussions that followed, it often became apparent, more than in earlier years, that a point did not register in his mind unless it fitted in with his own ideas. Moreover, an apt phrase was all too apt to divert his attention from the thread of the argument while his mind revolved round the phrase.

Although he was quick to foresee, and warn his countrymen of, the potential danger from Hitlerite Germany, he showed curiously little interest in the new military technique that gave this danger its penetrative power. During discussions in which I took part, and he was present, in the last few years before the war, he dwelled far more on the quantitative aspect than on the qualitative aspect. This out-of-date outlook led him to cherish, and to foster, illusions about the power of the French Army, which he described as 'the most perfectly trained and faithful mobile force in Europe'. That was the year before the war!

His pugnacity was predominant, and the reverse of prescient. From the first month of the war onward, he was agitating for action that meant violating the neutrality of the Scandinavian countries in the imagined aim of gaining an offensive advantage against Germany. This is made clear by his own account and the memoranda he includes, even though he omits some of his more inflammatory utterances at the time which all too obviously hinted at his intention. An example was his broadcast of 20 January 1940, to 'the neutral nations', specifically urging 'Scandinavia', 'Belgium', and 'the Dutch' to 'do their duty in accordance with the Covenant of the League' and 'to stand together with the British and French Empires against aggression and wrong'. After listening to it I predicted to various correspondents that it was likely to spell the early doom of these small countries close to Germany, so obvious were its implications as to what he was planning. To some extent he saw that this was likely to provoke Hitler to take forestalling action, but he laboured under the delusion that 'we have more to gain than lose by a German attack upon Norway and Sweden'.

Churchill regretfully records that at first the 'Foreign Office arguments about neutrality were weighty, and I could not prevail'. But his arguments were helped by Russia's invasion of Finland, and the wave of feeling it aroused in England: 'I welcomed this new and favourable breeze as a means of achieving the major strategic advantage of cutting off the vital iron-ore supplies of Germany.'

He was oblivious of the fatal consequences of pushing Russia and Germany closer together, and embroiling Britain in war with both – at a time when she was perilously weak everywhere, especially on the Western front. While Hitler talked of 'thinking with the blood', the leaders of the democracies unfortunately acted in accord with such emotional thinking.

Only the sudden collapse of Finland saved Britain from being at war with Russia, and thus doubly stretched and strained. Yet Churchill then reverted to the plan of action on the Atlantic coast of Norway, to gain control of that neutral area.

The captured records of Hitler's conferences show that until early in 1940 he still considered 'the maintenance of Norway's neutrality to be the best course for Germany', but that in February he came to the conclusion that 'the English intend to land there and I want to be there before them'. His definite decision to order a move into Norway was taken a few days after Churchill had sent a direct order to the British destroyer *Cossack* to push into Norwegian waters and board the German ship *Altmark*, carrying British prisoners, which had taken shelter there. The Norwegian Government protested against the inroad into Norwegian waters, but their gunboats' passive acceptance of it convinced Hitler that Norway was Britain's accomplice, and became the detonating spark of the forestalling action he now ordered.

Early in March, Churchill gained sanction for his scheme, helped by the French Government's eager support, but then it was temporarily upset by Finland's collapse on 13 March – which deprived the Allies of their primary pretext for going into Norway. However, the scheme was soon revived, and at the end of March it was agreed between the two Allied governments that the mining of Norwegian waters should be carried out on 5 April, backed by the landing of forces at the chief Norwegian ports, in the hope and belief that the Norwegians would acquiesce. But it was postponed until the 8th in order that Churchill might go over to Paris and make a further effort to persuade the dubious French to agree to his additional project of dropping by air a stream of mines into the Rhine and other German rivers. That three-day delay proved fatal to the prospects. For Hitler had ordered his move into Norway, and Denmark, to begin early on the 9th.

In the event, the small German invading force forestalled and upset Churchill's plan, capturing the chief ports of Norway at the moment when the defender's attention was absorbed by the British advance into Norwegian waters. The British were caught unready to meet this retort, and their own counter-moves were badly bungled. Churchill's dream-castles had thus tumbled down in succession. Yet the blame fell on Chamberlain, as Prime Minister, and his enforced resignation opened the way for Churchill to take his place. It was the irony, or fatality, of history that Churchill should have gained his opportunity of supreme power as the result of a fiasco to which he had been the main contributor.

His habit of miscalculation, made all the worse by his mis-understanding of modern mechanized warfare, was soon shown again during Germany's invasion of France – when his call to the armies to abandon the idea of defending water-lines and rely instead on 'furious assault' not only showed his failure to realize that the French Army lacked the modern means of effective counter-stroke, but encouraged the Allied forces to forfeit their last chance of stemming the German breakthrough. If they had concentrated every effort on holding the remaining water-lines, they might have had a chance – but they forfeited this through trying to concentrate their forces, inadequately mechanized, for a counter-offensive against the German flanks in 1914 style.

In that dark time of disaster, Winston Churchill shone by his fighting spirit. But although full recognition should be given to the example he set, it would be a mistake to equate this, in a historical judgement of events, with its influence on the situation. The British have always been less dependent than other people upon inspiring leadership. Their record embraces rela-tively few spectacular victories, but they have a unique record in winning 'soldiers' battles'. The fact of being 'up against it' with their backs to the wall has repeatedly proved sufficient to rally them. Thus, in their case, inspiring leadership may be regarded as an additional asset rather than a necessity. It may be a necessity when they are weary, but not when they have had a slap in the face. It was Dunkirk that braced them in June 1940, more than any individual influence.

Moreover, Churchill's fighting spirit favoured activity so profusely as to foster offensive moves inspired by fresh miscalculations. The first was the delusion about the early possibilities of winning the war by a bombing offensive. This brought, in its recoil, a danger out of all proportion to what it was able to inflict – like throwing pebbles against an opponent strong enough to throw boulders in reply. As a strategic policy it amounted to nothing better than slow suicide – from which Britain was saved only by Hitler's obsession with Communist Russia, and his decision to strike at her instead of concentrating his resources on building up bomber and submarine forces sufficient to finish off Britain.

Another rash step was the attack on the French fleet at Oran – a step taken contrary to the judgement of the admirals on the spot, which naturally drove the French in indignation towards collaboration with the Germans. In his anxiety to ensure that no accessible part of the French fleet was allowed to fall into German hands after France's capitulation, Churchill ordered drastic steps to be taken to avert any such risk – rather than trust in the French admirals' promises that they would never surrender their ships or allow the Germans to seize them. All the French ships which had gone to British ports were forcibly taken on the morning of 3 July, although without resistance except from the crew of one ship. Meanwhile Admiral Somerville's newly assembled force in the western Mediterranean was dispatched to tackle the French fleet at Oran that same morning, and present it with a choice of alternatives, failing acceptance of which the French ships would be bombarded and sunk 'before dark'. Somerville's pleas for more time were rejected by Churchill, so that evening, in default of speedy French acceptance of the conditions, his force opened fire, inflicting heavy damage on the French fleet, as well as heavy loss of life among its crews, although part of it escaped to Toulon – where, despite bitter resentment of British action, it honoured two years later the promise never to fall into German hands. At Alexandria, in the eastern Mediterranean, Admiral Cunningham secured the disarming of the French naval squadron the next day after more patient negotiation, and disregarding Churchill's impetuous messages. All three admirals concerned – Cunningham, Somerville, and North at Gibraltar – were horrified by Churchill's orders, and all three considered that if more time for negotiation had been allowed, a peaceful solution could have been achieved. That would have been a more effective outcome as it would not have caused the bitter resentment that for a time pushed Vichy France into the arms of Germany.

Churchill's best move in 1940, following the fall of France, was his bold decision to send reinforcements to Africa – even though it meant weakening the scanty defence of the homeland – and to take the offensive there against the Italian forces, numerically much larger but ill-equipped. That decision was justified both in principle and in result. It produced a tonic success, and a distraction to the principal opponent, while opening up a new avenue for future development. But in carrying out the strategy of indirect approach and pressure, he impaired the effect by excessive dispersion of effort – by pursuing too many diverse aims, with limited resources. His generals, who were apt to err on the side of caution, were to that extent justified in their criticism of his direction.

Audacity is a great asset in war. But to be profitable it must be calculated audacity. Bluffing on a weak hand is always perilous, as it provides both a provocation and a temptation to a stronger opponent.

For while the defeat of the Italian forces in Africa was incomplete, Churchill tried to open up another fresh avenue in the Balkans. The landing of a British force in Greece naturally precipitated a German invasion of that country. Yet the force was dispatched at a time when it was clearly recognized that Hitler did not intend to move against Greece. The outcome was a second 'Dunkirk', together with a reverse in Africa.

As a direct result of this rash move, Britain incurred a serious loss of prestige, and sacrificed a large part of the scanty equipment she then possessed. As an indirect result, she sacrificed the chance of completing her conquest of Libya – owing to the diversion of troops to Greece. By spurring the Germans on to establish themselves on the Greek coast, and the Aegean Islands, she also blocked the way for any subsequent Balkan move on her part when better prepared to undertake it.

Churchill's Greek venture cannot be justified by the retrospective argument that it delayed the invasion of Russia. For the Cabinet, as he himself admits, was not aware at the time that Hitler was planning such a step. Moreover, the postponement was not due to the British effort in Greece, with which Hitler had reckoned, but to his sudden fit of anger over the Yugoslav *coup d'état*. In any case, the weather in Russia ruled out an earlier start there.

The basic situation after the fall of France in June 1940 was far worse than was generally realized at the time – or has been recognized retrospectively, in the glow of final victory. On the lines that the war was running in the next twelve months, Britain's destination was a dead end. But reprieve came midway through 1941 when Hitler turned against Communist Russia, and away from Britain. That reorientation of his concentration brought a dramatic change of outlook for Britain.

The better prospect, however, was still far from being assured. If the Russian armies were overthrown, or even crippled, Hitler would be able to concentrate on finishing off Britain. Her reprieve began to look short-lived, as, month after month, the Russians reeled back under successive heavy blows.

The assurance of Britain's survival came late in the year, and in a different way. President Roosevelt had long been itching to come to the rescue – and to pursue Hitler's destruction in company with Churchill. But although he stepped further and further over the boundary of neutrality, and aided Britain more and more openly, he failed to provoke retaliatory action that would release him from 'the restraints of a Congress' under which he 'had writhed'. Hitler was determined to avoid war with the United States if he possibly could.

Before the end of 1941, however, Roosevelt achieved his purpose in an indirect way. By comparison with Hitler's Germany, Japan was extremely susceptible to economic pressure.

By putting an oil stranglehold on her, he overcame her leaders' reluctance to engage in a fight with the U.S. and drove them to strike back. Churchill's account makes the process vividly clear. Once Japan was at war with the U.S., Hitler could not avoid supporting his ally.

The extended war opened with initial disaster in the Pacific for the Anglo-Saxon powers. Strangely enough, neither was prepared, materially or mentally, to meet the obvious riposte, although they had reckoned on one. The bulk of the U.S. battle fleet was sunk or disabled at Pearl Harbor, in barely an hour, while the *Prince of Wales* and *Repulse* were sunk off the Malay Peninsula three days later, thus clearing the way for the Japanese capture of Malaya and the Dutch East Indies.

These disasters cast a deeper shadow on Churchill's strategy. For his boldness in the Middle East was accompanied by a blindness about the Far East. The Chief of the Imperial General Staff, General Sir John Dill, reminded him in May 1941 that 'it has been an accepted principle of our strategy that in the last resort the security of Singapore comes before that of Egypt. Yet the defences of Singapore are still considerably below standard'. Churchill replied: 'I do not take that view, nor do I think the alternative is likely to present itself.' In August he said: 'I feel confident that Japan will lie quiet for a while', and a little later expressed his belief that the dispatch to the Far East of a 'K.G.V.' battleship 'might indeed be a decisive deterrent'.

Yet on 26 July he had taken action with Roosevelt to impose economic sanctions which 'meant that Japan was deprived at a stroke of her vital oil supplies'. In earlier discussions it had always been axiomatic that such 'a stranglehold' was almost bound to cause war, but at this crucial time Churchill took the risk too lightly. 'I confess that in my mind the whole Japanese menace lay in a sinister twilight, compared with our other needs.' That is an honest admission. But in view of the very large forces accumulated, and also frittered away, in the Middle East, it is most unconvincing when he adds, 'I am sure that nothing we could have spared at this time . . . would have changed the march of fate in Malaya.'

*

The best that can be said about these events is that they led to America's entry into the war, which insured Britain against complete and final defeat more than anything else could have done. But her power and prestige suffered irreparable damage, entailing the loss of her empire.

Moreover, from that time onward Churchill inevitably counted less than Roosevelt and Stalin in the conduct of the war, because of the much greater weight of resources they wielded. He became 'President Roosevelt's lieutenant'.

The principal, and primary, issue for the Western Alliance after America's entry into the war was that of re-entry into Europe, for the creation of a 'second front' to relieve the German pressure on Russia and develop a combined offensive against Germany. This soon became, and has ever since remained, a very controversial matter.

Churchill and the British chiefs of staff were right in resisting the American desire, and the Russian clamour, for launching a cross-Channel attack in 1942. It would almost certainly have been a disastrous fiasco. This is very clear in the light of post-war knowledge of the inadequacy of the Anglo-American resources, especially in landing craft, for developing and maintaining an effective re-entry in face of the number of German divisions posted in France.

Moreover, since it was psychologically important, or even essential, for the Western Allies to take some striking action that year, there was no other course so practicable and impressive as a landing in French North Africa, the north-west corner of that continent, to start the process of liberation and of loosening Hitler's grip. It threatened the rear of Rommel's army in north-east Africa and promised to make the whole Axis position there untenable.

Although the move failed to fulfil expectations of an early clearance of Africa, this failure was a blessing in disguise for the prospects of what became the Allies' next move. For the very slowness of Eisenhower's advance in November 1942 from Algeria into Tunisia had the great compensation of drawing Hitler and Mussolini to rush large reinforcements across the Mediterranean, to hold their Tunisian bridgehead. There, six months later, they were trapped with the sea at their back, and the resulting 'bag' of the whole German-Italian Army in Africa cleared the way for the Allied re-entry into southern Europe – which might otherwise have been easily blocked.

On the other hand, the unexpected and increasing delay in clearing the enemy out of Africa led, by degrees, to the deferment and eventually, to the abandonment of a cross-Channel attack in 1943 – on which the American chiefs of staff, headed by General Marshall, had set their minds and hearts. Whether such a landing in Normandy could have succeeded that year is doubtful. In the light of what we know now about the narrowness of the margin by which the Normandy landing succeeded in 1944, despite the greatly superior resources then available, it seems likely that a cross-Channel attack in 1943 would have proved premature, but the balance of evidence is not definite enough to rule out the possibility of its success.

The landing in French North Africa, 'Operation Torch', was mainly due to Churchill and his persuasive influence on President Roosevelt. When it had been mooted in June 1942, the British chiefs of staff, headed by General Sir Alan Brooke, had agreed with the Americans in regarding it as impracticable. On the evidence of Alan Brooke's own diaries, he only came round to accept it in July. From then on his dominant aim was, after clearing North Africa, to concentrate the Allied effort of 1943 on the invasion of Italy and 'eliminate' her from the war. His diary entries for 30 November and 3 December have sharp complaints that Churchill's mind was 'again swinging back towards a Western Front during 1943'. The reason was that, besides American pressure, Churchill and the Foreign Office feared that Stalin otherwise might make a compromise peace.

But from now on Alan Brooke gained an increasing influence on Churchill by his strong personality and clear-cut views, combined with the way his views accorded with Churchill's innate preference for attacking the Axis from the southern flank, rather than risk the hazards and costs of a direct cross-Channel attack.

Brooke's next battle was with the American chiefs of staff. His diary for 11 December deplores that Marshall 'considers we should close down operations in the Mediterranean once we have pushed the Germans out, and then concentrate on preparing for re-entry into France. . . . I think he is wrong and the Mediterranean gives us far better facilities for wearing down German forces, both land and air, and of withdrawing strength from Russia'.

The argument was renewed at the Casablanca Conference in January 1943. Ironically, it was the failure of the Christmastide attack in Tunisia that tilted the scales in favour of Brooke's Mediterranean view, and the continued slow progress there that settled the matter. Not until May 1943 was the conquest of Tunisia completed. Meanwhile, Brooke had gained his way about making Sicily the next objective. But it was almost mid-July before the landing in Sicily took place, and mid-August before the island was cleared. The further delays that had occurred, coupled with the closeness of Sicily to the mainland, helped to determine that the Allies' next step should be into Italy, as Brooke desired. It was the logic of events resulting from loss of time more than logic of argument, which swung the Allied strategy into his channel instead of the more direct line of the English Channel.

The success of the Allied invasion of Sicily led to the overthrow of Mussolini, and its promised extension to the mainland produced Italy's capitulation. These results initially vindicated Brooke's line of strategy, although they entailed a postponement of the cross-Channel attack until 1944.

But the Germans were quicker in reacting to the emergency than were the Allies in exploiting the opportunity. The Allied advance up the mountainous Italian peninsula became sticky and slow. For the German forces, under Kesselring, speedily recovered from the shock of their Italian ally's change of sides, disarmed the Italian forces, and skilfully used the natural obstacles of the peninsula to impose repeated and prolonged checks on the Allied advance.

The claims that have been made for the value of the Italian campaign as an aid to the cross-Channel attack do not stand analysis. For the distracting effect caused by the Allies' amphibious flexibility diminished when the ubiquitous threat was translated into an actual landing. By June 1944, they were employing in Italy a strength in troops double that of Kesselring. That was not a good investment proportionately, and justified the American argument for breaking off the offensive there after the strategic airfields in the south were gained. Moreover, its continuance did not draw German reserves away from Normandy, nor prevent them reinforcing Normandy, as the British hoped – and have claimed.

The only claim that can be made for the strategic effect of the Italian campaign, as an aid to the success of the Normandy landing, is that without its pressure the German strength on the Channel front might have been increased even more. The scale of the assault and immediate follow-up forces there were limited by the number of landing craft available, so that the Allied forces employed in Italy could not have added to the weight of the Normandy landing during its crucial opening phase.

On the evidence of Brooke's diaries, both he and Churchill were half-hearted, as the American leaders suspected, about launching a cross-Channel attack into Normandy – and continued to seek ways of evading this commitment. As late as October 1943, Brooke records the receipt of a note from Churchill 'wishing to swing the strategy back to the Mediterranean at the expense of the Channel', and remarks: 'I am in many ways entirely with him.' The following week he records that Churchill argued the case for the Mediterranean 'as opposed to' the cross-Channel attack, and himself terms the latter 'very problematical'.

The British strategic plan, however, received a bad knock at the Teheran Conference at the end of November, through Stalin's reinforcement of the American arguments against it. That was ominous, and ironical. For the Americans, according to Harry Hopkins's diary, had expected the Russians to team up with the British at Teheran in favour of a Balkan rather than a Normandy operation in 1944 – an expectation which showed their blindness to the long-range political aims of Stalin's strategy. He naturally wished to see the British effort kept well away from Eastern Europe, and turned from Italy towards France.

So Churchill and Alan Brooke were pushed into a definite

commitment which neither of them liked. Indeed, almost on the eve of the Normandy landing, Brooke wrote in his diary that he was 'torn to shreds with doubts and misgivings. . . . The cross-Channel operation is just eating into my heart', and feared that it would prove 'the most ghastly disaster of the war'. Even after victory in Normandy was complete, he continued at successive stages of the advance into Germany to express pessimistic doubts about the prospect of early victory in that quarter.

But from the time the Normandy landing was achieved, he ceased, and Churchill too, to have any important influence on the course of the war – or on its sequel. Both strategically and politically, American influence became overwhelmingly pre-dominant, and dictated the Allies' course. Indeed, when the British Prime Minister began to see the ominous consequences of the 'unconditional surrender', he was powerless to modify it. He had in effect become, as he earlier proclaimed himself, merely the American President's 'lieutenant'.

In the British sphere, Churchill had continued to be the great animator of the war. The collection of minutes which fills the appendices of his volumes provides the best opportunity of seeing the genius of the man displayed in all its abundance. No one can read them without marvelling at his fertility, versa-tility, and vitality. He was constantly spurring or coaxing ministers, officials, and generals to greater activity and quicker progress. The characteristic use in his minutes of 'pray' – do this or that – was like a jockey showing the whip to a laggard racehorse. His minutes streamed out daily in all directions, urging that obstacles should be overcome, that red tape should be cut, that excuses should not be accepted, that objections should be searchingly questioned, that obstruction should be brought to book.

Yet his account leaves the analytical reader with the impression that his actual influence was much less than is commonly supposed. It is astonishing to find how often he failed to get his views accepted by the chiefs of staff, even when his views were most clearly right. His account also reveals a hesitation to insist on what he considered right, and a deference to officialdom, that run contrary to the popular picture of his dominating personality. How is it to be explained? Was it due to the carry-over effect of spending two years in the wilderness during the First World War as a penalty for putting himself in opposition to the weight of official opinion?

Although he had himself been slow to recognize some of the decisive new trends of warfare – with unfortunate effect on the earlier course of the war – his minutes from 1940 on show him as being usually in advance of his official military advisers and executants. Indeed, both in his minutes and in his later comments, he has some caustic reflections on their defective vision and time sense.

It may seem strange that he did not push his advisers along faster, or replace them by more forward-thinking men. He himself remarks in one place:

The reader must not forget that I never wielded autocratic powers, and always had to move with and focus political and professional opinions.

That view of his own limited powers hardly corresponds to reality, as created by his prestige and ascendancy since 1940, but it may represent the continued impress on his own mind of what he had suffered in the previous war for overriding professional opinion. If his bitter experience then had left him apprehensive, the effect was unfortunate in making him feel that he must take as a 'governor' the average pace of professional opinion – for that has always been a slow march.

The point is emphasized by a minute he wrote, after the Germans' airborne coup in Crete, regretting that the previous year a proposal for creating parachute troops had been whittled down from five thousand men to a mere five hundred:

This is a sad story, and I feel myself greatly to blame for allowing myself to be overborne by the resistances which were offered.

The same happened with tanks. He bitingly remarks: 'We ought to try sometimes to look ahead.' At the end he says:

I print these details to show how difficult it is to get things done even with much power, realised need, and willing helpers.

But they tend to show that, owing to some inhibition, he did not truly use his power to obtain helpers who realized what was needed and were really willing. At no time in the war did Churchill insist that any of the experts in mobile armoured warfare be given a chance in high command or in the higher direction of the Army. The absence of such knowledge accounted for many 'grievous errors'.

On the evidence of the records he prints, it would seem that he was not much helped by the guidance received from his official advisers. They repeatedly misjudged impending developments in many directions that were apparent to, and forecast by, outside observers who had no such elaborate machinery of intelligence. The evidence shakes confidence in the collective foresight of the combined staff organs in Whitehall.

A greater blindness was that which prevailed in the grand strategy of the war. Through it, the Western democracies have been in fresh and greater peril ever since the war ended. It was due to a too intense concentration on the short-term object, and a failure to take a long view. As epitomized by Churchill himself, the aim was 'the defeat, ruin, and slaughter of Hitler, to the exclusion of all other purposes'. The 'unconditional surrender' formula naturally tended to rally the German people behind Hitler, thereby prolonging their resistance – and the war. Churchill, as well as Roosevelt, seems to have been blind to the obvious fact that the complete destruction of Germany's and Japan's power of *defence* was bound to give Soviet Russia the chance to dominate Eastern Europe and Asia.

There is much significance in Lord Esher's 1917 verdict on Churchill:

He handles great subjects in rhythmical language, and becomes quickly enslaved by his own phrases. He deceives himself into the belief that he takes broad views, when his mind is fixed upon one comparatively small aspect of the question.

Churchill always had a deep-rooted tendency when concentrating on one problem to forget the other problems which were bound up with its solution. He lacked the power of relating one part to another, and the parts to the whole. A man may be successful as a tactician without that capacity for 'comparison', and the sense of proportion from which it springs – but he will be almost certain to go astray as a strategist and still more as a grand strategist.

Churchill's characteristics, and fascination for those who worked under him, are well epitomized by a passage in the memoirs of Sir George Mallaby, who was Under-Secretary in the Cabinet Office:

Anybody who served anywhere near him was devoted to him. It is hard to say why. He was not kind or considerate. He bothered nothing about us. He knew the names only of those very close to him and would hardly let anyone else come into his presence. He was free with abuse and complaint. He was exacting beyond reason and ruthlessly critical. He continuously exhibited all the characteristics which one usually deplores and abominates in the boss. Not only did he get away with it but nobody really wanted him otherwise. He was unusual, unpredictable, exciting, original, stimulating, provocative, outrageous, uniquely experienced, abundantly talented, humorous, entertaining – almost everything a man could be, a great man.

There is another significant comment on his attitude at the end of a passage by Lord Boothby about Churchill's method of control, and of keeping things in his own head as far as possible:

Churchill had derived two strong impressions from Lloyd George's premiership in the First World War. The first was the loss of political power which arose from lack of Party leadership; the second the continuing and disastrous clashes between the Prime Minister and his naval and military advisers. He judged that, on the whole, Mr Lloyd George had been right, and the sailors, and soldiers wrong. But he resolved, if possible, to prevent a repetition of any similar conflict. In war the civil power, which meant his own personal power, must be paramount and unchallenged.

Therefore, when he became Premier, in May 1940, he devised machinery to ensure an effective power relationship between the Prime Minister's office, the Chiefs of Staff and the great Departments of State. His chosen instruments for the execution of this task were General Ismay, Professor Lindemann and Mr Bracken. They worked, according to their very different lights, in the secret places where decisions of vital importance were taken and conferences held – often far into the night, and always far from public gaze.

Lord Snow has since drawn attention to the enormous dangers of confiding omnipotent scientific power to the hands of a single individual; and proved, conclusively, that upon at least two major issues of policy, Lindemann was wrong, and Sir Henry Tizard, whom he consigned to outer darkness, right. However, no one can say that the task itself was not accomplished to the satisfaction of their master.

Even so, there were difficulties from time to time. Winston Churchill could not only be tough in action, he could also be very rough in his personal dealings. There are, for example, various methods of sacking people. He did not always choose the kindest. This arose less from a streak of cruelty in his nature than from the ruthless egotism of his own sensibility.

In contrast to Lloyd George, who instinctively liked to surround himself with outstanding men – perhaps feeling sure that he could dominate and outshine them – Churchill seemed only to feel comfortable with men of lesser calibre than himself as colleagues and assistants, or, at any rate, as constant company.

An exception to this rule might appear to be his close association with T. E. Lawrence in 1921–2. But that lasted barely a year, and it was Lawrence who really initiated it, by suggesting to Lloyd George how a Middle East settlement might be brought about, and also by suggesting that Churchill should be used (instead of Amery) for the purpose. Churchill undoubtedly had a strong sentimental feeling for Lawrence – I remember how he shed tears at Lawrence's funeral in 1935.

But Lawrence on his part had no illusions about Churchill. One of the most illuminating things he ever said to me was in regard to the respective qualities of Lloyd George and Churchill. It arose from a remark of Lawrence's that Lloyd George was 'head and shoulders above anyone else at the Peace Conference'; that he was 'the only man there (in a big position) who was really trying to do what was right'. This comment rather surprised me, and I remarked that it was certainly very different to the popular idea, asking him: 'Would you really say that

Lloyd George would go so far as to follow such a standard if it meant endangering his political career?' Lawrence replied that that was too much to expect of anyone in political life – but Lloyd George's instinctive standard was to try to do what was right, if it were possible, and provided that it could be done without seriously damaging his political interests. To illustrate this point, Lawrence then went on to contrast Churchill with Lloyd George, remarking: 'If Winston's interests were not concerned in a question, he would not be interested.' Lawrence was as fond of Churchill as Churchill was of him – but no feeling of affection could cloud his clearness of sight. And the more closely I later observed Churchill, in the light of that reflection, the more I came to realize its profound truth.

In sum, the conclusion from this analytical study of Winston Churchill as a strategist is that in the First World War he received undue blame for initiatives that miscarried, and too little credit for contributions that were of key importance, whereas in the Second World War his importance and the value of his contributions were overrated.

In the first war, his vision excelled that of most of his contemporaries, and the main criticism that can be justified is that he was apt to mar brilliant conceptions by precipitancy, and a failure to calculate what was reasonably possible with the means available. In the second war, he showed the same tendency to precipitancy, and failure in calculation, but also a hesitancy about insisting on his own more prescient views that can be traced to his bitter experiences in the first war. While often an irritant to officialdom, and frequently a valuable one, he was never so dominant, nor dared to be, as popular opinion imagined or his official advisers apprehensively felt. Critics and admirers alike were fundamentally mistaken in regarding him as a revolutionary, either in thought or action.

Winston Churchill was a wonderful man, shining out from the gloom of an era of mediocrities in the democracies. He not only compelled admiration by his virtuosity, but inspired affection despite his intense egocentricity. At times he revealed a long view, helped by his historical sense, yet was inclined to act on a short view, prompted by his tactical sense as well as blinded by the force of his feelings. Once he went into action, his fighting instinct governed his course, his emotions swamped his calculations, and reason reasserted itself too late. In brief, his dynamism was too strong for his statesmanship – and his strategy. Thus, when he got his hand on the helm in 1939, too late to avert the danger that he had foreseen, events continued to move with the same inevitability of tragedy as in the preceding period, towards further danger that he did not foresee.

Boothby relates how, some years after the war, in a rather despondent mood, Churchill himself remarked that the final verdict of history would take account not only of the victories achieved under his direction, but of the political results which flowed from them, and added: 'Judged by this standard, I am not sure that I shall be held to have done very well.'

Anthony Storr THE MAN

The psychiatrist who takes it upon himself to attempt a character study of an individual whom he has never met is engaged upon a project which is full of risk. In the exercise of his profession, the psychiatrist has an unrivalled opportunity for the appraisal of character, and may justly claim that he knows more persons deeply and intimately than most of his fellows. But, when considering someone who has died, he is deprived of those special insights which can only be attained in the consulting-room, and is, like the historian, obliged to rely upon what written evidence happens to be available. In the analytical treatment of a patient, the psychiatrist is able to check the validity of the hypotheses which he proffers by the patient's response, and by the changes which occur in the patient as a result of his increased comprehension of himself. The psychiatrist may often be wrong or premature in his interpretation of his patient's behaviour and character; but, as the long process of analysis continues, errors will gradually be eliminated and the truth recognized by both parties in the analytical transaction. Deprived of this constant appraisal and reappraisal, psychiatrists who attempt biographical studies of great men are apt to allow theory to outrun discretion: with the result that many so-called psychoanalytic biographies have been both bad biography and bad psychoanalysis. The disastrous study of Woodrow Wilson by Freud and Bullitt is a case in point.

In this essay, I advance a hypothesis about Churchill which I think is warranted by the facts. But what I have to say must be regarded as tentative, for the possibilities of error in this complicated field are very great. Although Churchill himself provided many autobiographical details, especially in *My Early Life*, these are not the kind of details which are of much service to the psychiatrist. For Churchill showed as little interest in the complexities of his own psychology as he did in the psychology of others; and would have been the first to dismiss this essay as both futile and impertinent. Moreover, as C.P. Snow remarks in his essay in *Variety of Men*, Churchill's character was 'abnormally impenetrable to most kinds of insight'. His deeds, speeches, and career have been lavishly and repeatedly recorded, but very little of what has been written about him reveals anything of his inner life. Although Churchill can be rated as an artist, both as writer and painter, he was not, like many artists, introspective or concerned with his own motives. Indeed, if he had been, he could scarcely have achieved what he did, for introspection is the accomplice of self-distrust and the enemy of action.

Winston Churchill is still idolized, not only by those of us who remember his speeches in 1940, and who believe, as I do, that it was to his courage that we owe our escape from Nazi tyranny; but by men and women all over the world, to whom he has become a symbol, a personification of valour. But Churchill was also a human being, with the same needs, instincts, hopes, and fears which pertain to all of us. It is no disservice to a great man to draw attention to his humanity, nor to point out that, like other men, he had imperfections and flaws. Churchill, in spite of his aristocratic birth and social position, started life with disadvantages which he never wholly conquered; although his whole career was an effort to overcome them. Without these disadvantages he would have been a happier, more ordinary, better-balanced, and lesser human being. But had he been a stable and equable man, he could never have inspired the nation. In 1940, when all the odds were against Britain, a leader of sober judgement might well have concluded that we were finished. Political leaders are accustomed to dissimulation. Even when defeat at the polls is imminent, or the policies which they support have been shown to be futile, they will, until the eleventh hour, continue to issue messages of hope to their supporters. In 1940, any political leader might have tried to rally Britain with brave words, although his heart was full of despair. But only a man who had known and faced despair within himself could carry conviction at such a moment. Only a man who knew what it was to discern a gleam of hope in a hopeless situation, whose courage was beyond reason, and whose aggressive spirit burned at its fiercest when he was hemmed in and surrounded by enemies, could have given emotional reality to the words of defiance which rallied and sustained us in the menacing summer of 1940. Churchill was such a man: and it was because, all his life, he had conducted a battle with his own despair that he could convey to others that despair can be overcome.

For Winston Churchill, like his ancestor the first Duke of Marlborough, suffered from prolonged and recurrent fits of depression; and no understanding of his character is possible unless this central fact is taken into account. His own name for depression was 'Black Dog': and the fact that he had a nick-name for it argues that it was all too familiar a companion. For great sections of his life, Churchill was successful in conquering his depression; but old age and the narrowing of his cerebral arteries in the end undermined his resistance. The last five years of his protracted existence were so melancholy that even Lord Moran draws a veil over them. It was a cruel fate which ordained that Churchill should survive till the age of ninety; for the 'Black Dog' which he had controlled and largely mastered in earlier years at last overcame his fighting spirit.

Churchill is, of course, not a lone example of a great man suffering from recurrent depression. Goethe was of similar temperament; so were Schumann, Hugo Wolf, Luther, Tolstoy, and many others. The relation between great achievement and the depressive temperament has yet to be determined in detail, but there can be little doubt that, in some natures, depression acts as a spur. When depression is overwhelming, the sufferer relapses into gloom and an inactivity which may be so profound as to render him immobile. To avoid this state of misery is of prime importance; and so the depressive, before his disorder becomes too severe, may recurrently force himself into activity, deny himself rest or relaxation, and accomplish more than most men are capable of, just because he cannot afford to stop. We do not know how many men of exceptional achievement have this tendency towards depression, for it may often be well concealed. That some do, and that Churchill was one of them, admits of no possible doubt.

There is still dispute as to how far the tendency to suffer from recurrent depression is the product of heredity, and how much it is the result of early conditioning. Until the science of genetics is further advanced than it is at present, we shall not be able to answer this question fully. In Churchill's case, it is safe to assume that both factors played their part. For we know that at least two of Churchill's most distinguished ancestors were afflicted by swings of mood of some severity; and there is some evidence to suggest that they were not the only members of the family to be afflicted in this way. A. L. Rowse, writing of the first Duke of Marlborough, says:

Marlborough was *sensible* in the French sense, a most sensitive register of all the impressions that came to him. An artist by temperament in his ups and downs – the depression he got before the precipitant of action, the headaches that racked him at all the obstructions he had to put up with, and the self-control he exercised so habitually that it became second nature to him. It exacted its price.[1]

In 1705, the Duke wrote: 'I have for these last ten days been so troubled by the many disappointments I have had that I think if it were possible to vex me so for a fortnight longer it would make an end of me. In short, I am weary of my life.' This weariness is a recurrent theme in his letters: 'I am extremely out of heart', 'My dearest soul, pity me and love me'. Although it may be argued that many men might write like this in times of stress, Rowse is not the only historian to observe that the first Duke of Marlborough alternated between optimism and depression in a way which some people would not expect in one of England's most famous military commanders. Winston Churchill himself observed: 'Sometimes he was overdaring and sometimes overprudent; but they were separate states of mind, and he changed from one to the other in quite definite phases.'

The other Churchill forebear who exhibited the same kind of temperament was Lord Randolph, Winston's father. A. L. Rowse writes of him:

Though a very quick and piercing judge of a situation, his judgment was not really reliable. He was self-willed and impulsive, above all impatient. If he had only had patience all the rest would have come into line. But he had the defect of the artistic temperament, what we in our day of psychological jargon diagnose as the manic-depressive alternation – tremendous high spirits and racing energy on the upward bound, depression and discouragement on the down. This rhythm is present in a more or less marked degree with all persons of creative capacity, particularly in the arts. And clearly this strongly artistic strain we have observed in the stock came out in him, as it has done again in his son.[2]

Rowse is wrong in thinking that the manic-depressive alternation is present in all creative persons, some of whom belong to a very different temperamental group; but he is obviously right in his diagnosis of the Churchill family.

One other member deserves mention in this connexion, the Winston Churchill who was father of the first Duke of Marlborough. An ardent Royalist, he retired to his country seat in East Devon after the King's forces had been defeated in the Civil War. Here he occupied himself by writing history: '*Divi Brittanici:* being a Remark upon the Lives of all the Kings of this Isle.' Although we are not informed in detail of his temperamental constitution, A. L. Rowse describes him as follows: 'Sunk in glum resentment, he had, at any rate, the consolation that intelligent people have who are defeated and out of favour: reading and writing. . . . His spirit was not defeated: it burns with unquenched ardour in what he wrote.'[3] The later and more famous Winston adopted the same policy when he was out of office; and we may be thankful that creative activity can and does provide an effective defence against the depression which threatens to overwhelm those who possess this temperament when they are neither occupied nor sustained by holding a position of consequence.

Brendan Bracken, quoted by Moran, says five of the last seven Dukes of Marlborough suffered from melancholia; but it is difficult to confirm this even from Rowse's books, which Bracken alleges are the source of his information. There seems little doubt, however, that the cyclothymic temperament, that is, the tendency to rather extreme swings of mood, was part of the Churchill inheritance.

Before leaving the question of Churchill's heredity, we must take a glance at his physical endowment. It is probable, though not certain, that physique and character are intimately connected, and that the structure and shape of the body reflect genetic rather than environmental influences. A man's cast of mind is largely influenced by the way he is brought up and educated. His physical endowment, though modifiable to some extent, is more likely to be a datum of heredity.

It is clear that Churchill was possessed of enormous vitality. He survived to the age of ninety; and, by the age of eighty, he had surmounted a heart attack, three attacks of pneumonia, two strokes, and two operations. He habitually ate, drank and smoked as much as he wanted, and this much was a great deal. Until he was seventy, he hardly ever complained of fatigue. Yet, this extraordinary constitution was not based upon natural physical strength of a conventional kind. Indeed, he started life with considerable physical disadvantages. As Lord Moran puts it: 'I could see this sensitive boy, bullied and beaten at his school, grow up into a man, small in stature, with thin, unmuscular limbs, and the white delicate hands of a woman; there was no hair on his chest, and he spoke with a lisp and a slight stutter.'[4]

Winston Churchill himself, in a letter from Sandhurst written in 1893, claimed: 'I am cursed with so feeble a body, that I can scarcely support the fatigues of the day; but I suppose I shall get stronger during my stay here.' His height was only five foot, six-and-a-half inches; and his chest measured but thirty-one inches, which, by Sandhurst standards, was quite inadequate. When the poet, Wilfred Scawen Blunt, met Churchill in 1903, he described him as 'a little square-headed fellow of no very striking appearance.' The physical courage which he consistently, and sometimes rashly, displayed was not based upon any natural superiority of physique, but rather upon his determination to be tough in spite of lack of height and muscle. His search for physical danger in early youth, and his reckless self-exposure in France, even though his behaviour put others in danger, bear witness to the fact that his courage was not something that he himself took for granted, but rather something which he had to prove to himself; a compensation for inner doubts about his own bravery.

No man is immune from fear; but those who have been endowed by nature with exceptionally powerful physiques are generally less disturbed by physical danger than most of us. Churchill was uncommonly brave; but his courage was of a more remarkable and admirable variety than that which is based upon an innate superiority of physical endowment. He never forgot that, at his second preparatory school, he had been frightened by other boys throwing cricket balls at him, and had taken refuge behind some trees. This, to him, was a shameful memory; and, very early in life, he determined that he would be as tough as anybody could be. When he was eighteen, he nearly killed himself when being chased by his cousin and brother by jumping from a bridge to avoid capture. He fell twenty-nine feet, ruptured a kidney, remained unconscious for three days and unable to work for nearly two months. There is no doubt whatever that Churchill's physical courage was immense; but it rested upon his determination to conquer his initial physical disadvantages, much as Demosthenes' skill in oratory is said to have been the consequence of his will to overcome an impediment in his speech.

There have been many attempts to discern a relationship between physique and character, of which W. H. Sheldon's is both the most detailed and the most successful. Sheldon claimed that he could discern three main components in a man's physical make-up, to which he gave the somewhat awkward names of endomorphy, mesomorphy, and ectomorphy. He also constructed a scale of temperament comprising three sets of twenty basic traits which were generally closely allied to the subject's physique. The three main varieties of temperament are known as viscerotonia, somatotonia, and cerebrotonia.

When one comes to examine Churchill, it is obvious that his physique was predominantly endomorphic. His massive head, the small size of his chest compared with his abdomen, the rounded contours of his body, and the small size of his extremities were all characteristic. So was his smooth, soft skin, which was so delicate that he always wore specially obtained silk underwear. One would expect a man with this physique to be predominantly viscerotonic in temperament: earthy, unhurried, deliberate, and predictable. Churchill actually does rate high on eleven out of the twenty viscerotonic traits; but he also scores almost equally high on somatotonia – that is, the temperament which is allied to the powerful and athletic frame of the meso-morph. According to Sheldon, men whose temperament differs widely from that which accords with their physique are par-ticularly subject to psychological conflict, since they are at odds with their own emotional constitution.

Churchill was a very much more aggressive and dominant individual than one would expect from his basic physique. His love of risk, of physical adventure, his energy and assertiveness are traits which one would expect to find in a heavily muscled mesomorph, but which are unexpected in a man of Churchill's endomorphic structure.

In other words, we have a picture of a man who was, to a marked extent, forcing himself to go against his own inner nature: a man who was neither naturally strong, nor naturally par-ticularly courageous, but who made himself both in spite of his temperamental and physical endowment. The more one examines Winston Churchill as a person, the more one is forced to the conclusion that his aggressiveness, his courage, and his domin-ance were not rooted in his inheritance, but were the product of deliberate decision and iron will. 'I can look very fierce when I like,' he said to his doctor.[5] But the expression of bulldog defiance which appears in his most popular photographs was not evident upon his face before the war, and, as Moran hints, is likely to have been assumed when declaiming speeches in front of the looking glass, and thenceforth used on appropriate public occasions.

Before turning from the question of inherited physical and psychological characteristics to consideration of the environ-mental influences which shaped Churchill's character, it is worth glancing at one more typology. The Swiss psychiatrist, C. G. Jung, was responsible for introducing the terms 'extravert' and 'introvert' into psychology; most people are familiar with the broad outlines of what is meant by these two terms. The extravert is a person whose chief orientation is toward the events and features of the external world. The recesses of his

own soul are not of much concern to the predominantly extraverted person, nor is he much concerned with abstractions, ideas,
or the subtleties of philosophy. The main interest of the extraverted person is in action, not in thought, and when troubled,
he seeks to do things to distract himself rather than to explore
his inner life to determine the cause of his distress. Churchill was
undoubtedly highly extraverted. He showed little interest in
philosophy and none in religion, and he dismissed psychology
as irrelevant.

Jung's further subdivision of types into thinking, feeling,
sensation, and intuition has not been widely accepted; but his
delineation of the extraverted intuitive in *Psychological Types*
fits Churchill so accurately that it ought to persuade people to
take another look at the book. Jung writes:

Wherever intuition predominates, a particular and unmistakeable
psychology presents itself. . . . The intuitive is never to be found
among the generally recognized reality values, but is always present
where possibilities exist. He has a keen nose for things in the bud
pregnant with future promise. . . . Thinking and feeling, the indispensable components of conviction, are, with him, inferior func-
tions, possessing no decisive weight: hence they lack the power to
offer any lasting resistance to the force of intuition.

Hence, according to Jung, the intuitive's lack of judgement, and
also his 'weak consideration for the welfare of his neighbours'.
The intuitive is 'not infrequently put down as a ruthless and
immoral adventurer', terms often applied to Churchill in his
youth, and yet 'his capacity to inspire his fellow-men with
courage, or to kindle enthusiasm for something new, is unrivalled'.

In his extremely interesting essay on Churchill, C. P. Snow
refers to his lack of judgement. In fact, he says that it was
'seriously defective'. He goes on:

Judgment is a fine thing: but it is not all that uncommon. Deep insight is much rarer. Churchill had flashes of that kind of insight,
dug up from his own nature, independent of influences, owing nothing
to anyone outside himself. Sometimes it was a better guide than
judgment: in the ultimate crisis when he came to power, there were

times when judgment itself could, though it did not need to, become a source of weakness.

When Hitler came to power Churchill did not use judgment but one of his deep insights. This was absolute danger, there was no easy way round. *That* was what we needed. It was an unique occasion in our history. It had to be grasped by a nationalist leader. Plenty of people on the left could see the danger: but they did not know how the country had to be seized and unified.[6]

I think that the kind of insight to which C.P. Snow is referring might equally well be called intuition. Intuition is in many respects an unreliable guide, and some of Churchill's intuitions were badly wrong. In the First World War, his major strategic conception, the invasion of Gallipoli, was a failure, but his idea of the development of the tank, although it was not properly used at the time, was certainly a success. It is worth noting that as early as 1917 he described a project for making landing craft for tanks and also for something very like the transportable harbours used in the 1944 invasion of France. His intuition was at least as often right as it was wrong, and in his anticipation of the menace of Hitler, and later of the threat of Russian domination of Europe, he was intuitively right where others, who had better judgement than he, failed to see the important point. Jung's description of the extraverted intuitive has much which applies to Churchill. As Jung points out, this type is lacking in judgement. Churchill could never think for long at a time. Although he had brilliant ideas, he was hardly susceptible to reason and could not follow a consecutive argument when presented to him by others. His famous demand that all ideas should be presented to him on a half sheet of paper is an illustration of this point. Alanbrooke, in his wartime diary, wrote of him: 'Planned strategy was not his strong card. He preferred to work by intuition and by impulse. . . . He was never good at looking at all the implications of any course he favoured. In fact, he frequently refused to look at them.'[7] It is also true that he was, in many respects, deficient in feeling. He had little appreciation of the feelings of others. On three separate occasions, Churchill had promised Alanbrooke the supreme command of the Allied forces. Yet, when it was finally decided

that the invasion of Europe should be entrusted to the command
of an American, Churchill showed little appreciation of the
bitter disappointment which Alanbrooke experienced. 'Not for
one moment did he realize what this meant to me. He offered no
sympathy, no regrets at having had to change his mind, and
dealt with the matter as if it were one of minor importance.'[8]
As Jung says, 'Consideration for the welfare of his neighbours
is weak.'

All those who worked with Churchill paid tribute to the
enormous fertility of his new ideas, the inexhaustible stream of
invention which poured from him, both when he was Home
Secretary, and later when he was Prime Minister and director
of the war effort. All those who worked with him also agreed
that he needed the most severe restraint put upon him, and that
many of his ideas, if they had been put into practice, would have
been utterly disastrous.

In Jungian terminology, Churchill was an extraverted
intuitive. In W. H. Sheldon's classification, he was predominantly endomorphic, with a strong secondary mesomorphic
component. In terms of classical, descriptive psychiatry, he was
of cyclothymic temperament, with a pronounced tendency to
depression. These descriptive classifications, though overloaded
with jargon, are still valuable as an approach to character, but
they reveal very little about the dynamics of a person's inner
life. What follows will be an attempt, necessarily speculative,
to examine something of Churchill's psychological structure in
so far as this is possible.

Let us begin with a further consideration of Churchill's
'Black Dog'. Lord Moran, who, more than most people, realized
the importance of depression in Churchill's psychology, first
mentions this in the following passage from his book[9]:

August 14th 1944.
The P.M. was in a speculative mood today.
'When I was young,' he ruminated, 'for two or three years the
light faded out of the picture. I did my work. I sat in the House of
Commons, but black depression settled on me. It helped me to talk
to Clemmie about it. I don't like standing near the edge of a platform
when an express train is passing through. I like to stand right back

and if possible to get a pillar between me and the train. I don't
like to stand by the side of a ship and look down into the water. A
second's action would end everything. A few drops of desperation.
And yet I don't want to go out of the world at all in such moments.
Is much known about worry, Charles? It helps me to write down half
a dozen things which are worrying me. Two of them, say, disappear,
about two nothing can be done, so it's no use worrying, and two
perhaps can be settled. I read an American book on the nerves, "The
Philosophy of Fate"; it interested me a great deal.'

I said: 'Your trouble – I mean the Black Dog business – you got
from your forebears. You have fought against it all your life. That
is why you dislike visiting hospitals. You always avoid anything that
is depressing.'

Winston stared at me as if I knew too much.

Later in the book,[10] Lord Moran quotes a conversation with
the dying Brendan Bracken:

'You and I think of Winston as self-indulgent; he has never denied
himself anything, but when a mere boy he deliberately set out to
change his nature, to be tough and full of rude spirits.

'It has not been easy for him. You see, Charles, Winston has
always been a "despairer". Orpen, who painted him after the Dardanelles, used to speak of the misery in his face. He called him the
man of misery. Winston was so sure then that he would take no further
part in public life. There seemed nothing left to live for. It made him
very sad. Then, in his years in the wilderness, before the Second War,
he kept saying: "I'm finished". He said that about twice a day. He
was quite certain that he would never get back to office, for everyone
seemed to regard him as a wild man. And he missed the red boxes
awfully. Winston has always been wretched unless he was occupied.
You know what he has been like since he resigned. Why, he told me
that he prays every day for death.'

Many depressives deny themselves rest or relaxation because
they cannot afford to stop. If they are forced by circumstances
to do so, the black cloud comes down upon them. This happened
to Churchill when he left the Admiralty in May 1915, when he
was out of office during the thirties, when he was defeated in the
election of 1945, and after his final resignation. He invented
various methods of coping with the depression which descended
when he was no longer fully occupied by affairs of state, includ-

ing painting, writing, and bricklaying; but none of these were wholly successful. In order to understand why, we must venture some way into the cloudy and treacherous waters of psycho-analytic theory.

It is widely appreciated that psychoanalysis is chiefly concerned with the effect of environment, especially the very early environment, upon adult character. It is less generally realized that the psychoanalytic standpoint is not incompatible with the typological or constitutional approaches which we have hitherto adopted in our psychiatric scrutiny of Churchill. The two viewpoints are complementary, rather than contradictory. A man's genetic inheritance may predispose him to depression, but whether he actually suffers from it or not is likely to depend upon his early experiences within the family. Psycho-analysis does not assume that all individuals are born alike and would react in precisely the same way to the influences of the environment. There is no blueprint for an ideal upbringing, since no two individuals are the same. What psycho-analysis does assume, however, is that the psychological disturbances from which people suffer are related to the whole emotional climate in which they were reared, and that neurosis and psychosis in adult life are explicable in terms of a failure of the environment to meet the needs of the particular individual under scrutiny, at a time when those needs were paramount.

One salient characteristic of adults who suffer from depression is their dependence on external sources to maintain self-esteem. Of course, we are all dependent on externals to some extent. If a perfectly normal man is taken suddenly from his family, his job, and his social circle, and put into a situation of uncertainty and fear, he will become profoundly depressed. The Russian secret police know this well: which is why they arrest a suspect in the middle of the night without warning, place him in solitary confinement, and refuse him any communication with the outside world or any information about his future. It takes but a few weeks of solitary imprisonment in these circumstances to reduce most people to a state of profound dejection, an apathetic stupor in which both hope and pride disappear. We all need some support from the external world to maintain our sense of our own value.

Nevertheless, most of us can tolerate disappointments in one sphere of our existence without getting deeply depressed, provided the other spheres remain undamaged. Normal people may mourn, or experience disappointment, but because they have an inner source of self-esteem, they do not become or remain severely depressed for long in the face of misadventure, and are fairly easily consoled by what remains to them.

Depressives, in contrast to these normal folk, are much more vulnerable. If one thing in the external world goes wrong, they are apt to be thrown into despair. Even if people attempt to comfort them, they are likely to dismiss such efforts as futile. Disappointment, rejection, bereavement may all, in a depressive, pull a trigger which fires a reaction of total hopelessness: for such people do not possess an inner source of self-esteem to which they can turn in trouble, or which can easily be renewed by the ministrations of others. If, at a deep internal level, a person feels himself to be predominantly bad or unlovable, an actual rejection in the external world will bring this depressive belief to the surface; and no amount of reassurance from well-wishers will, for a time, persuade him of his real worth.

Psycho-analysis assumes that this vulnerability is the result of a rather early failure in the relationship between the child and his parents. In the ordinary course of events, a child takes in love with his mother's milk. A child who is wanted, loved, played with, cuddled will incorporate within himself a lively sense of his own value; and will therefore surmount the inevitable setbacks and disappointments of childhood with no more than temporary sorrow, secure in the belief that the world is predominantly a happy place, and that he has a favoured place in it. And this pattern will generally persist throughout his life.

A child, on the other hand, who is unwanted, rejected, or disapproved of will gain no such conviction. Although such a child may experience periods of both success and happiness, these will neither convince him that he is lovable, nor finally prove to him that life is worthwhile. A whole career may be dedicated to the pursuit of power, the conquest of women, or the gaining of wealth only, in the end, to leave the person face to face with despair and a sense of futility, since he has never incorporated within himself a sense of his value as a person; and no amount of external success can ultimately compensate him for this.

On one of his birthdays a few years before, in answer to my sister Diana's exclamation of wonderment at all the things he had done in his life, he said: 'I have achieved a great deal to achieve nothing in the end.' We were listening to the radio and reading the always generous newspaper eulogies. 'How can you say that?' she said. He was silent. 'There are your books,' I said. 'And your paintings,' Diana followed. 'Oh yes, yes, there are those.' 'And after all, there is us', we continued. 'Poor comfort we know at times: and there are other children who are grateful that they are alive.' He acknowledged us with a smile. . . .

Sarah Churchill, in her book *A Thread in the Tapestry*, begins her portrait of her father with these sentences; and it is surely percipient of her to do so. For she, and other members of the family, must have realized, in those last sad years, that in spite of the eulogies, the accolades, the honours, Winston Churchill still had a void at the heart of his being which no achievement or honour could ever completely fill.

It is interesting to compare this passage with another written by Churchill himself, emanating not from his old age, but from his early manhood. *Savrola*, Winston Churchill's only novel, was the first book upon which he embarked, though it was actually the third to be published. Though half-completed in 1897, it was not in print till 1900, since *The Story of the Malakand Field Force* and *The River War* intervened. Savrola, the orator and revolutionary, is, it has often been observed, a picture of Churchill himself. We are introduced to him in his study, surrounded by Gibbon, Macaulay, Plato, and St-Simon.

There were still some papers and telegrams lying unopened on the table, but Savrola was tired; they could, or at any rate, should wait till the morning. He dropped into his chair. Yes, it had been a long day, and a gloomy day. He was a young man, only thirty-two, but already he felt the effects of work and worry. His nervous temperament could not fail to be excited by the vivid scenes through which he had lately passed, and the repression of his emotion only heated the inward fire. Was it worth it? The struggle, the labour, the constant rush of affairs, the sacrifice of so many things that make life easy, or pleasant – for what? A people's good! That, he could not disguise from himself, was rather the direction than the cause of his efforts. Ambition was the motive force and he was powerless to resist it.

'Was it worth it?' The question recurs again and again in the lives of people who suffer from depression. At the end of *Savrola*, the query is reiterated. The revolution has been successful, but 'A sense of weariness, of disgust with struggling, of desire for peace filled his soul. The object for which he had toiled so long was now nearly attained and it seemed of little worth. . . .' Savrola has to go into exile, and looks back on the city he has liberated, now partially destroyed by shell fire. 'The smoke of other burning houses rose slowly to join the black, overhanging cloud against which the bursting shells showed white with yellow flashes.

'"And that," said Savrola after prolonged contemplation, "is my life's work."'

Even more interesting is the passage in which Savrola, 'weary of men and their works', ascends into his observatory to 'watch the stars for the sake of their mysteries'. He contemplates the beauty of Jupiter:

Another world, a world more beautiful, a world of boundless possibilities, enthralled his imagination. He thought of the future of Jupiter, of the incomprehensible periods of time that would elapse before the cooling process would render life possible on its surface, of the slow steady march of evolution, merciless, inexorable. How far would it carry them, the unborn inhabitants of an embryo world? Perhaps only to some vague distortion of the vital essence; perhaps further than he could dream of. All the problems would be solved; all the obstacles overcome; life would attain perfect development. And this fancy, overleaping space and time, carried the story to periods still more remote. The cooling process would continue; the perfect development of life would end in death; the whole solar system, the whole universe itself would one day be cold and lifeless as a burnt-out firework.

It was a mournful conclusion. He locked up the observatory

and descended the stairs, hoping that his dreams would contradict his thoughts.

The underlying despair, so characteristic of the depressive temperament, could hardly be better demonstrated. However successful Savrola is, he is still left uncertain as to the value of his achievement. His fantasy of life attaining 'perfect develop-ment' in some far-distant future is automatically cancelled by his belief that the universe must finally cool to a lifeless stop. The man who, a few years before his death, said to his daughter: 'I have achieved a great deal to achieve nothing in the end' is displaying an absolutely consistent emotional pattern, already evident in early manhood.

What were the childhood origins of Churchill's depressive disposition? Any answer must necessarily be partly a matter of guesswork, but certain obvious factors present themselves for consideration, of which parental neglect is the most striking.

Winston Churchill was a premature child, born two months before he was expected. No one can say with certainty whether prematurity has an adverse effect upon future emotional development, but we do know that the way in which a baby is nursed and handled affects the rate of its physical and mental progress, and that even the youngest child is sensitive to the environment. A premature child is unexpected and, therefore, something of an embarrassment. We know that preparations for Winston Churchill's appearance were incomplete, for there was a lack of baby clothes; and a first child, in any case, is apt to be somewhat of an anxiety to an inexperienced mother. How was Churchill handled as a baby? All we know is that, in accordance with the custom of those days, he was not fed by his mother, but handed over to a wet-nurse about whom we know nothing.

His mother, Lady Randolph, was only twenty when Winston was born. She was a girl of exceptional beauty, far too engaged in the fashionable social life of the time to be much concerned about her infant son. Lord Randolph, deeply involved in politics, would not have been expected to take more than a remote interest in his son and heir, and he more than fulfilled this expectation. In fact, Churchill received remarkably little affection or support from either parent in the vital years of early childhood. The person who saved him from emotional starvation was, of course, Mrs Everest, the nanny who was engaged early in 1875 within a few months of his birth, and who remained his chief support and confidante until her death when Churchill was twenty. Her photograph hung in his room until the end of his own life. She is immortalized as the housekeeper in *Savrola* and although Randolph Churchill makes use of the same quotation in his biography of his father, it is worth repeating here, since it reveals something of Winston Churchill's attitude to love.

His thoughts were interrupted by the entrance of the old woman with a tray. He was tired, but the decencies of life had to be observed; he rose, and passed into the inner room to change his clothes and make his toilet. When he returned, the table was laid; the soup he had asked for had been expanded by the care of his housekeeper into a more elaborate meal. She waited on him, plying him the while with questions and watching his appetite with anxious pleasure. She had nursed him from his birth with a devotion and care which knew no break. It is a strange thing, the love of these women. Perhaps it is the only disinterested affection in the world. The mother loves her child; that is maternal nature. The youth loves his sweetheart; that too may be explained. The dog loves his master; he feeds him; a man loves his friend; he has stood by him perhaps at doubtful moments. In all there are reasons, but the love of a foster-mother for her charge appears absolutely irrational. It is one of the few proofs, not to be explained even by the association of ideas, that the nature of mankind is superior to mere utilitarianism, and that his destinies are high.

Churchill's concept of 'disinterested affection' is worth comment. For it is surely not as astonishing as he implies that a nurse should love her charge. A nanny is a woman without children of her own, and without a husband. What could be more natural than that she should devote herself to the child who is placed in her care, and give him all the affection and love for which she has no other outlet? In the passage quoted above, Churchill is showing surprise at being loved, as if he had never felt that he was entitled to it. In the ordinary course of events, a small child receives from his mother and father love which he neither questions nor doubts. And he will generally extend his expectation of love to nannies, relatives, and other members of the family circle. As he grows up, he will find that not everyone loves him as he has come to expect; and this may surprise and disappoint him. But his surprise will surely be evoked by the discovery that some people do *not* love him, rather than by the fact that people other than his parents *do* love him.

Happy children do not ask *why* their mothers or anybody else love them; they merely accept it as a fact of existence. It is those who have received less than their early due of love who are surprised that anyone should be fond of them, and who seek for explanation of the love which more fortunate children take for granted. People who suffer from depression are always asking themselves why anyone should love them. They often feel entitled to respect, to awe, or to admiration; but as for love, that is too much to expect. Many depressives only feel lovable in so far as they have some achievement to their credit, or have given another person so much that they feel entitled to a return. The idea that anyone might give him love just because he is himself is foreign to the person of depressive temperament. In showing astonishment at Mrs Everest's disinterested love, Churchill is surely revealing what one would expect from his emotional disposition, that he had not experienced from his parents that total, irrational acceptance which we all need, and which is given by most mothers to a wanted baby. And although Mrs Everest's affection made up for what was missing to some extent, it could not replace the love of parents.

We cannot now obtain as much information as we would like about Churchill's very early childhood, but that his parents were neglectful is undoubted. As Randolph Churchill says in his biography[11]:

The neglect and lack of interest in him shown by his parents were remarkable, even judged by the standards of late Victorian and Edwardian days. His letters to his mother from his various schools abound in pathetic requests for letters and for visits, if not from her, from Mrs Everest and his brother Jack. Lord Randolph was a busy politician with his whole interest absorbed in politics; Lady Randolph was caught up in the whirl of fashionable society and seems to have taken very little interest in her son until he began to make his name resound through the world. It will later be seen how neglectful she was in writing to him when he was for three years a subaltern in India and when his father and Mrs Everest were dead. His brother Jack, more than five years younger, could not be a satisfactory correspondent and Winston was to feel exceptionally lonely and abandoned.

We are, I believe, entitled to assume that Winston Churchill was deprived by parental neglect of that inner source of self-esteem upon which most predominantly happy persons rely, and which serves to carry them through the inevitable disappointments and reverses of human existence. What were the ways in which he endeavoured to make up for this early lack and to sustain his self-esteem in spite of lack of parental affection?

The first and most obvious trait of character which he developed as a response to his deprivation was ambition. As he himself wrote of Savrola, 'Ambition was the motive force and he was powerless to resist it.' And in a letter to his mother, written in 1899 in India, he writes: 'What an awful thing it will be if I don't come off. It will break my heart for I have nothing else but ambition to cling to. . . .'[12] Children who have been more loved and appreciated than Winston Churchill do have something other than ambition to cling to. Ambition is, of course, a perfectly 'normal' trait, to be expected in any young man reared in the competitive climate of Western civilization. But Churchill's ambition was certainly inordinate; and it made him unpopular when he was young. Sir Charles Dilke is reported as writing that Rosebery was the most ambitious man he had ever met; but later he amended this opinion by writing alongside it, 'I have since known Winston Churchill.' Ambition, when, as in Churchill's case, it is a compulsive drive, is the direct result of early deprivation. For if a child has but little inner conviction of his own value, he will be drawn to seek the recognition and acclaim which accrue from external achievement. In youth, especially, success, or even the hope of success, whether financial, political, or artistic, can be effective in staving off depression in those who are liable to this disorder.

It is the inevitable decay of hope as a man gets older which accounts for the fact that severe attacks of depression become more common in middle age. It may be argued that very able people are always ambitious, since it is natural enough for a gifted man to require scope for his abilities and to want those ambitions to be recognized. In Lord Reith's phrase, to be 'fully stretched' is a pleasure in itself. But the compensatory quality of Churchill's ambition is not difficult to discern. Even his famous remark to Lady Violet Bonham Carter, 'We are all worms. But I do believe that I am a glow-worm', is revealing, in that it combines self-abasement and self-glorification in a single phrase.

Extreme ambition, of the Churchillian variety, is not based upon sober appraisal of the reality of one's gifts and deficiencies. There is always an element of phantasy, unrelated to actual achievement. This may, as it did with Churchill, take the form of a conviction that one is being reserved for a special purpose, if not by the Deity, then at least by fate. One of the most re-markable features of Churchill's psychology is that this con-viction persisted throughout the greater part of his life, until, at the age of sixty-five, his phantasy found expression in reality. As he said to Moran, 'This cannot be accident, it must be design. I was kept for this job.' If Churchill had died in 1939, he would have been regarded as a failure. Moran is undoubtedly right when he writes of 'The inner world of make-believe in which Winston found reality'. It is probable that England owed her survival in 1940 to this inner world of make-believe. The kind of inspiration with which Churchill sustained the nation is not based on judgement, but on an irrational con-viction independent of factual reality. Only a man convinced that he had an heroic mission, who believed that, in spite of all evidence to the contrary, he could yet triumph, and who could identify himself with a nation's destiny could have conveyed his inspiration to others. The miracle had much in common with that achieved by a great actor, who, by his art, exalts us and convinces us that his passions are beyond the common run of human feeling. We do not know, and we shall never know, the details of Churchill's world of make-believe. But that it was there, and that he played an heroic part in it, cannot be gainsaid. Before the invention of nuclear weapons, many a schoolboy had dreams of military glory which are hardly possible today. To be a great commander, to lead forces in battle against overwhelming odds, to make an heroic last stand, to win the Victoria Cross, are ambitions which have inspired many generations in the past. Churchill was born in an age when such dreams were still translatable into reality; and he sought to realize them in his early career as a soldier. But, unlike many soldiers, he did not become disillusioned. Even as an old man, it was difficult to restrain him from deliberately exposing himself to risk when he went out to France after the second front had been embarked upon. The schoolboy's day-dream persisted: and his search for danger was not simply a desire to prove his physical courage, a motive which was undoubtedly operative in early youth. It also rested upon a conviction that he would be preserved, that nothing could happen to a man of destiny – a belief which he shared with General Gordon, who likewise, throughout his life, exposed himself deliberately to death, and who inspired others by his total disregard of danger.

The conviction of being 'special' is, in psycho-analytic jargon, a reflection of what is called 'infantile omnipotence'. Psychoanalysis postulates, with good reason, that the infant has little appreciation of his realistic stature in the world into which he is born. Although a human infant embarks on life in a notably helpless state, requiring constant care and attention in order to preserve him, his very helplessness creates the illusion that he is powerful. For the demands of a baby are imperious. A baby must be fed, cleaned, clothed, and preserved from injury, and, in the normal course of events, these demands are met by a number of willing slaves who hasten to fulfil them. As the child matures, he will gradually learn that his desires are not always paramount, and that the needs of others must sometimes take precedence. This is especially so in a family where there are other children. The hard lesson that one is not the centre of the universe is more quickly learned in the rough and tumble of competition with brothers and sisters. Only children may fail to outgrow this early stage of emotional development; and, although Winston Churchill was not an only child, his brother Jack, born in 1880, was sufficiently younger for Winston to have retained his solitary position during five crucial years. Paradoxically, it is children who are deprived as well as solitary who retain the sense of omnipotence. A failure to meet a child's need for total care and total acceptance during the earliest part of his existence leaves him with a sense of something missing and something longed for; and he may, in later life, try to create conditions in which his lightest whim is immediately attended to, and resent the fact that this is not always possible.

In Churchill, this characteristic was evident. During one of his illnesses he required two nurses. His wife told Lord Moran[13]: 'Winston is a pasha. If he cannot clap his hands for a servant he calls for Walter as he enters the house. If it were left to him he'd have the nurses for the rest of his life. He would like two in his room, two in the passage. He is never so happy, Charles, as he is when one of the nurses is doing something for him while Walter puts on his socks.' Churchill's arrogance, impatience, and lack of consideration for others must have made him extremely difficult to live with; but these traits were softened by his magnanimity. How did so egocentric a man inspire devotion in those who served him, whose immediate needs he seldom considered, who might have to stay up till all hours to suit his own peculiar timetable, and who were often exposed to his formidable temper? It is not an easy question to answer; but it is often true that men who demand and need a great deal of attention from others are manifesting a kind of childlike helplessness which evokes an appropriate response, however difficult they may be. His wife recorded that the only time he had been on the Underground was during the general strike. 'He went round and round, not knowing where to get out and had to be rescued eventually.' As with a small child, omnipotence and helplessness went hand in hand. There are a good many characters in public life who would be totally nonplussed if they had to get their own meals, darn their own socks, or even write their own letters.

The fact that Churchill was an aristocrat must have been of

considerable service to him. However neglected he was by his parents, there was Mrs Everest to minister to him: and she was later succeeded by his wife, his valet, his doctor, and innumerable attendants and servants. Those of us who are old enough to remember the days in which the aristocracy and the upper middle class took it for granted that the ordinary details of living, food, clothes, travel, and so on would be taken care of by some minion or other, and who have since adapted to fending for ourselves, can without difficulty recall that the existence of servants did minister to our sense of self-esteem. Churchill was not rich in early life. He had to make his living by his pen. But he knew nothing of the lives of ordinary people, and, like other members of his class, grew up with the assumption that he was a good many cuts above the general run of the population. This assumption has stood many of his ilk in good stead. The English upper class have been notorious for handing over their children to the care of servants, and, in the case of boys, disposed to send them to boarding schools at an absurdly early age. The sense of belonging to a privileged class is some mitigation for the feeling of early rejection; and the Churchill family was, of course, of particular distinction within that privileged class. The young Winston Churchill may have felt lonely and unloved, but it cannot have been long before he became conscious that he was 'special' in another, less personal sense: the scion of a famous house with a long line of distinguished ancestors behind him. The fact that he chose to write biographies both of his father and of the first Duke of Marlborough shows how important this was to him.

When a child's emotional needs are not met, or only partially met, by his parents, he will generally react to this frustration by hostility. The most 'difficult', badly behaved children are those who are unloved; and they tend to treat all authority as hostile. Winston Churchill was no exception. But even the most rebellious and intransigent child retains, in imagination, a picture of the parents he would have liked to have. The negative image of authority as rejecting, cruel, and neglectful is balanced by a positive image of idealized parents who are invariably loving, tender, and understanding. And the less a child knows or has intimate contact with his real parents, the more will this double image persist. Real parents are real people: sometimes loving, sometimes impatient; sometimes understanding, sometimes imperceptive. The child reared in the intimacy of an ordinary family soon amalgamates the images of 'good' and 'bad', and comes to realize that, in other human beings as in himself, love and hate, goodness and badness, are inextricably intermingled. Psychiatrists have often observed that delinquent and emotionally disturbed children, who have parents who are actually neglectful or cruel, still maintain that these 'bad' parents are really 'good', and blame themselves for the parents' faults. This idealization of parents serves a defensive and protective function. A small child, being weak and defenceless, finds it unbearable to believe that there are no adults who love, support, and guide him; and if there are not, he invents them.

Winston Churchill showed this idealization very clearly. Of his mother, he wrote: 'She shone for me like the Evening Star. I loved her dearly – but at a distance.' This romantic view of his mother gave way to a more realistic appraisal of her, when, as a young man of twenty-three, he was compelled to recognize her financial irresponsibility, and to write to her about her extravagances. But the images formed in childhood are not so easily dispelled; and Churchill, at least in his early years, retained a romantic view of women which was derived from his idealization of his beautiful mother. Violet Bonham Carter draws attention to this:

This inner circle of friends contained no women. They had their own place in his life. His approach to women was essentially romantic. He had a lively susceptibility to beauty, glamour, radiance, and those who possessed these qualities were not subjected to analysis. Their possession of all the cardinal virtues was assumed as a matter of course. I remember his taking umbrage when I once commented on the 'innocence' of his approach to women. He was affronted by this epithet as applied to himself. Yet to me he would certainly have applied it as a term of praise.

Like many another romantic, Churchill was in youth somewhat awkward in his approach to women, although he was emotionally involved with at least three girls before he married. In his latter years he took little notice of women, and indeed would hardly speak to them. But the romantic vision persisted, attaching itself to the figure of Queen Elizabeth II. When contemplating the Queen's photograph, he is reported as saying: 'Lovely, inspiring. All the film people in the world, if they had scoured the globe, could not have found anyone so suited to the part.' Royalty never lost its magic for him; and, like his ancestor in the time of the Civil War, he remained an ardent Royalist throughout his life, despite the declining popularity of the monarchical principle amongst the sophisticated. When Churchill spoke of himself as a servant of the Queen, he undoubtedly felt that he was. His idealization of the monarchy, which extended itself to the kings and queens of other states besides Britain, meant that he seldom saw royalty as creatures of flesh and blood, any more than he saw his parents as human beings. It is a characteristic that he shared with many others in Great Britain.

Winston Churchill's idealization of his father was even more remarkable. It is not surprising that a small boy should see so beautiful and elegant a young mother as a fairy princess. But his father, though a notable public figure, and a highly gifted man, was so consistently disapproving of, or uninterested in, his small son, that Churchill's hero-worship of him can only be explained in terms of the psychological mechanism outlined above. As Violet Bonham Carter writes: 'The image remained upon its pedestal, intact and glorious. Until the end he worshipped at the altar of his Unknown Father.' And his father remained entirely unknown to him, never talked intimately with him, and seldom wrote to him except to reprove him. After Lord Randolph's death from general paralysis of the insane, when Winston Churchill was twenty, he learned large portions of his father's speeches by heart, and, in 1906, published a two-volume biography of him. Filial devotion could hardly go further; but it was devotion to an image, not to a real father whose life he had shared.

Children whose emotional needs have been insufficiently satisfied by their parents react to the lack by idealization on the one hand, and hostility on the other. Winston Churchill's obstinacy, resentment of authority, and wilfulness were manifest very early in his life. He was sent to boarding school before his eighth birthday; and it is evident from his earliest reports that the school authorities became the recipients of the hostility which he must have felt towards his parents, but which was never manifested because of his idealization of them. He was repeatedly late. 'No. of times late. 20. very disgraceful.' From being described as 'a regular pickle' in his earliest report, he is later designated as 'troublesome', 'very bad', 'careless', 'a constant trouble to everybody', and 'very naughty'. He remained at this school from November 1882 till the summer of 1884, and himself recorded how much he hated it. It is likely that he was removed because of the severe beatings he received, for the headmaster was a sadistic clergyman who would inflict as many as twenty strokes of the birch upon the bare buttocks of the little boys under his care, and who clearly enjoyed this exercise of his authority. But savage punishment failed to cow Winston Churchill, and probably served to increase his intolerance towards authority.

It is interesting to note that, in his early letters from school, he did not complain, but reported himself as happy; although, as he later admitted, this was the very opposite of the truth. Small boys who are miserable at boarding school very frequently conceal the fact from their parents. Ignorance of what the world is really like may lead them to suppose that ill-treatment and lack of sympathetic understanding is the expected lot of boys; and that, if they are unhappy, it is a sign of weakness and their own fault. This is especially true of those with a depressive tendency, for the hostility they feel towards parents and other authorities easily becomes turned inward against themselves. They therefore report themselves as happy because they feel they ought to be so, and easily deceive imperceptive parents who are not concerned to discover the truth.

There is, indeed, an intimate connexion between depression and hostility, which was not understood until Freud had unravelled it. The emotionally deprived child who later becomes prey to depression has enormous difficulty in the disposal of his hostility. He resents those who have deprived him, but he cannot afford to show this resentment, since he needs the very people he resents; and any hostility he does manifest results in still further deprivation of the approval and affection he so much requires. In periods of depression, this hostility becomes turned inward against the self, with the result that the depressive under-values himself or even alleges that he is worthless. 'I have achieved a great deal to achieve nothing in the end.'

It is this difficulty in disposing of hostility which drives some depressives to seek for opponents in the external world. It is a great relief to find an enemy on whom it is justifiable to lavish wrath. Winston Churchill was often accused of being a war-monger, which he was not. But there is no doubt that fighting enemies held a strong emotional appeal for him, and that, when he was finally confronted by an enemy whom he felt to be wholly evil, it was a release which gave him enormous vitality. Hitler was such an enemy; and it is probable that Churchill was never happier than when he was fully engaged in bringing about Hitler's destruction. For here, at last, was an opportunity to employ the full force of his enormous aggressiveness. Here was a monstrous tyranny, presided over by an arch-demon who deserved no mercy, and whom he could attack with an un-sullied conscience. If all depressives could constantly be engaged in fighting wicked enemies, they would never suffer from depres-sion. But, in day-to-day existence, antagonists are not wicked enough, and depressives suffer from pangs of conscience about their own hostility.

It is not decrying Churchill to state that his magnanimity and generosity to his many enemies rested upon this basis. People with Churchill's kind of early background know what it is to be insulted and injured; and, in spite of their internal store of hostility, they retain a capacity to identify with the underdog. It is unlikely that Churchill would have ever felt anything but hatred for Hitler, had the latter survived. But he showed an unusual compassion for the other enemies he defeated. Brendan Bracken reports that when Churchill sued Lord Alfred Douglas for making defamatory statements about him, he was not elated when he won the case. Indeed, he appeared depressed; and this was because he could not bear the thought of his defeated opponent being sent to prison. Although Churchill relished being in action against the enemies of England, compassion for them was equally in evidence, and he did not hesitate, at the age of twenty-three, to criticize Kitchener for the 'inhuman slaughter of the wounded' at Omdurman and to attack him in print for having desecrated the Mahdi's tomb.

This alternation between aggression and compassion is characteristic of persons with Churchill's character structure. No one could have had more pride in the British Empire; and yet, when Churchill was twenty-seven, he was writing of 'our unbridled Imperialists who have no thought but to pile up armaments, taxation and territory'. This criticism was prompted by his reading of Seebohm Rowntree's book *Poverty*, which engaged his compassion for the under-fed working class, neglected by Imperialist politicians. Churchill was highly aggressive, and in many ways insensitive, but he was far from ruthless, and when he could imaginatively enter into the distress of others he was genuinely concerned. This was especially so in the case of prisoners, with whom he could closely identify himself. Churchill's period of office as Home Secretary was notable for the improvements which he introduced in the treatment of 'political' prisoners, in his day the suffragettes; for the reform which allowed 'time to pay' in the case of those who would otherwise have been imprisoned for the non-payment of fines; and for the introduction of measures which reduced the number of young offenders sent to prison. He also advocated the introduction of lectures and concerts to prisoners, and insisted upon the provision of books for them.

Churchill's compassionate concern with prisoners originated in part with his generalized capacity to identify himself with the underdog, which we have already discussed. It also had a more particular root which sprang from his personal experience. During the Boer War he was captured by the Boers and incarcerated as a prisoner of war. Although his period of imprisonment was very brief, for he was caught on 15 November and escaped on 12 December, this experience made an

ineradicable impression upon him. In *My Early Life* he writes
of his imprisonment as follows:

Prisoner of War! That is the least unfortunate kind of prisoner to be,
but it is nevertheless a melancholy state. You are in the power of
your enemy. You owe your life to his humanity, and your daily
bread to his compassion. You must obey his orders, go where he
tells you, stay where you are bid, await his pleasure, possess your soul
in patience. Meanwhile the war is going on, great events are in
progress, fine opportunities for action and adventure are slipping
away. Also the days are very long. Hours crawl like paralytic centi-
pedes. Nothing amuses you. Reading is difficult; writing impossible.
Life is one long boredom from dawn till slumber.

Moreover, the whole atmosphere of prison, even the most easy
and best regulated prison, is odious. Companions in this kind of
misfortune quarrel about trifles and get the least possible pleasure
from each other's society. If you have never been under restraint
before and never known what it was to be a captive, you feel a
sense of constant humiliation in being confined to a narrow space,
fenced in by railings and wire, watched by armed men, and webbed
about with a tangle of regulations and restrictions. I certainly hated
every minute of my captivity more than I have ever hated any other
period in my whole life. . . . Looking back on those days, I have
always felt the keenest pity for prisoners and captives. What it must
mean for any man, especially an educated man, to be confined for
years in a modern convict prison, strains my imagination. Each day
exactly like the one before, with the barren ashes of wasted life
behind, and all the long years of bondage stretching out ahead. . . .
Dark moods come easily across the mind of a prisoner. . . .

Not all persons react to imprisonment like this. There are
some who actively seek prison as a refuge from the troubles of
this world. Others spend their time more or less contentedly
reading or engaged in solitary reflection. It is those who are
liable to depression who most suffer pangs of the kind that
Churchill described; for, deprived of the outside sources of
stimulation which sustain them and the opportunity for adventure and excitement which is a defence against their innate
tendency, they relapse into that state above all which they
most fear.

*

Churchill was never happy unless he was fully occupied, asleep, or holding the floor. He had no small talk. It is impossible to imagine him being cosily relaxed. He had to be perpetually active, or else he relapsed into 'dark moments of impatience and frustration', as Violet Bonham Carter describes his moods. As early as 1895 he was writing to his mother from Aldershot:

I find I am getting into a state of mental stagnation when even letter writing becomes an effort and when any reading but that of monthly magazines is impossible. This is of course quite in accordance with the spirit of the army. It is indeed the result of mental forces called into being by discipline and routine. It is a state of mind into which all, or nearly all, soldiers fall. From this slough of despond I try to raise myself by reading and re-reading Papa's speeches, many of which I know almost by heart. But I really cannot find the energy to read any other serious work.

Army discipline and routine had a constraining effect upon him, not unlike that of prison; and the realization that he became depressed as a result may have contributed to his decision to seek political, rather than further military, glory.

We have already mentioned Churchill's dislike of standing near the edge of a railway platform. He also admitted to Moran, while staying at Claridges, that he disliked sleeping near a balcony. 'I've no desire to quit this world,' he said with a grin, 'but thoughts, desperate thoughts come into the head.' He was also apprehensive about travelling by air, and was fond of quoting Dr Johnson on sea travel: 'Being in a ship is being in a jail, with the chance of being drowned.' An underlying pre-occupation with death, so characteristic of the depressive temperament, is easily detectable. In early youth, he was convinced that he would die young, as his father had. We can attribute this in part to an identification with his idealized father; but a conviction that time is short and an early realization of the ephemeral nature of human life is typical. His dislike of visiting hospitals belongs in this category of preoccupation, and so does his early tendency to hypochondriasis. Lucy Masterman reports of him in 1910: 'He thought he had got every mortal disease under heaven, and was very much inclined to dine off slops and think about the latter end.' When

Admiral Pound died, Churchill said: 'Death is the greatest gift God has made to us.' It is not argued here that Churchill was ever suicidal – there is no evidence on that point. But it seems likely that death had a kind of fascination for him against which he had to defend himself. Men who have to be hyper-active in order to protect themselves against depression gener-ally have a secret longing for total peace and relaxation; and the garden of Proserpina, 'where even the weariest river winds somewhere safe to sea', has a special appeal which has to be fought against.

Churchill at first reacted to authority by intransigent dis-obedience. This rebelliousness was not only a way of discharging his hostility, but a means of self-assertion – probably the only way of self-assertion available to a boy who, at that stage, felt himself to be weak physically, and who showed no disposition to excel in any school subject except history. Soon, however, another means of preserving, or rather gaining, self-esteem presented itself. Although he continued to perform inadequately in most school subjects, certainly far less well than his intelli-gence warranted, he discovered that he had a gift for words, a gift which became his principal asset, and which stood him in good stead throughout his life.

Before the use of words became his chief vehicle of self-expression, he had, at the age of eleven, shown a desire to learn the 'cello. Had this desire been granted, it is possible that music might have become important to him; for, as many musicians know, the world of sound can be a never-ending source of solace, and the ability to play an instrument is both a means of self-expression and a source of self-esteem. But Churchill's early interest in music was not encouraged, and soon died out; and his musical taste remained at the level of Sullivan and music-hall songs.

Churchill's attitude to words and the use of them is of interest psychologically. When he first met Violet Bonham Carter, he asked her whether she thought that words had a magic and a music quite independent of their meaning. For Churchill, they undoubtedly did. The magic of words became part of his inner world of make-believe. Sartre, in his autobiography, has recorded a similar process:

A Platonist by condition, I moved from knowledge to its object; I found ideas more real than things, because they were the first to give themselves to me and because they gave themselves like things. I met the universe in books: assimilated, classified, labelled and studied, but still impressive; and I confused the chaos of my experience through books with the hazardous course of real events. Hence my idealism which it took me thirty years to undo.

All through his life Churchill was a voluble fount of ideas. Smuts said of him: 'That is why Winston is indispensable. He has ideas.' His imagination was really creative; and it expressed itself in rhetoric, in an ornate phraseology which soon soared above the sober and often intransigent facts of reality. This was why he was always having to be restrained by his advisers; by his civil servants when he was Home Secretary; by his chiefs of staff, especially Alanbrooke, when he was Prime Minister.

The literary style which first attracted him was that of Gibbon, whom he frankly imitated: and he also owed much to Macaulay. It is not surprising that these authors appealed to him. Of the two, Gibbon is the wittier, the more realistic, and the better balanced. His sentences, beautifully constructed, have a strong appeal to the musical ear. The remarkable thing is that Gibbon did not abuse his literary gift to distort history or advance his own prejudices, with the possible exception of his intolerance towards Christianity. Gibbon's *Decline and Fall* remained a standard work for many years. The same cannot be said of Macaulay, who used the magic of words to persuade his readers of views which were often highly subjective.

Churchill knew that his imagination could mislead him into false appraisals, but he could always be brought back to reality, although it might take hours of argument to do so. Churchill's grasp of military strategy was considerable, but it was liable to be interfered with by his romantic imagination, which often led him to disregard the logic of the possible. And the fact that he could clothe his ideas in magnificent language must have made those ideas even more convincing to him. He was able to inspire himself as well as others by the magic of words, which indeed can take on a life of their own.

Artists and philosophers create worlds which may be, and often are, substitutes for the disappointing and stubborn facts of human existence. Had Churchill not been born into an aristocratic and political family, he might have become a writer of a different kind. Since his interest in other human beings was minimal, and his grasp of human psychology negligible, it is unlikely that he would have ever been a novelist of character. But he could have written good adventure stories, and did so in *My Early Life*, which, although true autobiography, has in places the pace and dash of a thriller. But Churchill's imagination was captured by dreams of military glory and of political power; and so, although he can be rated as a literary artist, his creativity also found expression in imaginative schemes of social reform, in military inventions like the tank, and in strategic conceptions like Gallipoli, for the failure of which he was made a scapegoat.

Even as an orator, Churchill remained essentially literary. As he said of himself: 'I am not an orator, an orator is spontaneous.'[14] In youth, his chief ambition was to be master of the spoken word, but it was an ambition which he never completely realized. Although some of his phrases, especially in his 1940 speeches, have become immortal, his was a literary rather than an oratorical talent. His speeches were carefully written out, and often learned by heart; and, in youth, he was extremely nervous before delivering them. He lacked the common touch which great orators like Lloyd George possessed: and his diligence in preparing his speeches is another example of his extraordinary determination to conquer his natural disadvantages, and to succeed in spite of, rather than because of, his native endowment.

One of the most successful of modern writers, Georges Simenon, says: 'Writing is not a profession, but a vocation of unhappiness.' Not all artists are depressive by temperament; but those that are habitually use their skill to ward off the 'Black Dog', and commonly go through a period of depression directly they have completed a new work. During this interval, before they can get started again, they often believe that they are finished, and that they will never have another original idea; but, in time, the creative impulse generally reasserts itself. It is likely that Churchill used his writing as a defence against the depression which invariably descended upon him when he was forced to be inactive. This psychological mechanism is clearly evident when we come to consider his painting. He did not start to paint until he was forty, and what initiated this new departure was a period of despair. Several observers have attested the severity of Churchill's depression after the failure of the Dardanelles expedition which he had initiated, and which led to his resignation from the Admiralty in 1915. Violet Bonham Carter records: 'He took me into his room and sat down on a chair – silent, despairing – as I have never seen him. He seemed to have no rebellion or even anger left. He did not even abuse Fisher, but simply said, "I'm finished."' Churchill himself wrote of this period:

I had long hours of utterly unwonted leisure in which to contemplate the frightful unfolding of the war. At a moment when every fibre of my being was inflamed to action, I was forced to remain a spectator of the tragedy, placed cruelly in a front seat. And then it was that the Muse of Painting came to my rescue – out of charity and out of chivalry, because after all she had nothing to do with me – and said, 'Are these toys any good to you? They amuse some people.'

And from that time onward, painting became a great resource to Winston Churchill: something to which he could always turn in time of trouble, something which would invariably engage his interest and provide a perpetual challenge.

Psycho-analysis has long recognized the relation between aggression and depression, and the difficulty which the depressed person has in the disposal of his aggressive impulses. Although creative activity frequently contains an aggressive component, this is not always easy to discern; nor do we habitually think of painting a picture or composing a symphony as an aggressive activity. Those who find my thesis unconvincing should turn to Churchill's own account of his approach to a canvas in his book *Painting as a Pastime*:

Very gingerly I mixed a little blue paint on the palette with a very small brush, and then with infinite precaution made a mark about as big as a bean upon the affronted snow-white shield. It was a challenge, a deliberate challenge, but so subdued, so halting, indeed so cataleptic, that it deserved no response. At that moment the loud approaching sound of a motor-car was heard in the drive. From this chariot there stepped swiftly and lightly none other than the gifted wife of Sir John Lavery. 'Painting! But what are you hesitating about? Let me have a brush – the big one.' Splash into the turpentine, wallop into the blue and the white, frantic flourish on the palette – clean no longer – and then several large, fierce strokes and slashes of blue on the absolutely cowering canvas. Anyone could see that it could not hit back. No evil fate avenged the jaunty violence. The canvas grinned in helplessness before me. The spell was broken. The sickly inhibitions rolled away. I seized the largest brush and fell upon my victim with berserk fury. I have never felt any awe of a canvas since.

He later compares painting a picture to fighting a battle. Indeed, this little book is one of the most revealing things he ever wrote about himself.

Churchill's predilection for rather grandiose, highly coloured language was related to the need of his romantic imagination to lighten the gloom into which he was apt to descend. His choice of colour in painting is strictly analogous:

I must say I like bright colours. . . . I cannot pretend to feel impartial about the colours. I rejoice with the brilliant ones, and am genuinely sorry for the poor browns. When I get to heaven I mean to spend a considerable portion of my first million years in painting, and so get to the bottom of the subject. But then I shall require a still gayer palette than I get here below. I expect orange and vermilion will be the darkest, dullest colours upon it, and beyond them there will be a whole range of wonderful new colours which will delight the celestial eye.

In psycho-analytic jargon, this is a 'manic defence'. The counterpart to the gloomy, subfusc world of the depressive is a realm of perpetual excitement and action, in which colours are richer and brighter, gallant deeds are accomplished by heroes, and ideas expressed in language replete with simile, ornamented with epithet, and sparkling with mellifluous turns of phrase. In

his book on painting, Churchill gives us a delightful glimpse
into his inner world of make-believe: a world where every
prospect pleases, but which is just as remote from reality as is
the downcast, hopeless hell of the man who feels useless and
'finished'.

Churchill's need of this manic realm is equally reflected in
his choice of friends. Holders of the Victoria Cross were immediately attractive to him, irrespective of their personalities; for
they were all real live heroes, who coincided with those in his
inner world. So were ebullient, energetic adventurers, like Lord
Birkenhead and Lord Beaverbrook. Churchill was a poor judge
of character. The sober, steadfast, and reliable seldom appealed
to him. What he wanted were people who would stimulate,
amuse, and arouse him. Lord Moran notes that he was unim-
pressed by many of the quietly distinguished doctors who were
sent to see him, but easily fell for the near-charlatans, the men
with the gift of the gab who were unrestrained by scientific
caution. The flamboyant extravert is life-enhancing, although
exhausting; he brings zest and vitality to life. Men like Birkenhead helped Churchill to find and sustain the manic side of his
own personality.

In an earlier passage we have taken note of the fact that
persons with Churchill's type of psychological structure find it
hard to learn that they are not the centre of the universe.
Because of the lack of intimate relations, first with parents, and
later with other people, they remain egocentrically oriented:
narcissistic. Every baby starts life in a predominantly solipsistic
state; most progress to a more mature emotional condition in
which it is realized not only that other people have desires and
needs, but also that one's own desires and needs interact with
them in such a way that one can both satisfy and be satisfied
simultaneously. The child who is early deprived forms no such
conception; with the result that he makes inordinate demands
on other people, but has little idea of being able to give them
much. Churchill was generous to defeated enemies, but remained
extremely demanding and insensitive to the requirements of
others. His principal love-object remained himself, because that
self had never, in childhood, been satisfied.

Psycho-analysts describe such a character as 'oral', because it is through the mouth that the baby's earliest needs are met; and, when they are not met, oral traits of character persist, both literally and metaphorically. It is interesting that, in one of his earliest school reports, Churchill is described as greedy; and it is also recorded that he was beaten for stealing sugar. All through his life, he needed feeding at frequent intervals; he was dependent on, though not necessarily addicted to, alcohol, and was a heavy smoker of cigars. He was also greedy for approval. His intimates knew that, if he showed them a manuscript of what he was writing, what he wanted was praise unadulterated with any tinge of criticism. 'You are not on my side' was the reproach levelled at friends who ventured any adverse comment upon his ideas or his creations. The part of him which still demanded the total and uncritical acceptance which he had never had as a child still divided the world into black and white, so that friendship and disagreement were regarded as incompatible. Because of this characteristic, his own relationship to friends was also uncritical. He was intensely loyal. As Brendan Bracken said, 'He would go to the stake for a friend'; and this was what he expected from his own friends. He remained hungry – hungry for fame, for adulation, for success, and for power; and although he gained all these in full measure, the end of his life showed that he never assimilated them into himself, but remained unsatisfied.

It is often said of Churchill that he 'lacked antennae'; that is, that he was insensitive where other people were concerned. There are several anecdotes which reveal that, quite unwittingly, he gave offence to other people on social occasions by neglecting them or taking no notice of them. This imperviousness to atmosphere is characteristic of the narcissistic person, who, like a small child, is still living in a private world which takes little account of other people except in so far as they provide what the child wants. We expect that small children will be 'selfish', intent on their own satisfaction, with little regard for what others are feeling. Churchill retained this characteristic in adult life; and it was directly related to his early deprivation. For the 'selfish' are those who have never had enough. It is only the child whose emotional needs have been satisfied who is later able to give as much as he takes. Churchill said of himself, quite accurately, 'I have devoted more time to self-expression than to self-discipline.' Had he been less egocentric he would not have achieved so much; had he been more self-disciplined, he would have been less inspiring.

We have discussed in some detail the methods which Churchill employed to prevent himself from relapsing into the depression which dogged him, and against which, as Lord Moran said, he was fighting all his life. Perhaps the most remarkable feature of Churchill's psychology is that, on the whole, the defences he employed against depression proved so successful. Although in youth he suffered long periods of depression, his various methods of dealing with this disability seem to have had the result that, in later life, he could generally extricate himself from the slough of despond and never let himself be overwhelmed by it until his old age. Those who knew him intimately during his years in the political wilderness may report differently. There are some hints that he drank more heavily during this period. But on the written evidence at present available, the success with which he dealt with his own temperament is quite extraordinary. Indeed, it is quite likely that some of those who were comparatively close to him never realized that he was liable to depression at all.

At the beginning of this essay, I suggested that the relation between great achievement and the depressive temperament was worth more attention than has yet been bestowed upon it. In psychiatric practice, it is not at all uncommon to come across men of great ability and dynamic force who have achieved far more than the common run of success, and who are generally supposed by their contemporaries to be, if not necessarily happy, at least free from any kind of neurotic disability. On the surface, such men appear to be more confident than the average. They often inspire those who serve them, set an example by their own enormous appetite for work, and appear to possess inexhaustible vitality. Those who follow in their wake regard such leaders as being superhuman, and merely envy their energy without stopping to inquire what it is that drives them. Yet, anyone

who has himself ventured along the corridors of power knows
that the extremely ambitious are often highly vulnerable, that
the tycoon may be lost if his luck deserts him, and that the
personal and emotion●l relationships of those who pursue
power are often sadly inadequate. Ambition, taken in isolation,
may be a trait of character which merely reflects a man's
desire to find adequate scope for his abilities. It can also be a
demonic force, driving the subject to achieve more and more,
yet never bringing contentment and peace, however great the
achievement. The degree to which the highly successful are able
to conceal, both from themselves and from others, that they are
tormented beings, is extraordinary; and it is often only in the
consulting-room that the truth emerges. Alanbrooke, weary of
the war and the enormous responsibility he carried, was content
to lay down his burden and retire to domestic happiness and
bird-watching. Churchill, on the other hand, was extremely
reluctant to abandon power, although, as early as 1949, after
his first stroke, some medical opinion considered that he should
no longer pursue high office. There is no doubt in my mind as to
which of the two men was the happier and the better balanced.
Yet Alanbrooke, as he would himself have been the first to
admit, could never have inspired the nation as did Churchill.

The end of Churchill's long life makes melancholy reading.
It is indeed a tragedy that he survived into old age. Moran
records that, after his retirement in April 1955, 'Winston made
little effort to hide his distaste for what was left to him of life',
and adds that 'the historian might conclude that this reveals a
certain weakness in moral fibre'. Any historian who does so
conclude will merely reveal his ignorance of medicine. For
cerebral arteriosclerosis, with which Churchill was seriously
affected, not only saps the will, as Lord Moran says. It also
makes impossible the mechanisms of defence with which a man
copes with his temperamental difficulties. In old age, most
people become to some extent caricatures of themselves. The
suspicious become paranoid, the intolerant more irritable, and
the depressives less able to rouse themselves from the slough of
despond. Moran brings his story to a close five years before
Churchill's death because he 'thought it proper to omit the

painful details of the state of apathy and indifference into which he sank after his resignation'. I think he was right, as a doctor, to do so. He records that Churchill gave up reading, seldom spoke, and sat for hours before the fire in what must have amounted to a depressive stupor. To dwell upon the medical and psychiatric details of Churchill's end would have exposed Moran to even more criticism from his medical colleagues than he received in any case. But the fact that the 'Black Dog' finally overcame an old man whose brain could, because of an impaired blood supply, no longer function efficiently, merely increases our admiration for the way in which, earlier in life, he fought his own disability. For he carried a temperamental load which was indeed an exceptionally heavy burden.

It is at this point that psycho-analytic insight reveals its inadequacy. For, although I believe that the evidence shows that the conclusions reached in this essay are justified, we are still at a loss to explain Churchill's remarkable courage. In the course of his life he experienced many reverses: disappointments which might have embittered and defeated even a man who was not afflicted by the 'Black Dog'. Yet his dogged determination, his resilience, and his courage enabled him, until old age, to conquer his own inner enemy, just as he defeated the foes of the country he loved so well.

We have often had occasion to comment upon Churchill's 'inner world of make-believe' in which, as Moran says, he found reality. At one period in his life, he was fortunate. For, in 1940, his inner world of make-believe coincided with the facts of external reality in a way which very rarely happens to any man. It is an experience not unlike that of passionate love, when, for a time, the object of a man's desire seems to coincide exactly with the image of woman he carries within him. In 1940, Churchill became the hero that he had always dreamed of being. It was his finest hour. In that dark time, what England needed was not a shrewd, equable, balanced leader. She needed a prophet, a heroic visionary, a man who could dream dreams of victory when all seemed lost. Winston Churchill was such a man; and his inspirational quality owed its dynamic force to the romantic world of phantasy in which he had his true being.

NOTES

1. A. L. Rowse, *The Early Churchills* (London, Macmillan, 1956), pp. 227–8.
2. A. L. Rowse, *The Later Churchills* (London, Macmillan, 1958), pp. 287–8.
3. A. L. Rowse, *The Early Churchills* (London, Macmillan, 1956), p. 29.
4. Lord Moran, *Winston Churchill* (London, Constable, 1966), p. 621.
5. op. cit., p. 621.
6. C. P. Snow, *Variety of Men* (London, Macmillan, 1967), p. 125.
7. Arthur Bryant, *The Turn of the Tide* (London, Collins, 1957), p. 25.
8. op. cit., p. 707.
9. Lord Moran, op. cit., p. 167.
10. op. cit., p. 745.
11. Randolph Churchill, *Winston S. Churchill* (London, Heinemann, 1966), vol. I, pp. 45, 46.
12. op. cit., vol. I, p. 441.
13. Lord Moran, op. cit., p. 433.
14. Lord Moran, op. cit., p. 429.

Chronology

WINSTON LEONARD SPENCER CHURCHILL
(1874–1965)

1874. 30 September. Winston L. S. Churchill, elder son of Lord Randolph Churchill and Lady Churchill (an American, born Jessie Jerome), is born at Blenheim Palace, residence of his grandfather, the 7th Duke of Marlborough.

1888–93. During four and a half years at Harrow, Winston Churchill shows no signs of ability at work or games.

1893. After six months at a special coaching establishment and at his third attempt, Churchill just passes entrance into the military college at Sandhurst.

1894. Finding work to his taste, Churchill develops rapidly and graduates eighth out of 150.

1895. Lord Randolph dies, admired but barely known by Winston Churchill. Commissioned in the 4th Hussars, Churchill is granted permission to visit the Spanish Army then fighting rebels in Cuba. He is under fire for the first time. He begins his career as a journalist by sending articles to the *Daily Graphic*.

1896–7. Churchill serves as 2nd lieutenant in India. At Bangalore he begins serious reading: Gibbon, Macaulay, Schopenhauer, Darwin, Plato and Aristotle. He sees action on the N.W. Frontier and sends dispatches to the *Daily Telegraph*.

1898. Joining Kitchener's army in Egypt, he takes part in the charge of 21st Lancers at Omdurman. He writes dispatches for the *Morning Post*. His first book, *The Malakand Field Force*, is published.

1899. Churchill, resigning from the Army, stands as Conservative candidate for Oldham but is defeated. In South Africa as correspondent for the *Morning Post* he is captured by the Boers but, escaping, rejoins the Army and takes part in the relief of Ladysmith. *The River War* – on the reconquest of the Sudan – and his only novel, *Savrola*, are published.

1900. Churchill is returned as M.P. for Oldham in the 'khaki election'. His lecture tours in Great Britain, Canada and the U.S.A. bring in £10,000. *London to Ladysmith* and *Ian Hamilton's March* are published.

1901–4. After opposing government policy of Army reforms, Churchill finally crosses the floor (1904) and joins the Liberals in defence of Free Trade.

1906. Appointed Under-Secretary for the Colonies in Campbell Bannerman's Liberal ministry, he is elected M.P. for Manchester North-West. He supports the policy of conciliation in South Africa. His biography of *Lord Randolph Churchill* is published.

1908–10. He serves as President of the Board of Trade in Asquith's ministry. He supports strongly Lloyd George's radical measures, being responsible for establishing Labour Exchanges and setting up a Board to prevent 'sweated' labour. He joins in the attack on the House of Lords. He marries Miss Clementine Hozier. *My African Journey* is published.

1909. Diana Churchill is born.

1910. He becomes Home Secretary. He incurs blame for sending Metropolitan Police and troops to maintain order during a Welsh mining strike.

1911. He appears in person to watch a mixed force of police and troops which he had dispatched to capture two anarchists who had barricaded themselves in a house in Sidney Street. In October he is appointed First Lord of the Admiralty. His only son, Randolph Churchill, is born.

1912–14. Active in modernizing the Navy, he also shows interest in aviation and authorizes the construction of the first 'tank'. He supports the Government's policy of Home Rule for Ireland.

1914. Churchill dispatches the Home Fleet to war stations on his own responsibility in July. In October he organizes and accompanies the expedition to defend Antwerp. In November he recalls Fisher as First Sea Lord. In December he writes to Asquith raising the possibility of an attack on Gallipoli. Sarah Churchill is born.

1915. With the sanction of the war Cabinet and the half-hearted support of Fisher, Churchill directs a naval attack on the Dardanelles at the end of February even when Kitchener declines to promise military support. Naval delay in following up early successes and the

lack of troops to effect a surprise landing result in reverses and ulti-
mate failure. Fisher resigns and, in the coalition government which
Asquith is now forced to form, Churchill is removed from the Ad-
miralty and given the sinecure post of Chancellor of the Duchy of
Lancaster. In November he resigns to command a battalion in
France.

1916. Churchill returns to civilian life.

1917. On the fall of Asquith, Churchill becomes Minister of Munitions
in Lloyd George's ministry. Though active in his own department he
has little say in the over-all conduct of the war.

1918. Marigold Churchill is born (died 1921).

1919–20. As Minister of War and Air, he organizes demobilization
and prevents spread of discontent and mutiny. Though strongly anti-
communist and in favour of intervention in Russia, he organizes the
withdrawal of the British forces from that country.

1921. He becomes Colonial Secretary, makes a treaty with the Irish
Free State and negotiates a settlement with the Arabs in the Middle
East with T. E. Lawrence as adviser.

1922. Though he opposes Lloyd George's pro-Greek policy at the
expense of the Turks, Churchill supports him in his threat of war
when Kemal Ataturk advances on the British garrison at Chanak in
the neutral zone near the Straits. His bellicose attitude contributes to
the fall of the coalition ministry in October and causes the loss of his
own seat in Parliament at the election a few weeks later.

1923. Churchill is defeated in a by-election at Leicester West. The
first volume of *The World Crisis* is published (work completed 1931).

1924. After being defeated at Westminster, Churchill is elected M.P.
for Epping in October, becomes Chancellor of the Exchequer in
Baldwin's ministry and rejoins the Conservative party.

1925. Churchill returns to the gold standard in his first budget. He
introduces an insurance scheme for widows and orphans.

1926. He is active in opposing the general strike.

1927. Visiting Mussolini in Rome, he expresses admiration for him
and the régime.

1929. On the fall of Baldwin's ministry, Churchill is re-elected for
Epping. Out of office for the next ten years.

1930. My Early Life, his autobiography, is published.

1930–35. Believing that it would be a fatal mistake to grant dominion status to India, Churchill had opposed the 'Irwin Declaration' of 1929. Between 1931, when he resigns from Baldwin's 'shadow cabinet' on this issue, and 1935, he becomes the leading spirit of the India Defence League. The alarmist speeches he makes on this subject weaken the impact of his later warnings on German rearmament. *Marlborough, His Life and Times* is published (completed 1938).

1935. Churchill makes his 'hostages to fortune' speech, warning Mussolini of the dangers involved by attack on Abyssinia. He joins the Committee of Imperial Defence on Air Defence Research and is re-elected at Epping.

1936. He criticizes sanctions as imposed by Baldwin and the League of Nations in an attempt to deter Mussolini. During the abdication crisis he is shouted down in the House of Commons when he advocates delay in dealing with the problem. He now becomes more isolated than ever, without influence or followers. He goes to Paris to confer with French civilian and military leaders.

1938. He protests against handing over naval bases in southern Ireland. In October, he describes the Munich agreement as a 'defeat without a war'.

1939. On 3 September Churchill becomes First Lord of the Admiralty.

1940. In April Churchill is made President of Military Co-ordination Committee. On 10 May he becomes Prime Minister and forms an all-party coalition with himself as Minister of Defence. He offers 'blood, toil, tears and sweat' and commits his government to 'victory at all costs'. He successfully appeals to Roosevelt for old American destroyers, stops sending fighters to France and orders the Dunkirk evacuation. In June he delivers his Dunkirk speech, visits France to save the French fleet and patronizes De Gaulle. His offer of Anglo-French union is rejected. As the British face Hitler alone Churchill declares: 'This was their finest hour.' His determination is shown by his order to destroy the French fleet at Oran in July. He declares his faith in a bombing offensive against Germany. In August he decides to reinforce the Mediterranean and in September pays his famous tribute to 'the few' R.A.F. pilots who have frustrated the German air force's attempt to gain control of the air over Britain.

In October he becomes leader of the Conservative party. His letter to Roosevelt in December inspires the Lend-Lease Bill.

1941. In March Churchill sends forces to Greece and proclaims the 'Battle of the Atlantic' against the U-boat menace. On 22 June, when Hitler attacks Russia, Churchill instantly pledges aid. In August he risks the Atlantic crossing to Newfoundland for the first of his nine meetings with Roosevelt; they publish their war aims in the 'Atlantic Charter'. On his return, the decision to develop an atomic bomb is taken. On 7 December, after Pearl Harbor, Churchill declares war on Japan; the *Prince of Wales* and the *Repulse* are sunk by Japanese planes. Churchill meets Roosevelt at the first Washington Conference to correlate plans; the U.N. Pact is signed. He suffers a minor heart attack.

1942. To Churchill's surprise and dismay, Singapore, Britain's bastion in the Far East, falls in February. After the Battle of the Santa Cruz Islands in October reduces American carrier strength in the Pacific to one vessel, Churchill sends the carrier *Victorious* in support. In March Churchill offers India dominion status after the war. He rejects a 'second front' in France in 1942. In June he suggests the Mulberry Harbour. At the second Washington Conference Roosevelt and Churchill discuss a landing in North Africa, decided on in July. At home Churchill survives the censure debate occasioned by the fall of Tobruk. In Cairo in August, he gives Montgomery the Eighth Army command and goes on to Moscow where he establishes cordial relations with Stalin in the first of their five wartime meetings. Churchill accepts the Beveridge Plan, published in December, as the basis for the post-war welfare state.

1943. In January, Churchill and Roosevelt discuss their strategy at the Casablanca Conference and announce the policy of unconditional surrender; in May, at the third Washington Conference, they agree to invade France in May 1944. They confer again in Quebec in August and at Cairo in November, going on to meet Stalin at Teheran and reach agreement on future Allied operations.

1944. On 6 June Churchill announces *D-Day*; he visits the beachhead on the 10th, Montgomery's headquarters in July, Italy in August and Roosevelt at the second Quebec Conference in September. In October, Churchill meets Stalin again in Moscow agreeing zones of influence in the Balkans. He recognizes the De Gaulle government, visiting Paris in November. In December Churchill intervenes in Greece.

1945. In February at Yalta, Churchill, Roosevelt and Stalin discuss post-war settlement; Churchill is alarmed by Russian designs and tries to moderate Stalin's claims in Poland and Germany. On 8 May he announces victory in Europe; on the 23rd he forms a 'caretaker government' until the general election. He cables Truman about the Russian 'Iron Curtain'. In July he assents to the use of the A-bomb and has his first meeting with Truman at the Potsdam Conference, where Churchill again challenges Stalin. On 26 July, defeated in the general election, Churchill resigns, to become leader of the Opposition.

1946. Churchill receives the Order of Merit. At Fulton, Missouri, in March he makes his 'Iron Curtain' speech. He advocates a United States of Europe at Zürich in September.

1947. The Royal Academy accepts two of Churchill's pictures.

1948. In May he opens the Congress of Europe at the Hague. Publication of Vol. I of *The Second World War* (sixth and last volume completed 1953), and of *Painting as a Pastime*.

1949. In August he suffers the first of six strokes.

1950. In February he suggests a summit conference with Russia. He is re-elected for Woodford.

1951. On 26 October Churchill becomes Prime Minister again with a small majority. In December he meets Truman in Washington.

1952. In January he addresses Congress and meets Eisenhower in Jamaica in December.

1953. In April Churchill is created Knight of the Garter. In May, after Stalin's death, Churchill revives the idea of a summit meeting. In October he receives the Nobel Prize for Literature. He attends the Bermuda Conference in December with Eisenhower.

1954. Churchill visits the American President in Washington.

1955. On 5 April Churchill reluctantly resigns the premiership. He is returned for Woodford in the general election.

1956. In April he meets Bulganin and Khrushchev on their London visit. He goes to Germany in May. The first two volumes of *History of the English-Speaking Peoples* are published (completed 1958).

1963. Honorary American citizenship is conferred on Churchill.

1964. He is returned as M.P. for Woodford.

1965. On 25 January Churchill dies. He is given a state funeral and buried in Bladon churchyard.